£4.50

POLITICAL ISSUES
IN BRITAIN TODAY

POLITICAL ISSUES
IN BRITAIN TODAY

edited by
Bill Jones

SECOND EDITION

MANCHESTER UNIVERSITY PRESS

Published by
Manchester University Press,
Oxford Road, Manchester M13 9PL, UK
and 27 South Main Street, Wolfeboro,
New Hampshire 03894-2069, USA
First edition 1985; second, revised edition 1987

British Library cataloguing in publication data

Political issues in Britain today. — 2nd
 ed. — (Politics today)
 1. Great Britain — Social conditions —
 1945–
 I. Jones, Bill II. Series
 941.085'8   HN385.5

Library of Congress cataloging in publication data applied for

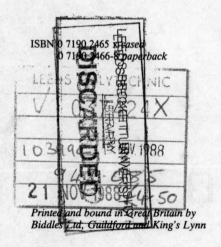

ISBN 0 7190 2465 X *cased*
 0 7190 2466 8 *paperback*

Printed and bound in Great Britain by
Biddles Ltd, Guildford and King's Lynn

Contents

Introduction

It was Peter Byrd from Warwick University who first pointed out to me the dearth of books which cover a range of current political issues. The studies which do exist tend to be weighty investigations into single issues which are too long and complex for most students of politics, whether at advanced or undergraduate level. Their need, it seemed to me, is for a shorter treatment which conveys the important facts and arguments and places them in the context of the present political debate. This book is designed to do just that.

Political issues develop and change rapidly, so to help reduce preparation time a number of contributors were invited to write their chapters during the months of August and September 1984. Contributions to this second edition were produced in July 1986. The format used follows that of the MUP's successful 'Today's series: students seem to appreciate this fleshed out note form which is crisp, concise and highlights the major points. As with the other volumes in the series the aim is to provide a complement rather than a substitute for the more comprehensive studies. We hope that the brief, clear introductions provided here will encourage students to follow up and deepen their knowledge via the further reading suggestions which appear at the end of each chapter.

Are the issues dealt with in an unbiased fashion? Total objectivity, of course, is an impossible ideal, especially in the teaching of politics, and I have always felt that too earnest an aspiration towards it robs the subject of much intrinsic interest. Contributors have their own views which will have played a part in the selection and presentation of their material, but the aim has been to offer a balanced approach which explains and discusses all the major arguments and value positions.

This is not to say that on occasions in the book certain values or positions – for example the chapter on Racism – are not explained, elaborated and defended.

The seventeen issues covered are loosely organised into four sections: institutional questions, economic issues, social policy, and keeping the peace. Inevitably the coverage is not comprehensive but it is as wide as the length of the volume allows and certainly takes in a wide range of political controversy. Interestingly, following the example of certain university departments, a number of examination boards have moved away from the traditional institutional approach to one which also embraces issues. This trend can only be applauded: issues are the stuff of politics and more attention must be paid to them by teachers if they want to interest, challenge and truly involve their students. Elections, after all, are not fought over delegated legislation or the office of the Comptroller and Auditor General but over the economy, social policy, law and order – those subjects which influence the way we live, think and cast our votes. I said in my introduction to the first edition that I hoped this book would nudge the movement a little further along its way. The fact that a second edition has followed so swiftly suggests that perhaps it has indeed achieved a degree of success in this area.

Finally, thanks are due to all the contributors for producing their material so efficiently and delivering it so promptly, and to Ray Offord at Manchester University Press for all his expert help.

Bill Jones,
Manchester, August 1986

Notes on contributors

Bill Jones is Senior Staff Tutor in Government and Politics, Department of Extra-Mural Studies, University of Manchester. He is editor of Manchester University Press's 'Today' series.

Peter Byrd is Lecturer in Politics at the University of Warwick and publishes in the areas of defence, the Labour Party and foreign policy.

John Delaney was a part-time tutor for the University of Manchester Department of Extra-Mural Studies and for the North-West district of the WEA. He now works for a computer firm in West Germany.

Andrew Gray is Senior Lecturer in Administrative Studies at the University of Kent at Canterbury.

Karen Hunt is a Woman's Education Officer for Manchester LEA and teaches Women's Studies in adult and higher education.

Geoff Lee formerly lectured in Government and Management at Manchester Polytechnic and is currently working in management training in industry.

John McIlroy is Staff Tutor in Industrial Relations, Department of Extra-Mural Studies, University of Manchester.

Lynton Robins is Senior Lecturer in Politics at Leicester Polytechnic and is editor of *Teaching Politics*.

Paul Wilding is Professor of Social Administration, University of Manchester.

INSTITUTIONAL ISSUES

Chapter One   *Bill Jones*

The Thatcher style

Just before the 1983 general election, *The Economist* lead editorial read: 'The Issue is Thatcher'.[1]* This provided the theme for the chapter which I wrote for the first edition of this book in August 1984. Astonishingly, two years later, as the second edition goes to press, 'The Issue' still *is* Thatcher – only much more so. On 7 July 1984 *The Economist*, scarcely a left-wing publication, observed that 'Mrs Thatcher's second government is stepping out to become Britain's most inept since the war' and 'most of what is wrong ... is rooted in the Prime Minister's own personality'. On 18 January 1986, in the middle of the Westland crisis, the same journal judged: 'Her style is no longer her asset. It is her biggest liability'. Indeed, Mrs Thatcher's personality and style of government have so dominated the political agenda in 1986 that Ian Aitken was moved to comment (*Guardian*, 28 July 1986) that 'the real issues' of unemployment, social policy, and so forth, had been relatively ignored.

As in the first edition this chapter will consider the pros and cons of seven critical propositions which encapsulate the chief charges against her style of government. The events of the two years since the first edition will be taken into account but, because of its fascination and significance, the Westland crisis – a saga which continues to unfold – will be addressed separately at the end of the chapter.

---

* Notes do not appear in other chapters but are used here to indicate the wide range of newspaper articles upon which this chapter has drawn and which may be of interest to readers.

1. **Mrs Thatcher pursues an excessively ideological line**

The case for

An *Observer*/Harris poll in 1984[2] indicated that a fair proportion of
the public think Mrs Thatcher is 'too right-wing': 59% agreed with this
statement whilst only 29% disagreed. But the charge of excessive
ideology is made particularly within the Conservative party itself.
'Wets' like Pym and Gilmour argue that Conservatives never hold fast
to any specific set of policies. Whilst seeking to defend and promote
principles like freedom, competition, property and patriotism, they
employ whatever policies are appropriate given the circumstances:
pragmatism has always been their overriding principle. Mrs Thatcher,
however, has turned this fundamental tenet of Toryism on its head. She
has expounded, passionately, a view of Conservatism which is closer
to nineteenth-century liberalism: drastically reduce the role of government in the economy; let market forces liberate the economy from the
dead hand of high taxes and bureaucratic state intervention. To this
she has added her own Grantham shopkeeper version of Victorian
middle-class values: thrift, hard work, getting on, acquiring property,
self reliance and the central importance of family life. She treats the
nation's economy like the family budget, preaching, in her own words,
'the homilies of housekeeping' and 'the parables of the parlour'.[3] But
the biggest mistake, say her critics, was to lay such store by the ideas
of Milton Friedman, the economist who enshrined the idea that
inflation could only be cured by controlling the money supply: the
circulation of cash and credit in the economic system. The principal
means of control − high interest rates − caused massive industrial
failure and helped produce a 2½ million increase in unemployment.

To make matters worse for the non-ideologically inclined members
in her party, Mrs Thatcher's belief in herself seems to survive, nay grow,
in spite of the disasters which attend her actions. 'I am politics', she
declared in September 1984, 'because of the conflict between good and
evil, and I believe that in the end good will triumph'.[4]

The case against

As with so many of the criticisms levelled against her, Mrs Thatcher
would accept parts of this one proudly. She freely admits she is a
'conviction politician' who wishes to 'change the heart and soul' of
the nation.[5] She shared Lord Blake's view, expressed in 1976, that
'Nothing less will suffice than a major reversal of the trends which ever

since 1945 Labour has presented and Conservatives have accepted.[6] She realised she was a 'rebel amidst a government of squares',[7] that her enthusiasm and commitment disturbed and even embarrassed the complacent scepticism of the Conservative establishment but declared to Hugo Young, 'If I give up we will lose', adding (perhaps wisely), 'I hope that doesn't sound arrogant'.[8]

A clear message, frequently and passionately delivered was necessary for it to have any chance of acceptance, but 'Thatcherism' is wrongly named in one sense, her defenders would say, for it incorporates the ideas of some of the best and brightest Conservative brains. And just because she holds strong views does not mean that she cannot change her policies when necessary or back away when the occasion requires.

According to her view, and that of her Chancellor, Nigel Lawson, the economy has never been in better shape. Despite the world recession of the early eighties, over one million *new* jobs have been created during the Thatcher years; economic growth since 1981 has been steady at about 3% per annum; and with an inflation rate of around 3% (in the autumn of 1986), British industry has never been better placed to expand strongly. Moreover, Mrs Thatcher can claim, with some justice, that her mission to change our political culture is succeeding. Her instinct that the centre ground of British politics was further to the right than Edward Heath supposed has been vindicated. She has catalysed a drift to the right into a major shift in popular attitudes on issues like the economy, defence and law and order. Even a crticial writer like the *Guardian's* Hugo Young (10 July 1985) allowed that 'a substantial process of national education has taken place in the past few years ... Thatcherism remains the body of belief which dominates political thinking ... Up to a point, we are all Thatcherites now'.

2. Mrs Thatcher protects middle-class interests and is insensitive to the suffering caused by her policies

The case for
The Prime Minister is often reported as referring to the Conservative voting middle class as 'our people'. Critics point out that whilst 'her people' have generally prospered since 1979 − high earners have benefited substantially from tax cuts − the average wage-earner's tax bill has actually increased from 34% to 40% of salary. For those

at the bottom of the pile life has become infinitely more miserable. In July 1986 the DHSS revealed that the numbers living in poverty had increased from 11.5 million in 1979 to 16.3 million in 1983.

The public judges accordingly. Only 19% in a Marplan survey believed she was 'in touch with ordinary people' (50% felt Neil Kinnock was).[9] Francis Pym thinks 'the public tone of the government has often sounded unattractive and unsympathetic' and is sure 'this causes immense harm'.[10] Ferdinand Mount perhaps expressed the essence of it in 1979 when he noted in Mrs Thatcher 'a certain impatience with subtlety of feeling, a lack of sympathy with people unlike her and a definitely limited range of experience'.[11]

The case against

Mrs Thatcher's defenders would argue that tax cuts for high earners were necessary incentives to effort and that much of the unemployment has been caused by the international recession and by companies shedding superfluous manpower in an effort to become competitive. Once the economy starts to expand – and the cure was always going to take at least ten years – then not just the middle classes but *all* sections of society will benefit. Some suffering will be inevitable but, says Mrs Thatcher, in the long term it is the best and only way. She denies the charge of insensitivity, telling Hugo Young that every time a business closes down 'I think gosh, what would I have done if my husband had come home and said we've got notice and there just don't seem to be any places to go'.[12] In the same interview she pointed out the advantages she had received through being brought up in a small town: 'We knew everyone, we knew what people felt. I sort of regard myself as a very normal ordinary person with all the right instinctive antennae.' Her supporters can also point out that her preferences lie not with the aristocratic elements in the Conservative Party but with those from humble origins like herself, who have worked hard for their success: Geoffrey Howe, Norman Fowler, Norman Tebbit and others. And if she is so uncaring to the working class, how come 40% of skilled workers voted for her in 1983 compared with only 32% for Labour?

3. Mrs Thatcher is stubbornly confrontationist

The case for

Some of her critics maintain that Mrs Thatcher came to power spoiling for a fight with the trade unions: 'My God, I'll confront them', she once said, 'should it prove necessary'. This confrontationist approach with its concomitant division and bitterness violates the traditional Conservative approach which, argue the 'wets', has been to strive for harmony and balance in the nation. Even worse, Mrs Thatcher is stubborn, making a fetish of getting her own way. Examples abound. Over the GCHQ issue, Mrs Thatcher was so determined to ban trade union membership in Britain's top-secret communications establishment that she refused a trade union offer giving her virtually all she asked and forced through the ban in the face of outrage in the opposition, trade unions and her own party.

The 1984 miners' strike is another good example: Thatcher's appointment of Ian McGregor and her own inflammatory rhetoric elevated Arthur Scargill into a left-wing mirror image of herself. Yet another example was her opposition to economic sanctions against South Africa in the summer of 1986. In direct contradiction to the views of the Commonwealth, not to mention the front line states and black leaders within South Africa itself, she insisted on roundly condemning such measures as 'immoral'. Her defense of such divisive action? 'If I were the odd one out and I were right, it wouldn't matter would it?[13]

In retrospect, say her critics, her promise upon her election to office in 1979 that 'where there was discord' she would 'bring harmony' now seems to be the most grotesque piece of hypocrisy. Since the Falklands war she has tended to see every opponent − at home as well as abroad − as a Galtieri to be defeated and destroyed. Unsurprisingly the Marplan poll revealed that 78% thought Mrs Thatcher 'stubborn'; 33% thought Kinnock so. More worrying for Mrs Thatcher though was the 1986 'Gallup Survey of Britain' revelation that 74% of people interviewed believed that she 'divides the country' compared with 37% in April 1979.[14]

Her abrasive style makes matters worse. Francis Pym's book *The Politics of Consent* begins with a pointed quotation from Nietzsche: 'We often refuse to accept an idea merely because the voice in which it has been expressed is unsympathetic to us'. He should know: no one will forget Mrs Thatcher's public humiliation of him at a pre-1983 press conference. The various nicknames bestowed upon her − 'the Boss', 'Leaderene', 'Attila the Hen', all reflect her fearsome reputation. This is not the way, say her critics, the English way, to conduct government. When projected each week from the despatch box it offends unnecessarily, provoking angry responses at home and abroad.

The case against

Again, Mrs Thatcher would probably accept much of this criticism as praise. She is proud of her ability not to turn, not to compromise, to stick to a task until it is complete. 'I am extremely patient', she says, 'provided I get my own way in the end'. She has always, quite openly, rejected consensus politics as the insidious process which has protected uneconomic industries and hastened our relative national decline. Rather, like her left-wing opponents, she believes conflict to be necessary, for antiquated socialist ideas to be called out into the open and defeated. Only then can Britain begin to build on a new consensus built around her own economic ideas.

Her critics fail to realise that these qualities are the inevitable complements of those which have singled her out for leadership. As Harold Wilson observed, 'I have no doubt Margaret was elected [leader of the Conservatives] because of her courage'. In the Falklands crisis where national humiliation and tragic loss of life threatened, it was her willingness to confront the fascist military junta in Argentina, her stubborn refusal to evade the conflict and compromise, which eventually won for us a famous and honourable victory. Her perfect composure under great stress was again demonstrated in the wake of the 1984 Brighton bomb explosion. The 78% of respondents in the *Observer*/Harris poll who saw Mrs Thatcher as 'Britain's toughest Prime Minister since Churchill' were surely paying her a compliment. But whilst determined and resolute Mrs Thatcher is not blind to political realities. As Anthony King has noted, 'Thatcher not only respects power, she is unusually adept at weighing it'.[15] Thus she gave in to the miners in 1981 but fought them in 1984 when she felt a big majority, plentiful coal reserves and a divided NUM enabled her so to do.

Naturally she loses her temper occasionally – few Prime Ministers maintain their equanimity indefinitely – but the fact that so many of the complaints emanate from ex-Cabinet members perhaps helps explain – say Thatcherites – why they lost their jobs in the first place.

4. Mrs Thatcher is excessively authoritarian

The case for

Soon after her elevation to power one political correspondent wrote, 'whilst not actually surrounded by sycophants she gives the impression that she would like to be'. Some would say that by 1984 this unspoken wish had come to pass. In 1981 a showdown with the 'wets' in her

Cabinet shifted the balance of power finally in her favour; she used the Falklands war and her crushing election victory to put the finishing touches to the removal of all her major opponents. Pym describes the atmosphere pervading her government in grim terms: 'To be loyal means one hundred per cent acceptance of Government thinking: any dissent, or even admittance of doubt is treachery and treason.'[16] Regular checks are kept on loyalty: twice a year the whips meet to discuss the voting record and opinions of every Tory MP. 'All this is sifted and considered when she makes her appointments; nothing is forgotten and little forgiven.'[17] The public seem to have gained a similar impression; 62% of respondents in the *Observer*/Harris poll agreed 'she acts too much like a dictator'.

For several years she has seemed not to listen. According to Whitehall folklore civil servants have at most four minutes (some say less than a minute) to explain an issue to her, however complicated. 'Beyond that point, unless her interest is awakened, Mrs Thatcher's eyes glaze over. To continue is to jeopardize future promotion'.[18] And she delivers endless lectures to visitors, colleagues and public alike. The Canadian Prime Minister, Brian Mulroney, complained she had spoken to him as if he were a six-year-old child! Her public style is a kind of authoritarian populism which is reflected, aided and abetted by the *Sun*'s style of journalism. Not content with the shift to the right which Rupert Murdoch's entry into Fleet Street has caused she has used her power to manage the press to a worrying degree. Indeed, some students of the political personality have seen in some of Mrs Thatcher's behaviour signs of the paranoia widely recognised as a symptom of the disease Lord Acton diagnosed so memorably: the corruption of power. An example occurred during July 1984 when Mrs Thatcher's leadership was suffering a mini crisis. No. 10 put it about that Francis Pym had convened a meeting of MPs to organise opposition to their leader – when Pym proved to be perfectly innocent, No. 10's accusations appeared not only foolish but sinister.

The case against

Mrs Thatcher's supporters have no difficulty in dismissing these criticisms as the resentment of sacked ministers, passed over MPs and the predictable bias of left-of-centre journalists. It is absurd to compare Mrs Thatcher to a dictator: as Prime Minister she works purely within the parliamentary system and is dependent upon the support of her party, a formidable array of ability and intellect in which groups of

MPs regularly assert their independence by abstaining or voting against the government. But over its overwhelming support for Mrs Thatcher there has never been any doubt and for this support she has worked hard and democratically. Harry Greenway, a Tory MP, puts it like this: 'A Prime Minister gets the authority he or she can command by brilliance at the job and personality and above all by dominance of the House of Commons; in this Margaret Thatcher is quite exceptional.'[19]

According to this view, Mrs Thatcher is no dictator but a tough, determined, very successful Prime Minister who so dominates the democratic process that she appears more authoritarian than she really is. The weakness of the Labour opposition and tribal loyalties of the 'wets' merely enhances this effect. Her supporters also deny she is as grim as her critics like to present her. She can relax and laugh at politics — as she did when she wrote and performed in a televised *Yes Minister* sketch — and has a genuine warmth and concern for family and friends.

5. The Prime Minister is poorly advised

The case for

For some time now a vacuum of policy advice in No.10 has been discerned by Whitehall watchers. Whilst previous prime ministers had teams of able political advisors Mrs Thatcher has none. According to *The Economist* (7 July 1984): 'No. 10 Downing St., the epicentre of Britain's political life is a curiously empty place. The Prime Minister flaps round its corridors like a solitary hawk looking for prey.' Her advisors are often part-time and transient and real influence is given to shadowy figures, like Bernard Ingham (press secretary), David Wolfson (Chief of Staff) and Chief Whip John Wakeman: scarcely a heavyweight line-up. After the Westland débâcle *The Economist* pointed out that most of the crucial misjudgements had been made by incompetent 'kitchen courtiers'. 'This is a portrait of high office reminiscent of the Watergate hearings', remarked the journal reminding her of the advice tendered seven years earlier that she would need 'a strong private office of politically astute advisers' (25 January 1986).

The problem seems to lie in the fact that Mrs Thatcher recognises only her own immovable certainties. 'We have', writes Hugo Young, 'the most politically confident government of modern times.'[20] He points out that Mrs Thatcher has dispensed with Royal Commissions and lengthy enquiries in favour of short investigations, often undertaken by accountants. She is so sure of the answers she does not see the need for advice. The consequences of this illusion were manifest in the series of misjudgments and errors following her reaccession to power in 1983: GCHQ, the top people's pay award in July 1985, Westlands, the failure of the important Shops Bill in April 1986 and so on, and so on.

The case against

Against this charge, it can be pointed out that the size of Mrs Thatcher's office in January 1983 was in fact 'slightly larger than the staff of 69 which was in place when Mr. Callaghan departed'.[21] She has always had a policy unit, first led by Sir John Hoskyns, then by Ferdinand Mount and currently by Brian Griffith: since 1983 the unit has doubled in size. In addition, a number of very distinguished experts – often drawn in from the outside world – have tendered their advice e.g. Sir Alfred Sherman, director of the right-wing Centre for Policy Studies (why fund a think tank when the Conservative Party has its own?), Professors Douglas Hague and Alan Walters and on diplomatic matters, Sir Anthony Parsons. And why waste public money if their contributions can be effectively made part-time? Remember also that in 1982 Mrs Thatcher proposed that all the advisers and assistants at No. 10 be gathered together into a 'Prime Minister's Department' but this idea was criticised on the grounds that it would make her office too powerful. Notwithstanding, Mrs Thatcher would probably accept one element of the charge against her: she *is* sure of what she wants to do and is determined to go straight for it; an overwhelmingly majority in the 1983 election is her authority for doing so. As *The Economist* puts it, 'The Prime Minister herself is the guardian of the government's strategy. She knows in broad outline what she wants done. What she needs is advice on how to do it.'[22]

6. Mrs Thatcher has subverted the constitution

The case for

The Duke of Wellington wrote to a friend after his first Cabinet meeting, 'I gave them their orders and they wanted to stay behind and discuss them'. He had not yet realised that in parliamentary government, military style decision-making is not possible. Since his day the conventions have been strengthened so that it became accepted that all important interest groups are consulted before decisions are taken, all major decisions are taken collectively in Cabinet, and implementation is by a politically neutral civil service. The charge against Mrs Thatcher is that she has ignored these conventions by:

(*a*) *Downgrading the Cabinet as a decision-making body*   The Iron Lady is cleverer than the Iron Duke: she avoids bringing important matters before the cabinet in the first place. Take economic policy: 'The single most important fact about Mrs. Thatcher's first period in government', writes Burch 'is that the main thrust of economic policy was effectively hived-off from the scrutiny of the whole Cabinet. Apart from discussions on expenditure reviews, the Cabinet as a body did not consider the general economic strategy until July 1980: 14 months after entering office.'[23] All this, combined with her abrasive style, her habit of eschewing calm discussion for what David Howell has called 'high pitched argument';[24] her tendency to state her own view at such great length that none dared challenge her, proved too much for her Defence Minister, Michael Heseltine, in January 1986. When a Cabinet committee meeting scheduled to discuss the Westland issue on 13 December 1985 was cancelled, it was the last straw. 'I resigned', he told Fred Emery on *Panorama*, 'on my judgement of a breakdown of constitutional procedures'. There has been an 'affront to the constitution'. Later in the year on the Terry Wogan chat show he was asked his opinion of the *Spitting Image* satirical puppet show. He recalled a sketch in which Mrs Thatcher was supposedly dining out with her Cabinet colleagues. Having ordered her meat course, the waiter asked 'And what about the vegetables?' 'Oh they'll have the same as me' replied the Prime Minister with weary contempt. That sketch Heseltine thought would come to be seen by historians as symbolic of politics in the eighties.

Even so, according to Jim Prior, the Cabinet worked reasonably well until the crucial dishing of the 'wets' in the September 1981 reshuffle. After that, 'There was more and more control by the Prime Minister ... I don't think it was as good a Cabinet and certainly the debates on economic policy really ceased to exist.'[25]

In his important book, *Cabinet*, Peter Hennessey reveals that Mrs Thatcher has relied less and less on Cabinet meetings, halving their number compared with Attlee and Churchill, the flow of Cabinet papers being only one-sixth of the annual totals during the fifties and sixties.[26] And whilst she has utilised the device of Cabinet committees – as Richard Crossman noted, the classic way in which modern prime ministers divide and rule Cabinet – she has not used them as much as some of her predecessors. Her favoured *modus operandi* is the *ad hoc* grouping of ministers and civil servants, specially convened to report on a problem or solve it, and responsible directly to her rather than via the Cabinet network. She had always made it clear that she was going to be in charge. 'As Prime Minister', she said, in February 1979, 'I could not waste any time having internal arguments'.[27]

When things go well there are few complaints about this dominant style and, as the Falklands War proved, this is a quick and direct way of making policy. However, when things go badly this prime ministerial style means that there is no one to blame but Mrs Thatcher herself. When her judgement is sound she is vindicated but when it is not she must accept heavy criticism, and not just from enemies. Paul Johnson, the ex-socialist turned Thatcherite, for example, believed she was wrong not to support Reagan's invasion of Grenada in 1983. Without her hitherto good judgement, he wrote, Mrs Thatcher 'is a very ordinary woman occupying a position where ordinary virtues are not enough'.[28]

(*b*) *Politicising the civil service*   The charge here is that civil servants are being appointed on the basis of their political views, rather than their ability. Largely as a result of retirement, eleven out of the twenty-five top permanent secretary posts became vacant between 1981 and 1983. Mrs Thatcher took a close interest in the new appointments and, it is alleged, did her best to fill them with civil servants who had either worked for her or were thought sympathetic to her views. Thus her ex-private secretary, Clive Whitmore, went to Defence, Peter Middleton, who helped design the Medium Term Financial Strategy, to the Treasury and David Hancock, who had worked on EEC matters in the Cabinet Office to Education. 'The permanent secretaries at most major departments', writes *The Economist*, 'are now known as Mrs. Thatcher's personal appointments, often promoted over the heads of more senior candidates.'[29] The case is further strengthened by the example of Bernard Ingham who fills the highly political office of press secretary; he too is a civil servant. Civil servants have, moreover, been asked to work in a different way. Mrs Thatcher requires results: she wants departments to 'execute policy without constant reference back to the centre and without wasting time and effort on elaborate Cabinet Office coordination'. Civil servants are expected to have one overriding loyalty: to the objectives set by No. 10. This alleged politicisation of the civil service has been offered by some as an explanation for the constant series of leaks from within the government machine which has plagued the Thatcher government from the outset and which have gathered momentum since June 1983.

(c) *Overcentralising government decision making*   Mrs Thatcher claims that she wants to return responsibility to the individual, to take government out of their lives. In practice, say her critics, she has achieved the opposite: 'central government', says Pym, 'now exercises direct control over more and more aspects of our lives'.[30] Two important examples illustrate this point. Firstly, local government has been progressively brought under central control: Whitehall now decides how much local councils can spend and seeks to penalise those who levy what are regarded as excessive rates. And in April 1986 the Labour controlled GLC and the six other metropolitcan counties were formally abolished. Secondly, Mrs Thatcher has ceased to pay the respect traditionally accorded to pressure groups which seek to influence specific policies. The trade unions, of course, she has systematically weakened – some say crushed – by ignoring them and passing restrictive legislation.

The case against

(a) In her defence it can be argued that Mrs Thatcher has not broken any rules: none of the conventions about prior Cabinet discussion of important issues and the formulation of a consensus have any legal status at all. Heseltine's complaint that a constitutional outrage had occurred over Westlands is dismissed by Hugo Young as 'a total absurdity ... The rules of Cabinet in my view are largely determined by the balance of political power between the different forces which exist'.[31] In other words, if the Prime Minister enjoys the overall support of party in Parliament than it matters not how decisions are reached. Sir Frank Cooper, outspoken former Permanent Under-Secretary in the Ministry of Defence, in an interview with Peter Hennessey, did not believe that she had put 'severe dents in the traditional model of collective cabinet government'. 'I think she's changed a number of things', judged Sir Frank, 'She believes it's the duty of any prime minister to lead from the front and I would have a great deal of sympathy with that view quite frankly'.[32]

(b) Both Hennessey and Young deny that Cabinet government has been dismantled by Mrs Thatcher. 'Cabinet government undoubtedly still exists despite rumours sometimes heard to the contrary', says Hugo Young. He discerns 'a collective mood of those who are in Cabinet which acts, maybe often, as an inexplicit veto on what Prime Ministers may want to do'.[33] Hennessey cites examples of issues which Mrs Thatcher did not take to full Cabinet for fear that they would be defeated, e.g. 'the total abolition of the closed shop, the radical breaking-up of the National Health Service, student loans, rates, vouchers for schools ...'.[34]

Her defeat in the Cabinet (spring 1986) over the sale of parts of BL to American buyers is surely further evidence that Cabinet government is alive under Mrs Thatcher, if not particularly well. After the débâcle of Westlands she simply could not get her own way and had to back down.

(c) Inevitably any Prime Minister will run things with the help of a small, possibly informal, group of colleagues. As David Howell pointed out, 'This country, really since the sixteenth century has basically been run by five or six people. I don't think its very different today: five or six is what you need and that's what any prime minister tends to form around them.'[35]

(d) Burch argues that it would be 'misleading to suggest' that Mrs Thatcher intervenes more in the work of individual departments than previous Prime Ministers. Her style is interventionist; she wants to influence policy in its formative stage and quite naturally seeks to involve and encourage the civil servants concerned. Anthony King argues that Mrs Thatcher is uninterested in the 'nuts and bolts of government. Faced with a problem she instinctively asks not "what organisation shall I create?" but "who can help me?"'[36] Ignoring bureaucratic procedures she then assembles those people who can produce the desired results quickly and efficiently.

(e) She is less interested in the political views of civil servants – professionally trained to serve any master – than their energy and ability. It is understandable that she should seek to advance those whose abilities she admires.

(f) It is the spendthrift councils which intervene so unjustifiably into our lives, argue Thatcher loyalists: it is necessary to curb them. The public will also benefit from the removal of metropolitan county councils which have proved to be an unnecessary, expensive and bureaucratic tier of government.

(g) Pressure groups have a right to tender advice but governments are not obliged to take it. Mrs Thatcher believes that the practice of consulting myriad pressure groups in the hope of creating some kind of consensus tends either to prevent the right decisions being made or to produce immobilism.

7. Mrs Thatcher has become a president rather than a prime minister

The case for

This criticism is really a synthesis of all those discussed earlier. From the original idea of a British Prime Minister as first among equals within the Cabinet, Mrs Thatcher seems to have travelled a long way. Her style of government is intensely personal — more so than any Prime Minister within living memory. As Pym says, 'she would ideally like to run the major Departments herself and tries her best to do so.' It is *her* will which dominates, not the cabinet's. By degrees she has gathered all the threads of power into her own hands, bypassing Cabinet and its committees in a number of crucial areas; if Cabinet has no collective force it is little different from its American equivalent which is purely the creature of the President.

The corollary of this is that Mrs Thatcher tries to do too much. *The Economist* criticises her hectic schedules, her short attention span, her tendency to be 'not quite in intellectual control'.[37] Other commentators regularly discern a desperately tired Mrs Thatcher, looking drained and grey: Mr Edward Du Cann MP in March 1984 even had the temerity to suggest that a deputy should be appointed to help carry her excessive workload. Interestingly, the suite of rooms in the Grand Hotel, Brighton, used by Mrs Thatcher at the time of the 1984 bombing, has been rebuilt and renamed 'The Presidential Suite'!

The case against

(*a*) A 'presidential tendency' in the British premiership has been noted ever since Richard Crossman's famous introduction to Bagehot's *English Constitution*. It was inevitable that a strong character like Mrs Thatcher would help this tendency develop.

(*b*) Unlike the American President, Mrs Thatcher was not elected directly for a fixed term. She is always beholden ultimately to her party in parliament. As long as they loyally support her, it is arguable that she has more relative power than the US President who always faces opposition from Congress but, if her party deserts her, then, unlike the President, she is lost. The point is that she has to *earn* this support. The fact that she commands the kind of support which enables her to act like a president should not be held against her: it is really a compliment rather than a criticism.

A century ago Sir William Harcourt said that 'In practice the thing very much depends on the character of the man ... The office of Prime

Minister is what its holder chooses and is able to make of it.' In the present day Joe Haines, a former aide to Harold Wilson, dismisses 'presidential' descriptions of Mrs Thatcher as an exaggeration: 'If you have a powerful man like Churchill was, or MacMillan was, or Mrs Thatcher is, then they tend to dominate their colleagues.'[38] Hennessey also holds well back from claiming that Mrs Thatcher has 'privatised' the Cabinet from the Constitution.

(c) Mrs Thatcher is human and of course becomes tired though her energy is prodigious. She rises at 6.00 am each day and stays up into the small hours dealing with her red boxes and reading the first editions of the national newspapers. Each day is highly organised and involves a gruelling schedule of high level meetings, interviews, visits and appearances in the House of Commons. Her supporters would claim she has a genius for making decisions – the vast majority of them good ones. These special abilities enable her to do more than the normal Prime Minister: she overflows the boundaries of the office and consequently appears to be presidential. But again, it is her achievement.

Concluding comments

From the Falklands triumph in 1982, Mrs Thatcher's public standing has slipped badly. Hugo Young suggests that governments perish either because their ideological force is spent or discredited – like the Callaghan government in 1979 – or through inefficiency. As we learnt earlier Young did not believe Thatcherism had lost any of its relevance; it was its record of incompetence which had laid its reputation low. The 'banana skins' of the immediate post-1983 period were followed by more serious perceived policy failures in the economy, education, health and the inner cities. And then in January 1986 the Westland Affair exploded onto the public stage.

The Westland Affair seemed to prove the truth of most or all of the critical propositions surveyed in this chapter and add a few more besides. The defence and economic issues involved in the financial failure of the Yeovil-based company were important but not that crucial. Michael Heseltine at Defence favoured the European rescue package which he himself had co-ordinated; Brittan at Trade and Industry at first claimed to be neutral but in reality supported the Westland board's own preference for the American Sikorsky (United Technologies) bid. Heseltine was furious when he realised that Mrs

Thatcher, despite claims to be even-handed, was manipulating the Cabinet committee system against him, finally cancelling that key meeting in December 1985 in which Heseltine hoped to win wider Cabinet backing for his European proposal.

Both sides engaged in intensive lobbying over the Christmas and New Year holiday period. Heseltine defied the Prime Minister by publicly writing to a prominent member of his proposed consortium that a Sikorsky-owned Westlands would be at a disadvantage regarding European contracts. Mrs Thatcher countered this ploy by asking the Solicitor-General to offer a legal view on Heseltine's letter. Sir Patrick Mayhew duly obliged by writing a rather vague letter which spoke of 'material inaccuracies' in Heseltine's advice. It is what happened next which is still the subject of much acrimonious but very intriguing debate.

Sir Patrick's confidential letter expressing a legal opinion damaging to Heseltine's case was leaked to the press within two hours of its despatch on 6 January. Who did it? Mrs Thatcher ordered her most senior and closest adviser, the Secretary to the Cabinet, Sir Robert Armstrong, to find out. The enquiry took two weeks but in the meantime Tam Dalyell, MP, revealed that Miss Colette Bowe, Director of Information at the DTI, was the author of the leak.

In the subsequent furore Leon Brittan admitted authorising the leak with the agreement of Mrs Thatcher's personal staff at No.10. Heseltine had stage-managed his resignation on 9 January in an atmosphere of fine moral indignation; Brittan's resignation was more an admission of guilt. But was he really guilty? Was it conceivable that Mrs Thatcher, with her reputation for close personal attention to detail and her intimate interest in the Westland issue could *not* have known about the leak and, at least tacitly, have authorised it? And why did Sir Robert take two weeks over an enquiry the answer to which he had always known? Parallels with Watergate, when all the roads of enquiry lead relentlessly to the President's office, began to be made.

The Select Committee on Defence, comprising a majority of Conservative MPs and chaired by Mrs Thatcher's old friend, Sir Humphrey Atkins, conducted a six-month enquiry into the Westlands affair. Mrs Thatcher did not give evidence personally and refused to allow Bernard Ingham or her private secretary, Charles Powell – widely rumoured to have managed No.10's side of the leak operation – to give evidence either. Instead Sir Robert Armstrong gave what was generally regarded as an evasively bland performance, whilst

Leon Brittan, in his evidence, repeatedly refused to answer certain key questions.

When it finally appeared in July 1986 the committee's report accepted Mrs Thatcher's assurances that her aides had approved the leak without her knowledge but it described her early explanations of the leak as 'flimsy to say the least'. The leak itself was condemned as 'disreputable' and her staff were roundly criticised. In the House of Commons Mrs Thatcher rejected these criticisms and stoutly defended Sir Robert and her personal staff. *The Economist* (2 August 1986) neatly summarised the damaging implications of the report.

> If Mrs. Thatcher intended to leak a private letter written by one of her colleagues discrediting another, she should accept responsibility for a serious offence. If she did not, she should have asked those involved to resign. The effective dismissal (which is what it was) of ... Mr. Leon Brittan, is looking more and more like the shooting of a hired gun after he had performed the planned contract. The refusal to let a number of the officials involved testify before the Commons select committee was deeply suspicious ... In their place went ... the hapless Sir Robert Armstrong, who had conducted the 'leak enquiry' that the select committee has shown to be a charade to deflect blame from the prime minister. (See also pp. 33–4.)

Nineteen eighty-six has not been a good year for Mrs Thatcher. Echoes of Westland will dog her until the next election and beyond. And after her climbdown over the British Leyland sale, her extraordinary defeat over the Shops Bill, her massively unpopular decision to allow US planes to bomb Libya from British bases, her flouting of Commonwealth – and according to rumour – Royal opinion over South African sanctions and her retreat in a number of key policy areas, it is hardly surprising that her personal rating has dropped dramatically. In 1983 over 50% of people polled were satisfied with Mrs Thatcher's performance as Prime Minister; in August 1986 her 26% rating trailed that of her party by several points. John Biffen suggested in the early summer of 1986 that she should encourage other colleagues to take more responsibility rather than continue to run the whole show herself. Number 10 unofficially poured scorn on the idea.

Crystal ball-gazing is always dangerous in a publication like this, but in the autumn of 1986 two aspects of the future seem reasonably clear. Mrs Thatcher will lead her party into the next election. But if she loses, the history of the Conservative party suggests that the accumulated slights and resentments produced by her abrasive, domineering 'conviction' style politics will ensure she will not for long survive as its leader.

Notes

1   *The Economist*, 14 May 1983.
2   *The Observer*, 29 April 1984.
3   Her words to the Lord Mayor's banquet 1982, quoted in Peter Riddel, *The Thatcher Government*, Martin Robertson, 1984, p. 9.
4   Quoted in *The Observer*, 23 September 1984.
5   Interview with Ronald Butt, *Sunday Times*, 3 May 1981.
6   Quoted in Arthur Aughey, 'Mrs Thatcher's philosophy', *Parliamentary Affairs*, autumn 1983, p. 393.
7   Quoted in Simon Winchester, 'You see before you a rebel', *Sunday Times*, 3 May 1981.
8   Interview with Hugo Young, *Sunday Times*, 3 August 1980.
9   *The Guardian*, 21 November 1983. A *Sunday Times* MORI poll (7 October 1984) produced similar findings.
10 Francis Pym, *The Politics of Consent*, Hamish Hamilton, 1984, p. 14.
11 Riddel, *op. cit.*, p. 2.
12 Young, *Sunday Times*, 3 August 1980.
13 Hugo Young, *The Guardian*, 8 July 1986.
14 *Observer* leader, 27 July 1986.
15 Professor Anthony King, *The Sunday Times*, 15 April 1984.
16 Pym, *op. cit.*, p. 2.
17 Simon Hoggart, 'Mrs Thatcher: five years on', *The Observer*, 29 April 1984.
18 Peter Hennessey, *Cabinet*, Blackwell, 1986, p. 98.
19 Interview given to Tyne Tees TV 'Is Democracy Working?' 16 April 1986.
20 Hugo Young, *The Guardian*, 24 September 1984.
21 Martin Burch, 'Mrs. Thatcher's approach to leadership in government 1979–June 1983', *Parliamentary Affairs*, 36, 4, p. 408.
22 *The Economist*, 'No other gods but Mrs. T.', 10 March 1984.
23 Burch, *op. cit.*, p. 411.
24 Hennessey, *op. cit.*, p. 97.
25 *Ibid.*, p. 95.
26 *Ibid.*, p. 99.
27 Interview in *The Observer*, 25 February 1979.
28 Paul Johnson, *The Sunday Times*, 24 November 1983.
29 *The Economist*, 10 March 1984.
30 Pym, *op. cit.*, p. 17.

31 Interview for Tyne Tees TV, 'Is Democracy Working?', 19 April 1986.
32 Hennessey, *op. cit.*, p.105.
33 Interview with Tyne Tees TV, *op. cit.*
34 Hennessey, *op. cit.*, p.111.
35 *Ibid.*, p.96.
36 Anthony King, *The Sunday Times*, 11 April 1984. See also A. King's 'Margaret Thatcher: The Style of a Prime Minister', in *The British Prime Minister*, Macmillan, 1985, pp.96–133.
37 *The Economist*, 7 July 1984.
38 Interview with Tyne Tees TV, 16 April 1986.

Secrecy and openness in government

Open Government is a contradiction in terms. You can be open – or you can have government.
(Cabinet Secretary in *Yes Minister*)

Even those with a distaste for such *Alice in Wonderland*-type quotations at the heads of chapters will have to admit to the lure of a quip such as this. As on so many other occasions, the series *Yes Minister* captured the essence of the issue. In this chapter, therefore, we shall examine the forces for secrecy and openness and identify the purposes served by freedom of information and the problems faced by would-be reformers. But first the issues must be placed in their historical context.

Cases and confusions

In George Orwell's *1984* the Ministry of Truth is of course really the Ministry of Falsehood. Its job is to present an interpretation of the world which protects the Party. Oceania may be a fiction but it illustrates issues which have exercised minds not only in the real 1984 when the Campaign for Freedom of Information was mounted, but both before and since. Indeed, Des Wilson's campaign, which has been supported by such establishment figures as Sir Douglas Wass and Sir Patrick Nairne, both former permanent secretaries in the civil service, and Sir John Hoskyns, former policy adviser to Mrs Thatcher, is only a part of a notable saga.

Legal landmarks

(*a*) *Marvin and The Globe, 1878* At least as far as the past century or so is concerned the saga begins with Marvin, a clerk who worked for the diplomatic service. In 1878, in preliminary discussions for the Berlin Peace Conference, the British and Russian governments were hatching a secret deal. Marvin simply took some of the drafts to representatives of *The Globe* newspaper who rewarded him for his services and published what they saw. As Marvin had not actually stolen the documents the government found they had no case for a prosecution under the existing legislation. This was one of the reasons for the first Official Secrets Act of 1889.

(*b*) *German spies, 1911* In summer 1911 anxiety grew about German espionage, especially after some of its nationals were found drawing pictures of fortifications at Dover. As a result, the government hurriedly passed the Official Secrets Act of that year. It is this Act which is still in force and of which Section II causes so much controversy for the way it proscribes the passing of *any* unauthorised information.

(*c*) *The Sunday Telegraph Case, 1971* More recently, in 1971, a prosecution arose out of a *Sunday Telegraph* article about British government involvement in the Nigerian civil war. The article cited a government document which elaborated the nature and extent of British military equipment being sent to help the federal Nigerian government in its struggle with the secessionist state of Biafra. It also contained an analysis of the prospects of the federal government in which it was not exactly complimentary about military standards in the Nigerian army. After a four week trial the journalist (Jonathan Aitken, now an MP), the editor, and the army colonel who leaked the document, were acquitted. In one of the more robust judgements of British legal history, the judge said that Section II of the Official Secrets Act, 1911, should be pensioned off. This case was important, therefore, for the way it appeared to make Section II inoperative.

(*d*) *The Crossman Diaries, 1975* A few years later another case appeared to confirm the liberalising tendency of the judiciary at this time. It concerned the diaries of the former Labour Cabinet minister, Richard Crossman. The interest of this diary for political history has been not so much for what it contained (which was anyway rather too verbose) as the issue raised by its very publication. An attempt was made by the Attorney-General, the law officer of the Labour government of 1974, to prohibit publication in both serialised form by the Sunday Times and in full by Jonathan Cape Ltd. This attempt eventually failed in the Court of Appeal.

(e) *Civil Servants and the Ministry of Defence, 1984*   Yet, for some, these steps towards greater openness were reversed by two prosecutions brought in 1984. Both concerned civil servants in the Ministry of Defence. The first was a junior official who was convicted for passing to the *Guardian* documents relating to decisions about the installing of Cruise missiles in the UK. The second was a senior civil servant who was acquitted of leaking to an MP documents about the sinking of the Argentinian battleship *Belgrano* during the Falklands War of 1982. This acquittal implied that an MP might be an authorised person to whom under Section II information could be passed.

An administrative landmark

(f) *The Westland Affair, 1985–6*   The latest prosecutions were brought in a climate of almost unprecedented leaks by officials. More recently still, of course, the Westland Affair confirmed that ministers may be just as prone to leaking as their officials. Judging from the hearings of the Select Committee on Defence, this long and complex series of incidents involved ministers, their press officers and regular civil servants in a good deal of underhand activity. Even the Prime Minister and Head of the Civil Service themselves appear to have been guilty of at best midjudgement if not actual collusion in the manipulation of disclosure and withholding of information. In the end it was Mr Leon Brittan as Secretary of State for Trade and Industry who resigned over his part in the affair. Ostensibly, this resignation arose from Mr Brittan's disclosure of part of a letter from the Solicitor-General which impuned the validity of the arguments of the Defence Secretary (Mr Heseltine) in the debate on whether the Westland Helicopter Company should be rescued financially by a consortium led by the American competitor Sikorsky. In part, however, the resignation arose from the manner in which Mr Brittan failed to present a credible account to the House of Commons (see Chapter 3). In any event the story suggests a very fine dividing line between what consti-tutes official and unofficial disclosure (a line which often disappears altogether behind our private system of government) and, according to Alan Watkins of *The Observer*, a new conjugation of an English verb: I bring matters into the public domain, you leak, he/she betrays a colleague!

The history which these cases present indicates that both the law and administration of government information are based very largely on chance and political discretion. Before we consider the forces which shape this practice, however, we should consider the objectives and potential beneficiaries of greater openness.

Objectives and beneficiaries

Objectives of greater openness

Perhaps one of the reasons for the rather sterile discussion of open government in recent years has been the scant attention paid to what objectives it would promote. It has been as though the obvious links between power, liberty and openness were justifications in themselves. The consequence, however, has often been a confusion of ends and means. One way to resolve this is to consider the objectives in terms of Birch's characterisation of *Representative and Responsible Government*. By representative, Birch understands three notions: election as the means by which governments are chosen, government by representatives of the people, and government as representative or reflective of the people. By responsible government he understands three further notions: responsive government, considered and unarbitrary government, and accountable government. In this context the objectives of open government relate primarily to government by representatives, the promotion of responsive and accountable government, and the protection against arbitrary government.

Specifically these objectives may be expressed as three propositions:

(1) *The civil rights objective*: secrecy should be relaxed to allow the individual to see files containing his personal records and thereby protect his individual rights.

(2) *The policy-making objective*: governments should be obliged to outline in greater detail the nature of the problems it faces and provide for public use the information thought relevant to the search for solutions.

(3) *The accountability objective*: governments should be obliged to provide more detailed accounts not only of their decisions but also the reasons for them and the conduct of their implementation.

Whether these objectives have equal weight in the current debate is not easy to determine. What is clear, however, is that each might have its own implications for the development of greater openness and that these might even be mutually inconsistent.

Beneficiaries of openness

As secrecy is about the protection of information and openness about its dispersal, we might expect the potential beneficiaries of greater openness to be MPs and other representatives of the public, whether groups or individuals, who presently depend on government disclosure. This generalisation, however, conceals a complex pattern.

(*a*) *Members of Parliament*   This complexity is reflected in the attitudes of front benches in the House of Commons: in opposition each has been broadly in favour of greater disclosure, while in government each has resisted progress. Backbenchers of all parties, however, appear to be prime beneficiaries; at least they make such claims in the support for private members' bills on the subject, based on their requirements for more information in the performance of their various parliamentary functions.

(*b*) *The mass media*   There is a story about one senior civil servant who told his colleagues in a Civil Service College seminar that the only real demand for greater openness came from one jouranlist (a reference to Peter Hennessey, formerly of *The Times*)! This is somewhat mischievous, for my own researches in the 1970s gave the clear impression that the press does collectively regard itself as a major beneficiary. This has been expressed formally in terms of its ability to enhance its dignity and freedom which, in the words of a famous *Times* leading article as long ago as 1852, 'are trammelled from the moment it accepts an ancillary position' to government. In some quarters the position of the lobby correspondent is clearly regarded as corruptly ancillary. No doubt, also, the press hopes (perhaps unrealistically) to obtain good copy from less secrecy.

(*c*) *Interest groups*   A further beneficiary is suggested by the experience of the Freedom of Information Acts in the USA where corporate business has gained perhaps more than any other group. Some commentators have described legislation as providing for legalised industrial espionage and the largest corporations have benefitted most.

But not all interest groups would appear to gain equally; those without established and institutionalised links with government might certainly gain, but those already close to the policy making process in this way might actually see their positions in jeopardy.

(*d*) *Individual members of the public*   This category of beneficiaries would appear directly affected only by systematic and effective attempts to promote the civil rights objective outlined earlier, either by allowing individual access to personal files or by enhancing the access of officers such as ombudsmen.

From the above discussion it is clear that the issues in the secrecy and openness of government are not as straightforward as some have supposed. This is unfortunate for the student seeking to encapsulate them in a few pithy (and preferably memorable) lines. But it is nevertheless the reality of things.

Forces for secrecy and openness

The variability of these issues and the practice of secrecy is rather reinforced by the ambiguous influences of many of our political institutions and processes which can act as forces both for and against secrecy.

Forces for secrecy

(*a*) *The unwritten constitution*   The absence of a written document which lays down the rights of governed and government and the very dependence on custom and practice for the operation of so much of our system of government are themselves important sources of secrecy. The fact that it is for a prime minister, for example, to decide how much shall be revealed about the structure of Cabinet committees is reflective of an inbuilt inertia towards secrecy which only conscious and active attention can prevent pervading the whole system.

(*b*) *Statutes*   Those parts of the constitution which are written as legislation tend to reinforce this tendency. Two sets of statutes are significant here: those relating to official secrets and the publication of official records. Of the Official Secrets Acts that of 1911, and especially Section II, is the most important. As we have seen earlier, it is this section which makes it an offence to pass unauthorised information. The all-embracing nature of these provisions are so restrictive in theory as to make government unworkable. The Public Records Act of 1958 (as amended) stipulates that official information may not be published for at least thirty years. We are almost unique in this country in having such a rule and in many countries it is possible to inspect personal files upon application and to see documents relating to a decision or policy once it has been made. This Act, then, helps to keep a prying public (not to mention academia) at bay.

(c) *Parliament*   Many of our parliamentary arrangements also constitute a force for secrecy. At the heart of this is the party system itself. The divisions of government and opposition and the attendant constraints of party discipline and the management of the party game have tended to provide obstructions to those seeking information. The fact, for example, that no incoming government may see the papers relating to its predecessors is characteristic. But this is also reflected in parliamentary questions which many textbooks refer to as a cornerstone of Parliament's ability to scrutinise the Government. Yet this function is constrained by the sets of questions which ministers can refuse to answer. Some of these are very properly not dealt with as they relate to matters of security, the confidentiality of individuals, or areas outside the minister's direct responsibility (e.g. the activities of nationalised industries or local government). It is not difficult, however, to see how such definitions might be stretched so as to prevent unfavourable revelations. Indeed, so secretive was this tendency that it was not until the late 1970s that the Speaker allowed an MP even to ask about the sorts of questions which a minister could refuse to answer!

Another constraint here, of course, is the inadequacy of a political and parliamentary system which neither attracts the most talented and informed members of the community nor provides them with the facilities once elected for gaining information on their own account. This is underwritten by a part-time ethic amongst many MPs and reinforced in much of the regular cycle of parliamentary business. MPs are thus dependent on the government for information.

(d) *The mass media*   In general, relations between the Government of the day and the mass media are controlled by the various press officers in the departments and especially that of No. 10, Downing Street. But of special note here is the 'D' (for defence) Notice Committee. This comprises journalists and civil servants and represents an instrument for the voluntary censorship in the media of defence matters.

Each notice suggests whether or not the media may publish matters relating to the issue in question. It is described by those who have researched the area as working tolerably well. If it did not exist legislation would certainly takes its place. Nevertheless, in so far as the Press accepts the guidelines laid down it represents an unaccountable force against disclosure and in favour of secrecy.

In other areas the media is almost totally dependent on the lobby. This is essentially a system of government handouts supported by unattributable briefings by press officers, the secrecy of which is probably unmatched in the Western world.

(*e*) *Civil service*   It is also true that the organisational development of the civil service, i.e. its hierarchical tendencies, division of tasks, rules and procedures, helps to induce a bureaucratic organisation and mind which are both structurally and attitudinally unsympathetic to openness.

(*f*) *Wider cultural forces*   Perhaps this attitude in the civil service reflects more general cultural traits in our society. Even if it is now rather old-fashioned to speak of a deferential political culture in this country, it is still perhaps true that we have a tendency to be trustful of government and that our political institutions and practices are built on an assumption of trust. Nevertheless, this can support a relative invisibility and inaccountability of government, a world of private and secretive government.

Forces for openness
All the above illustrations have been drawn rather starkly in order to clarify the tendencies at work. That the reality is more ambiguous, however, is indicated by the fact that each of the above features of our constitution and practice can also act as a force for openness.

(*d*) *The unwritten constitution*   As we saw earlier, a responsible government is a responsive government, i.e. responsive to the demands and interests of the public. It can demonstrate its responsiveness only by informing the people what it is doing and how. Thus it provides data about houses built, people unemployed, money spent, and so on. But this provision of information is also a facet of accountable government in the sense that it is part of the obligation to give an account (see chapter 3 on ministerial accountability). Similarly, in order to show that they have not been arbitrary, governments are obliged to bring groups into the decision-making processes such as in enquiries and other participatory mechanisms. In short, the government can open itself up as part of the process of displaying its responsibility.

(*b*) *Statutes*   Even the legislation which we have seen as a force for secrecy can work two ways; law is only effective if it is enforced. In the case of the Official Secrets Act of 1911, we may have been witnessing (notwithstanding recent prosecutions) the passing of Section II into the dignified (rather than effective) parts of the constitution. Even the most recent cases suggest how much depends on the desire of ministers to want to apply it. In addition, some of the provisions of relevant legislation can be used for openness. The Public Records Act, for example, contains an important discretionary provision (Section V) whereby the Lord Chancellor may extend or *shorten* the thirty year rule.

(*c*) *Parliament*   Changes in parliament have also had their effects. The break-up of the two-party system has given rise to an increasingly numerous band of MPs unwilling to accept the old order of things as arranged by the two front benches. The new select committee system has also provided an opportunity for MPs to dig out the information they need as well as to specialise and become more expert in chosen fields of policy. There are signs too that a number of MPs have established their own networks of contacts within the civil service and other public organisations which can provide them with useful ammunition on such committees. In short, there is evidence of a new professionalisation of MPs which, whatever its drawbacks, will act as a force for openness.

(*d*) *Mass media*   These MPs' activities have been much supported by the development of investigatory journalism and the public's interest in it. This is a field made notable by the *Sunday Times* Insight Team but now more widespread. Granada television has also over the years gained a similar reputation from its early series of *The State of the Nation* and *Decision* to its use of 'hypotheticals' to simulate government activities in particular contexts. Perhaps this development falls behind that in other countries such as the USA but it is nevertheless contributing to the opening up of government.

(*e*) *Civil service* Both the MPs and the journalists now enjoy closer links with the civil service. This has been an area of important developments, from provisions in the Establishment Officer's Guide (the civil service 'bible' on conduct) and the Croham Directive of 1977 which encourages the publication of background papers, to the development of consultative Green Papers on government thinking, and the in some ways more substantial developments in the experience and attitudes of more recent generations of civil servants. The latter are now less anonymous both in public and parliamentary contexts and have been brought up administratively in a time of greater experience of the more open ways of the European Economic Community and other supranational organisations. It has also been observed that the civil service is increasingly less prepared to accept the secrecy of a government which itself so publicly criticises the administrative machine on which it depends.

(*f*) *Wider cultural forces* If this last point suggests a rising anti-authoritarianism, this reflects a changing attitude to government in the country as a whole. Some have 'blamed' this on the educational system, others on an increasing affluence and therefore independence generally. Whatever the cause, there does appear to be less willingness to accept what governments say at face value. The sagas of the Belgrano and Westland affairs are perhaps indicative here.

Problems in the pursuit of openness

It is with these forces for openness that successive campaigns for greater freedom of information have been launched to promote the sort of objectives cited earlier. Yet each campaign has faced four sets of practical problems which it has been obliged to resolve.

(1) *The subject matter of disclosure*
What to exempt from disclosure presents problems not so much in the matter of *real* secrets (matters of genuine national security) as in drawing the line in a feasible way between what is to be disclosed and what protected.

(2) *Decisions about disclosure*
The fuzziness of the dividing line may mean that we have to depend on some agency or other to decide whether matters should be disclosed

on their merits. This is liable to rest finally with ministers. The problem then would lie with the clash between their own and the public interest. As a result some have suggested a kind of ombudsman for secrets to check up on ministerial decisions.

(3) *The form of disclosure*

The simple availability of files, even if this were feasible, would be helpful to few other than those familiar with the workings of the system. Perhaps, therefore, special documents should be prepared. The problem is who by and at what cost. Many doubt the value of such an exercise.

(4) *Effects of disclosure*

Some fear that the consequences of greater disclosure would be a distortion of the democratic process as, for example, institutions with the resources necessary for capitalising on the opportunities of greater openness came to wield greater influence.

These are not inconsiderable problems; often they raise fundamental questions about the nature of our political system.

Conclusion

The issues in government secrecy and openness are many and varied, the objectives and beneficiaries sometimes conflicting and the problems faced by reform difficult to resolve. Des Wilson, the founder of the 1984 Campaign for Freedom of Information, was confident that it would lead to a successful repeal of Section II of the 1911 Official Secrets Act as a committee chaired by Lord Franks recommended as long ago as 1972. The movement assembled such respected figures behind it that *The Economist* was moved to ask 'could the idea be turning respectable?' (1984). Recent events such as those during the Westland affair have confirmed that it is not only the legal but also the administrative arrangements which need to be sorted out. Public opinion appears to favour reform. A MORI opinion poll in July 1986 found that over 65% supported a Freedom of Information Act subject to safeguards for national security and personal confidentiality. Nevertheless, with Mrs Thatcher still totally unsympathetic to liberalisation, *The Economist*'s conclusion, that 'for the present there is little hope of a Tory government accepting freedom of information in any guise', is justified. The question remains whether another government would be prepared to tackle reform.

Reading

A. H. Birch, *Representative and Responsible Government*, Allen & Unwin, 1964. (Good on the constitutional context.)

The Economist, 'It's a free country − isn't it?', 10 March 1984, p. 31.

J. Lynn and A. Jay, 'Open Government', Ch. 1 of *Yes Minister*, Vol. 1, BBC 1981.

C. Seymour-Ure, 'Great Britain', in I. Galnoor (ed.), *Government Secrecy in Democracies*, New York University Press, 1977. (A good general account sympathetic to the approach adopted here.)

R. Wraith, *Open Government: the British Interpretation*, RIPA, 1977. (A history of the subject.)

The individual accountability of ministers

When a small group of Argentinian scrap metal workers landed on the tiny island of South Georgia in March 1982 they set off a chain of events which, following their country's invasion of the Falkland Islands on 2 April, led eventually to the resignation of Lord Carrington, the British Foreign Secretary. Then in January 1986 Mr Leon Brittan, Secretary of State for Industry, resigned over his part in the Westland affair, in particular the unofficial disclosure of a confidential letter from the Solicitor General to the Secretary of State for Defence, Mr Michael Heseltine. For many, these cases have shown that the principle of ministerial accountability, that for every policy or action of a department its minister is accountable, answerable and if necessary culpable, is still alive and well in the British constitution. After a gap of nearly thirty years ministers have accepted the ultimate responsibility for the policy and conduct of their department.

Is such an interpretation justified? This chapter will attempt to answer this not only by reference to the circumstances of these cases but of others of the past few decades and by setting them into an analysis of what accountability is and how it is exercised. This will involve an examination of *stewardship*, which is at the heart of accountability, and the different *codes* which govern its form and content. We will also explore the way *accounts* are presented, noting a distinction between judicial and theatrical settings. All these considerations will be important for our understanding of what has been going on.

The story so far

Carrington and the Falklands

Before their departure on Sunday 28 March 1982 for an EEC meeting in Brussels, the Foreign Secretary (Lord Carrington), and the Prime Minister considered intelligence reports of Argentinian forces who were threatening the security of the British Falkland Islands in the South Atlantic. The next day saw the Prime Minister herself order three nuclear-powered submarines to the region. By Thursday, when Lord Carrington returned from Tel Aviv (whence he had flown after Brussels), all who were privy to these discussions knew they could do nothing to prevent what Carrington later called a 'humiliating affront to this country', the Argentinian invasion of the Falklands.

During the evening of Friday 2 April, Carrington and John Nott (Minister of Defence) gave a press conference and confirmed what most of the world already had gathered, that the invasion had taken place and that the Argentinian forces were secure. The full Cabinet then met and implemented the contingency plans, including the launching of the counter-invasion task force. Richard Luce suggested to Carrington that as junior minister responsible for the negotiations with the Argentine government he should resign. But Carrington played it down. On the following day, in a unique Saturday session of Parliament, Nott took a pounding in the Commons. With Carrington in the Lords, Nott was the obvious target for the vengeance seekers who promptly made the most of his inept performance. He had previously offered his own resignation but the Prime Minister had rejected it on the grounds that it had not been *his* department's responsibility.

Perhaps unwittingly, the Prime Minister had thereby pointed the finger at the Foreign Secretary. This and his absence from the Commons appeared to persuade Carrington that it was he who should go. To his surprise, Carrington found the Prime Minister exerting great pressure on him to stay. But the Press was hostile over the weekend and not even the counsels of former premiers Home and Macmillan could prevail: Carrington resigned and with him his deputy, Humphrey Atkins, and his junior minister, Luce.

Brittan and the Westland affair

On 13 and 14 December 1985 the Board of Directors of Westland plc resolved to reject a financial rescue package from a consortium of European companies and to accept that from the American Sikorsky

Company. Despite Mr Heseltine's recorded protest at the 12 December Cabinet meeting, Mrs Thatcher must have hoped that this was the end of the matter as far as the government was concerned. Yet within a month or so two of her colleagues had resigned and her own position was as much under threat as at any time in her premiership.

That the issue would not lie down was much the result of Mr Heseltine's determined and unusually public lobbying on behalf of the European Consortium. In the end, he walked out of the Cabinet on 9 January, unable to accept a collective responsibility for the decision-making process and its outcome. Thus far, the main issue was therefore that of collective responsibility.

Yet even as Mr Heseltine resigned, Mr Brittan's department, Trade and Industry, was under suspicion for having leaked to the Press Association selected passages from a letter written by the Solicitor General, a government law officer, to Mr Heseltine which referred to 'material inaccuracies' in the latter's own communications to Lloyds Bank, the European Consortium's bankers. After two presentations to the House of Commons by Mr Brittan of accounts of this and related handling of the case which were not only unacceptable to the Opposition parties but also to large numbers of his own back-benchers, Mr Brittan resigned. Thus, at this stage, an affair which had begun as important for collective responsibility became significant for individual ministerial accountability.

This however was not the end of the affair for it became clear that the Prime Minister's press officer, private office and the Cabinet Secretary had been involved in the decision to disclose the Solicitor General's letter. The subsequent accounts both to the House of Commons itself and its Select Committee for Defence suggested first a certain lack of co-ordination between the Department and the centre over the decision and second evidence of collusion in concealing the real state of affairs from the House of Commons and the wider public. The latter included the most dead-bat performance from the Cabinet Secretary that one is likely to witness from an official and the non-appearance before the Committee of the Prime Minister's press officer and other officials involved in the disclosure decision. Thus a third issue arose, that of Parliament's right to examine civil servants.

The story is full of paradoxes. Mr Brittan resigned probably only because first, he was found to have improperly disclosed a law officer's letter and second, he gave such inadequate accounts to the House. If the matter had remained a strictly internal departmental error, history suggests he would have been able to pass responsibility down the hierarchy. Mrs Thatcher's misjudgements do seem to have been protected by deflecting responsibility to members of her private office while she protected them from the Select Committee.

Hoare and Abyssinia

The above reference to historical precedents suggests the value of an appreciation of the way the principles involved have developed. As we saw earlier, many have found in the Carrington and Brittan resignations the restoration of the principle that for every policy or action of a department the minister is responsible and if necessary culpable. The previous occasion when a Foreign Secretary had resigned in similar circumstances to those of Lord Carrington had been in 1935 when Sam Hoare, after secretly negotiating a deal with the French relating to the fate of Abyssinia, returned to find that the details had been leaked and there was a press outcry over them. The Cabinet felt the need to disassociate itself from the deal and Hoare resigned.

Dugdale and Crichel Down

Of course, the previous occasion on which *any* minister resigned over the policy or actions of his department was in 1954 in the case of Crichel Down. Then, Sir Thomas Dugdale, Minister of Agriculture, found himself the inheritor of a long-running saga involving a number of departments and relating to some private land which had been compulsorily purchased for war department needs in the Second World War and which the original owner had found difficult to buy back, despite assurances to the contrary. A subsequent committee of enquiry found negligence on the part of Agriculture officials and Dugdale resigned on the grounds that 'I, as Minister, must accept full responsibility to Parliament for any mistakes and inefficiency of officials in my Department'.

Amery and Ferranti

However, apart from a few who have resigned over their personal misconduct (one of the latest of whom was Cecil Parkinson in 1983), ministers have not been exactly leaping over themselves to follow Dugdale's example. In 1964, for example, Julian Amery did not resign as Minister of Aviation over the excess profits which were later discovered to have been made by the Ferranti company from contracts with the Ministry to make the Bloodhound missile. Amery's defence was that the fault lay with cost accountants and not with himself. This was accepted by a hard-pressed government of the day and the large Conservative majority in the House of Commons.

Davies and Vehicle & General

A similar case arose in the 1971 Vehicle and General affair. The V&G was an insurance company which had struggled with liquidity problems for a decade. Under the Insurance Acts the Department of Trade and Industry (the successor in these matters to the Board of Trade) had the discretionary powers to intervene in a company's affairs if it had reason to doubt the company's solvency. When the V & G was suddenly and compulsorily wound up in March 1971 there was a good deal of outcry over the conduct of the Department in leaving stranded so many members of the public, a situation which the Acts were designed specifically to prevent.

The Tribunal of Enquiry which followed named and blamed certain officials, in particular the under-secretary whose division was directly responsible for monitoring the affairs of such companies. The tribunal reported negligence and incompetence in the handling of the V&G case. Ministers, however, remained unmentioned; indeed, they were not even asked to give evidence. And when the Secretary of State, John Davies, made a statement to the House on the tribunal's report he made no comments about his own or his colleagues' positions. Mr Davies had joined the government in 1970, after serving as Director-General of the Confederation of British Industry. He was an inexperienced politician with a huge and complex department to control. Nevertheless, the question of his resignation was barely touched on in the whole affair.

Callaghan and devaluation

The closest parallel in recent years with the Falklands case, however, was the devaluation crisis of 1967. On this occasion James Callaghan had been Chancellor of the Exchequer since the Labour victory of 1964. The economy had been in some difficulty throughout this time eventually leading to a run on the pound sterling from the summer of 1966. (In those days governments took the protection of the value of the pound much more seriously than they do today.) When the government was in the end obliged to devalue the pound in 1967, Callaghan's personal policy was defeated and he immediately offered his resignation to the Prime Minister, Harold Wilson. Wilson, however, felt that at such a time it was important for the government to stick together. Callaghan therefore stayed on to introduce the package of measures designed to help the devaluation achieve its desired effects but later that year, in a minor Cabinet reshuffle, he changed places with Roy Jenkins at the Home Office.

What can be made of these stories? On the one hand there is the principle of ministerial accountability so clearly stated and (admirably?) followed by Dugdale; on the other is the trend of later cases which supports Lord Hunt's evidence to the Expenditure Committee of the House of Commons in 1977 when he was Secretary to the Cabinet: 'The concept that because somebody whom the Minister has never heard of, has made a mistake, means that the Minister should resign, is out of date, and rightly so.' Although much has been written about accountability, including these cases, there have been very few attempts to *understand* what accountability is and how it is exercised. In the remainder of this chapter, we will attempt to do this by setting these incidents into an analysis of accountability.

Ministerial accountability and stewardship

Definitions

(1) *To be accountable* is to be liable to present an account of and answer for the discharge of responsibilities to the person or group entrusting those responsibilities. Thus, at the heart of accountability is stewardship.

(2) *Stewardship* is a relationship where one party is entrusted with the property and/or resources of another.

(3) *There are three parties involved* in stewardship and accountability.

(a) *The steward* (or accountor) is the party to whom the responsibilities are entrusted and who is obliged to give an account of their execution.

(b) *The principal* (or accountee) is the party entrusting those responsibilities and to whom the account is presented.

(c) *The code* (or set of codes) is the collection of understandings that govern the content and conduct of these responsibilities as well as the manner in which the account shall be presented.

A minister is thus a steward in the way he is responsible to parliament (the principal) for the discharge of his duties and for presenting an account of this. In turn civil servants are stewards in the way they are responsible for accounting to ministers for their duties. This idea of ministers and civil servants as stewards is a very old one in British government. In the Middle Ages, for example, sheriffs were the king's stewards responsible for, among other things, the collection of revenues. They were held accountable when they were summoned to appear before the king's commissioners (the Exchequer). If they satisfied the Exchequer as to their activities on the king's behalf they were literally 'discharged'. Much more recently, Mrs Thatcher's government has sought to enhance the accountability of the civil service. Since 1982 the Financial Management Initiative (FMI) has been trying to install a system of accountable management whereby civil servants are made responsible for more clearly defined resources and operations. In the way that the FMI is dealing with the content and conduct of stewardship it represents a new code of accountability.

Codes of accountability

These codes are often overlooked in traditional discussions of accountability mainly because they are not obvious, unlike ministers and civil servants. But they are important, for they define the nature of the relationship between (say) parliament and minister, minister and civil servant, the content and manner of the execution of the responsibilities, and the terms in which the account is presented and evaluated. Further, they give rise to what some refer to as different types of accountability, i.e. political, legal or financial. But there are many different codes at work.

(1) *Specific codes* are those designed to relate to a specific relationship.

(2) *General codes* are those which already exist (e.g. professional codes of conduct) and are applied to a general set of relationships between stewards and principals.

(3) *Outcome codes* refer to the expectations principals have about the results of the stewardship.

(4) *Process codes* refer to the methods by which these outcomes are to be achieved.

(5) *Symbolic codes* are those which stewards and even principals might acknowledge but which have no practical effect on the conduct of the stewardship even if they are alluded to in the account itself.

(6) *Substantive codes*, on the other hand, often have a direct practical effect in the way that they seek to promote in the execution

of responsibilities a particular style of reasoning in the decisions taken, for example economic, social or legal reasoning.

You will notice that these types of code appear here as contrasting pairs. This is deliberate. Of the first pair there is a tendency in ministerial accountability for *general* codes to predominate over specific ones. One of the features of our relatively unwritten constitution is that the responsibilities of ministers are rarely made explicit; rather they are based on the development of practice in often widely differing fields and contexts of government. The ambiguities which arise may allow an individual minister to escape censure because principals may be unclear in the end as to what the steward was actually entrusted with (see the cases of Amery and Davies above).

Of the second pairing there has been an emphasis on *process* codes rather than those relating to outcomes of accountability. Thus concepts such as due process and equity of treatment are stressed in the conduct of government as much as its results. At one point in the saga of the Government and the General Communications Headquarters (GCHQ) the courts found that the Government had neglected due process by not adequately consulting the trade unions involved. Similarly, in the accounts which departments present to Parliament about public expenditure more attention has been paid in their evaluation to what is called *regularity* (whether what has been spent has been so authorised) as to the effectiveness or efficiency of that expenditure.

Reference to *symbolic* codes draws attention to the whole doctrine of ministerial responsibility itself, for many have commented that it is a myth. Parliament, ministers and civil servants may all symbolically acknowledge it but it has little practical effect on these stewards and principals either in the execution of responsibilities or in the adjudication of accounts. On the other hand, there clearly are codes which do affect accountability in the way that they encourage decisions and actions embodying certain types of reasoning (such as complying with the law or making greater use of financial resources).

Stages of accountability

For analytical purposes we can see accountability as passing through several stages.

(1) *The establishment of stewardship* arises when one party entrusts the other with resources and/or responsibilities. Almost certainly, the steward takes on this trusteeship in return for some reward. In this

way accountability can impose a reciprocal obligation upon the principal.

(2) *The execution of the trusteeship*, whether this be the guardianship of public assets, the use of such assets for some mutual gain, or the performance of general or specific duties, is followed by:

(3) *The presentation of the account* and its examination in accordance with the codes by which the stewardship was struck.

(4) *The adjudication of the account* confirms, modifies or terminates the stewardship.

These stages thus constitute the *cycle of accountability* and are repeated for each stewardship struck in turn by a steward with substewards (as between ministers and civil servants). They show how the obligation to give an account arises and how the account may be examined with a view to establishing responsibility for desired and undesired outcomes and activities. The trouble with ministerial accountability, of course, is that these stages are not so neatly distinct, so that not only may the terms of the minister's responsibilities (the codes) be unclear to both parties (Parliament and minister) but the occasion when they are laid down is most uncertain. The moment when a minister accepts his trusteeship, for example, is formally when he receives his seals of office from the monarch; parliament is only remotely involved. Further, these ambiguities may be exploited in the presentation of ministers' accounts.

The presentation of the account

This stage of accountability may be regarded in at least two ways:

(1) as a *quasi-judicial process* in which the account is presented and examined as evidence might be in a court of law; and

(2) as a *dramatic performance* in which the account is presented and examined as a script or play in a theatre.

Originally, the process of accountability in government *was* judicial: sheriffs, for example, were charged and (all being well) discharged in a king's court. In the passage from the courtroom to other arenas, however, the possibilities for theatrical performance (already present in the courtroom) multiplied. Thus ministers presenting their accounts to parliament may be seen as actors in the way, for example, they rehearse their scripts in order to prevent any embarrassing and revealing incidents. Similarly, parliament (as the audience) adopts devices to help the minister sustain his performance such as signals of appreciation during and at the close of the performance, warnings when it is less happy with the performance and wants it altered in some way, and the disregarding of errors or obvious acceptance of ministers' explanations. In short, there may be a collusion between minister and parliament (steward and principal) more appropriate to theatrical than judicial settings.

Such a view of ministerial accountability may help to explain why so many ministers appear to escape censure. One of the reasons for the collusion we have identified is that the style of parliament is more appropriate to some of its functions (e.g. debating and legislating) than to others (holding the executive to account). It may also be, of course, that parliament has come to be filled by those who *wish* to collude (at least in this arena). Perhaps this also explains why the various reforms in this area, e.g. ombudsmen, select committees and tribunals, have all been attempts to get backstage to break down the performance.

The changing accountability of ministers

So far in this chapter we have seen from the selected illustrations that ministerial accountability has been changing. We have also observed from our analysis of how accountability is established and maintained that it is not as straightforward as many have supposed. From these discussions it is now possible to draw some conclusions about our definition of ministerial accountability, its changing form and content, and the different arenas in which it is now discharged.

Ministerial accountability

In speaking of this we have been referring to the individual responsibility of ministers for the policy and conduct of themselves as ministers and of their departments (and not, therefore, for their actions as private individuals however much these may affect their suitability for office, nor for their share of the collective responsibility of the government as a whole).

The form and content of ministerial accountability

The character of ministerial responsibilities has changed over the years as different *codes of accountability* have come to be adopted and discarded. Traditionally, three substantive codes characterised the responsibilities:

(a) *Financial* codes originally stipulated that ministers (or the monarch's servants) were responsible for using financial resources in the way authorised by king and parliament. More recently, economic constraints have extended these codes to encompass a responsibility for the effectiveness and efficiency of the expenditure as well.

(b) *Legal* codes have for centuries subjected ministers to the rule of law (even if they have sometimes been in a handy position to say what it is) and thereby charged them to act both within their powers and in the way stipulated. An important characteristic of such codes was the anonymity of departmental officials when acting on behalf of the department.

(c) *Political* codes came to be important when parliament and the electorate replaced the monarch as the source of ministerial patronage. Ministers' policies and actions came to require the general support of colleagues and parliament and ministers remained in office only so long as this support was maintained. This too implied an anonymity of the ministers' officials.

While these codes (or types) of accountability have continued to be significant, ministerial accountability has more recently been affected by the rise of different codes, both administrative and professional.

(d) *Administrative* codes have bestowed a public responsibility and accountability on *officials* for their activities on behalf of ministers and their departments. Thus civil servants are increasingly obliged to account before all sorts of bodies (as in the cases of Crichel Down, Ferranti, and Vehicle & General above). Thus this administrative accountability has weakened the anonymity of officials. Further, there has been the development of a process for allocating administrative responsbilities (for example, for finance and operations) in a specific way. This process is sometimes referred to as *accountable management* and is at the heart of the Conservative government's Financial Management Initiative. Together, these two aspects of administrative acountability have made officials more publicly accountable for more precise sets of responsibilities.

(e) *Professional* codes have developed in government as its activities have become both more specialised in themselves and required the practice of professions to undertake them. The incorporation of groups of professions such as doctors, lawyers and, more recently, accountants imports sets of codes developed originally outside government and without recognition of its requirements (including the judgement of electors as opposed to fellow professionals).

The effect of these two sets of codes has been to lessen the direct responsibility of ministers for detailed work in their departments, though not for its general conduct and oversight.

The arenas in which accountability is discharged

Traditionally, there have been only two arenas in which ministers have been obliged to give accounts directly: parliament and the courts. The latter remain significant. However, as the political (and especially governing) parties have come to dominate the membership and conduct of parliament so the theatrical tendency of this arena has been intensified. Reformers have, therefore, sought to subject ministers and departments to alternative arenas in which the latter have less control. The development of the select committee system and the use of the tribunal of enquiry provides evidence of this, as does the rise of the institution of ombudsman. We may call these arenas *quasi-judicial* for the way they seek to subject accounts to a more judicial type of scrutiny. But their enhancement of more detailed examination paradoxically allows for more detailed specification of the responsibility of *officials* rather than of ministers.

Conclusions

Ministerial accountability is a complex process involving a complex set of relationships. There have been changes to the form and content of this accountability and to the arenas in which it is discharged. As a result, and despite the two cases described at the beginning of this chapter, the principle that for every policy or action of a department a minister must answer has been replaced by a practice which limits this responsibility.

Reading

You will find sections on ministerial accountability in almost any textbook on British government. They will contrast with the way the issues are presented here. The ideas are developed in more detail in:
A. G. Gray & W. I. Jenkins, *Administrative Politics in British Government*, Wheatsheaf, 1985, chapter 6.

Town Hall versus Whitehall

The traditional tension between central and local government reached an unprecedented pitch of intensity under the Thatcher government. This chapter examines the idea of local democracy, the constitutional perspective, local government finance and the abolition of the metropolitan counties.

Background

Local democracy

Democratically elected local representatives have the responsibility of controlling local government. The benefits are:

(i) Participation − by the people in their own governance. As a by-product they become educated about the process.

(ii) Responsiveness to local needs by local representatives who will control the administration and frame policies accordingly.

(iii) A training ground is created for those who wish to enter national politics.

(iv) Political parties are able to test candidates, policies and their own procedures and maintain morale and effectiveness between general elections.

Advocates of local autonomy, such as the council associations, the Alliance parties and other opponents of centralising policies usually refer to the threat to the first two factors.

Critique

This ideal model is cast into doubt by:

(i) the low turnout in local elections − often below 30%;

(ii) the incursion of party politics and the salience of national issues in local elections. In June 1986 the Widdicombe inquiry said that politics could be a 'malign influence' leading to a distribution of spoils. It recommended a larger role for the ombudsman and Audit Commission, party balance on committees, a register of councillors' interests, national party rules and no officials to be politically affiliated above principal officer.

(iii) the lack of accountability for spending decisions. Only a third of voters pay full domestic rates, which in turn contribute less than a quarter of local income — business rates and government grant make up the rest.

This last factor was used strongly by the business community and the Conservative government as the premise for further control over waste and deliberate irresponsibility.

(iv) the secrecy in decision-making. Following a court case against Hackney Council in 1984 the government supported a Freedom of Information bill in 1985 (though critics pointed to the retention of secrecy in Whitehall).

Agents of central government

(i) *the constitutional relationship* Local authorities require statutory authorisation, through public, private or adoptive Acts of Parliament, provisional orders or statutory instruments, for all that they do. If they exceed their powers, they can be judged *ultra vires*, and sued in the courts. This judicial control was exercised against the GLC fares policy reviewed later.

Government, through parliament, has the power to remove powers or even abolish a tier of government — as it did in Northern Ireland. In a unitary state it has to be accepted that national policy prevails. Local government has suffered a steady erosion of its influence, as energy provision, water, health and some education functions were transferred to *ad hoc* agencies, public corporations or central government. Indeed in 1982 it was suggested that a separate block grant would remove the control of education to central government completely. This can become a self-fulfilling prophecy — in 1983 the GLC's loss of water, ambulance services, housing planning and transport were cited as reasons for its abolition, its role having diminished so much.

(ii) *Uniformity of services* Public demand for a relatively equal level of services, and concern that one authority should not disadvantage its neighbours all foster central intervention. The 1975 Layfield Committee had prophetically explained the logic − if more government control was exerted, it would have to ensure equity and to do that more detailed intervention would follow.

(iii) *Finance* Government have varied the proportion of specific grants to services and block grants, but the overall position is clear − even after government cutbacks they were still providing 53% of council spending in 1983−4. The Layfield Committee had wanted to align responsibilities for decision-making and fund-raising − that central government should assume control directly or local authorities be allowed to raise a local income tax (LIT). But in addition to the technical problems of change it is politically convenient for both sides that responsibility and blame cannot be clearly apportioned.

Dialogue

The truth lies somewhere in between. Councils are clearly not autonomous, nor can a partnership exist when the power, including dissolution, is on one side. But neither are local authorities mere agents:

   (i) There are policy differences and local initiatives are possible.

   (ii) It is significant which party is in power − government circulars have been ignored, and policies delayed − on comprehensive schools, council house sales and rate levels.

   (iii) Government grants allow different patterns of allocation.

   (iv) Since reorganisation in 1972, attempts have been made to loosen controls over the appointment of officers, auditors, over planning authority and entertainments (300 controls were scrapped in 1979 and legislation passed in 1981).

   (v) Though the Department of the Environment is of central importance, there is no single ministry for local government. Different departments, themselves interest groups, deal with councils collectively or individually. The process of consultation and bargaining was institutionalised in 1975 when a Consultative Council was created. And through their Associations the councils can command media attention.

   (vi) *Rates* This independent source of revenue brings councils over £5 billion each year. It has been heavily criticised as a regressive tax, falling heavily on businesses and bearing no relation to services used. But it is a simple system and neither the Conservative Green Paper of

1971, nor that of 1981 could find a viable alternative. Sales tax, poll tax or local income tax would be evaded, resented or incur expense and none would improve accountability to electors. The 1974 Conservative pledge to abolish rates was therefore dropped, to the delight of Labour who adopted it as their own in 1981 in favour of LIT.

The balance upset?

It was contended that the Conservative government upset this balanced relationship in favour of ever-tightening control because its priorities, controlling public expenditure and unburdening industry, so dictated. The case of one interest group – the business community – was accepted, i.e. that rates increased costs, destroyed jobs and recovery. They pressed for rate-capping, compulsory consultation on rate levels and abolition of rates on empty buildings – all of which were incorporated into the 1983 Rates Bill. The process described later of Whitehall calculating individual councils' spending needs by service items and imposing rate limits and penalties was too extreme for many Conservatives.

Process

(i) *Spending crisis 1974–6*

By 1975 there were fears that local government spending was out of control; it was consuming 16% of Britain's gross domestic product, with an overspend of 5.4%. This was a function of:

(*a*) Reorganisation: in reducing 1390 English and Welsh councils to 422, staffing had risen by 4.7% or 100,000 people. Larger populations helped to increase salaries and costs as did the duplication of functions.

(*b*) Demand: intentions to provide better services, developed in the 1960s, led to increased staffing e.g. 500,000 more in education in a decade.

(*c*) Inflation: salaries grew to be 60% of local spending with many groups being made 'special cases'.

(*d*) Government requirements: e.g. in 1973, 64 new Acts and 2229 ministerial orders required action. (*Sunday Times*, 23 February 1975)

In 1974–5 rates rose 30% on average and as high as 138%, as rate-payers' organisations complained of town hall overstaffing and incompetence and challenged the rises in court. As Britain approached a financial crisis, Secretary of State, Anthony Crosland, declared that 'the party' was over.

48 *Institutional issues*

(ii) *Stabilisation 1976–9*

By 1976–7 there was a 1.8% underspend, and NALGO and NUPE produced a booklet 'Breakdown – the crisis in your public services'. The 1978 Public Expenditure White Paper allowed for modest 2% to 5.5% growth.

(iii) *Retrenchment 1979–83*

The economic policy of the Conservative government elected in May 1979 was based on the premise that expansion would be facilitated by reducing public expenditure, of which local government claimed a quarter.

(*a*) Cutback: in the June 1979 budget, local authorities were told to reduce spending by £360 million in addition to an overbudgeted £450 million – a 7% cut in nine months. The reaction to this first collision was more vociferous than during later, more fundamental confrontations – the Institute of Municipal Engineers asserted that sewage could swill through the streets and NALGO promised strike action against redundancies.

(*b*) Rate Support Grant: the 1979 RSG settlement was supposed to cover 61% of spending, but it was said to be a reduction to 58%.

(*c*) Hit list: the first list of 'overspending councils' was produced to pressurise them.

(*c*) Legislation: the Local Government Planning and Land Act 1980 altered the whole framework of financial support by replacing the old RSG formula with a block grant calculated on Grant Related Expenditure (GRE).

(*e*) Holdback: in 1981 local authorities were deprived of £300 million to ensure government monetarist targets were achieved and it threatened to hold back £450 million more unless cuts were made.

The Association of Metropolitan Authorities (AMA) thought compliance would cost 150,000 jobs. The government, however, had already declared the 2% cut in manpower over the previous year to be insufficient.

(*f*) Rate referenda: encouraged by the example of Coventry City Council's referendum in August 1981, when electors chose cuts rather than rate increases, the government moved to establish such a process nationally. Pressure from Conservative peers, backbenchers and councillors forced its abandonment, but

(*g*) The Local Government Finance Act 1982 banned supplementary rates and increased the grant withdrawal powers of government.

The atmosphere was one of uncertainty; there were discrepancies between disciplinary and GRE targets, pay awards increased cuts beyond planned percentages, and the Treasury based its 1982 plans on only cash figures − implying 7% cuts and 120,000 lost jobs.

Confrontation

(*a*) Legal: the right of government to send in agents to sell Norwich City Council's housing went to the High Court where the 'bullying' powers were criticised and both Strathclyde Regional Council and the London Borough of Hackney took ministers to court for withholding grants.

(*b*) Propaganda: by 1982 the AMA was conducting a £½ million advertising campaign and interest groups were using official reports detailing the damage done to services. The government responded by stretching the powers of the new 1982 Act to compel publication of spending league tables to embarrass the 'profligate'.

(iv) *The second attempt 1983−6*

The process described above did not satisfy the government whose targets had been exceeded every year, with a total overspend in 1983−4 of £770 million. The overall expenditure figures, they conceded, concealed the massive rise in current spending given a 50% decrease in capital expenditure between 1978−9 and 1982−3. While local authorities managed a 4% reduction in their 2½ million total manpower from June 1979 to March 1983, this trend had reversed. Noting that three-quarters of the overspending was incurred by sixteen authorities, the 1983 Conservative manifesto promised to legislate to control them and introduce a general scheme.

The Scottish example

The Scottish Office, since 1929, has had the power to penalise authorities for levying excessive rates. In 1981 this was changed from a retrospective to an immediate response and in 1982 rate-capping was introduced. The main target became the rebellious Lothian Regional Council which had to reduce its rate from 116p to 100p and then to 86p in the pound. These powers and their successes acted as an example and a spur and countered objections that they were incompatible with local government in Britain.

Rate limitation

Following its White Paper in August, the government published its Rates Bill in December 1983. It contained two main elements:

(*a*) A selective power to single out 'extravagant' authorities and control their spending and rate levels.

(*b*) A reserve general power to control the spending of all councils. The government were at pains to point out that this would only be used with the approval of parliament.

Excluded from the selective scheme are district councils spending less than £10 million or below the GRE assessment. The government claimed only twelve to twenty councils would be caught.

Opposition

(*a*) *Conservatives* Some twenty to thirty MPs, backed by Francis Pym, attacked the rate-capping proposals and particularly the general reserve powers as 'dangerous and unconstitutional' (*Sunday Times*, 18 December 1983). The Conservative-controlled Association of District Councils had declared its opposition in June 1983, and doubts were expressed in the House of Lords. But while this coalition had stymied referenda in 1981 and was to embarrass the government again in 1984, on this occasion the manifesto commitment was fulfilled. Conservative shire councils, such as Buckinghamshire and Essex, made no attempt to disguise their anger in July 1984 when cuts were made in their grants for 'overspending'. In 1985 the government eased the system of penalties to remove the pressure from 'low spending' shires, but encountered fury in 1986 for moving £224 million to the inner cities.

(*b*) *Labour 'hit list' councils* Of the 18 councils singled out for rate-capping, only Brent and Portsmouth were Conservative. They were chosen for spending 4% above their 1983–4 target and 20% above GRE assessments. Most were told to make a cut the size of inflation.

In July 1984 the sixteen Labour councils agreed on non-compliance, in refusing to cut jobs or services and boycotting the new derogation procedure of renegotiating their spending limits. Labour's local government conference discussed options which included:

(i) mass resignations;

(ii) illegally refusing to make a rate, to create a crisis for councils and government, by losing interest payments and having to borrow more to pay workers.

(iii) deficit budgeting – making a legal rate and illegally failing to reduce expenditure accordingly.

Councillors pointed to their own mandates, and statutory obligations to provide services. This resistance was endorsed by the Labour NEC and TUC Conference. In September 1984 the AMA set up a £175,000 fighting fund.

Labour councils employed (ii) and some moved to (iii) during 1985, but eventually withdrew their opposition until only Liverpool was left. Despite Mr Jenkin's embarassment in trying to avoid explaining how his figures were calculated, there was never any question of the government conceding. At the same time, no major cuts were made as the limits were set reasonably high initially, and public support was not forthcoming as anticipated, with 3 out of 5 electors opposed to rate-capping (Mori poll, *Sunday Times*, 7 May 1985).

By 1986 the Comptroller and Auditor-General had condemned capital spending controls while he and the Audit Commission had damned the rate support grant system and its effects on the rates and spending. Mr Jenkin had by now resigned, unhappy at being a scapegoat for unpopular legislation, and it was reported that his successor, Mr Baker, did not have much faith in the system. In fact rate-capped authorities accounted for only 8% of the total overspend.

In July 1986 the government added another £1 billion, bringing local authority current account spending to £25.2 billion, while at the same time stopping deferred payment of capital funding, rate-capping another 9 authorities and stopping the aid given to compensate for metropolitan county abolition. By setting realistic targets in line with inflation it was seeking the appearance of 'control', no rate rises to damage Conservative electoral prospects, and to show that any blame for overspending was apportioned to (mainly Labour) councils.

(c) *Liverpool* Labour took control of Liverpool City Council in 1983. It was left with no rate as 'hard' left councillors tried to pass 'no cuts' budgets and confront the government. As Labour made gains in the 1984 elections, the government prepared to take over the council functions with commissioners and surcharge councillors. Instead a package was agreed in July 1984 which involved a 17% rate rise. Labour leaders there claimed a victory and £8 million new money from central government, as assessment with which *The Times*, in its editorial 'Danegeld in Liverpool', disgustedly agreed (11 July 1984). As a result, when the council refused to set a rate in 1985 and then did so at a level that ensured the money would run out, the government did not intervene. The council had to withdraw redundancy notices and the six-month confrontation ended in November as the 31,000 work-force would not support a closure of all but emergency services. By this time Labour councils were reluctant to help after the Liverpool leaders rejected the Stonefrost Report recommendations and Neil Kinnock condemned the 'Tendency tacticians'. By 1986 47 councillors had been surcharged, Militant leaders expelled from the Labour Party and the city, according to the district auditors, was in financial chaos with large financial commitments, poor budgetary control, high costs and overmanning.

Capital spending curbs

To further undermine goodwill, the government announced restrictions on capital spending in July 1984, less than two years after criticising councils for underspending. While avoiding the complete moratorium of 1980, cuts of up to £1 billion were involved. Doubts were raised about the legality of preventing reinvestment of 80% of funds from the sale of council houses and the short-term stop—go treatment of a long-term issue.

In 1981–2 and 1982–3 councils underspent by 17% and 14%, but in the following 3 years they overspent by 15%, 30% and 36% respectively. The Audit Commission severely criticised the DOE's long-winded vetting of capital projects (March 1985).

Statistics in doubt

From the outset a war of figures began as local government leaders in 1979 claimed to have been deliberately misled by government's omission of specific grants from totals. Grants for pay rises were said to be too low and councils on 'hit lists' claimed they were there on bogus figures having earlier been called underspenders. 1981 targets were chosen on national averages related to spending in 1978–9, so arbitrarily some councils faced 20% cuts.

Local government came to believe that the Treasury in particular could not be trusted: in 1981 they were said to be planning a surreptitious cut of £1,500 million by technical changes, and their July 1982 figures were so unrealistic that the cuts were quickly reduced from 7% to 2% (redundancy payments had been forgotten). The GREA target system, based on its fifty-six items of spending needs, was queried in December 1983 when the DOE was forced to release its figures.

One reason for the discrepancies on cuts and grants is that they were based on councils' reporting of spending, and some had disguised the true level by 'creative accounting'.

Most serious was the report of the government-appointed Audit Commission in August 1984 whcih complained of the complexities and uncertainties of the grant system which had caused ratepayers to be charged £1.5 billion more than necessary over three years. Described by Labour as 'dynamite' which discredited the whole basis of government policy, the report advocated three-year grants and no individual targets.

The metropolitan dimension

Discrimination

The retrenchment described above was not uniform in its application, but was more severe upon the metropolitan authorities. The Association of County Councils served notice that they wanted money from the inner cities by a change in the calculation of the needs element of grant when the Conservative government took office in 1979.

The AMA believed that the new block grant formula would be detrimental to its members, and their confidence was not heightened when the county councils were granted concessions to win their support and help the 1980 Bill through the House of Lords. The Labour Party's Environment spokesman mounted a detailed attack on the switching of grants worth £1,445 million from district to county councils. This was said to increase the latters' share from 32% to 53%.

To add insult to what urban Labour councils described as the injury of grant 'gerrymandering', the government proposed to cover only 60% of the costs of the 1981 inner city riots, leaving them to find another £18 million.

Abolition

Background Prior to May 1981 the Labour Party controlled the metropolitan county councils of Tyne and Wear and South Yorkshire. In the elections that month they won West Yorkshire, Greater Manchester, Merseyside, West Midlands and, by a narrow majority, the Greater London Council. Only the Liberal Party consistently demanded abolition of this tier of government during the campaigns. The Conservatives, as their creators and as incumbents, were more disposed to defend their achievements. The Labour Party showed signs of ambivalence; while they saw and wanted the opportunity to take control, many district councillors resented county level interference. On the other hand, at the time of reorganisation in 1970–2 Labour had favoured stronger metropolitan authorities with responsibility for education and social services, and some still advocated incremental or radical restructuring of local government.

After 1981 these councils, and in particular the GLC, emerged as strident opponents of government policy. Two months after taking office Mr Ken Livingstone called for a campaign of disruption in parliament and a general strike to stop legislation designed to curb councils' spending. Pronouncements followed on Northern Ireland, nuclear weapons and unemployment – large banners on County Hall reminded parliament across the river of the number of London unemployed. As Mr Livingstone turned into a major public figure the Conservatives raged against the GLC's grants policy which saw donations to 'Babies Against the Bomb', 'The Southall Black Sisters' and 'The Irish Women's Group' (e.g. *Daily Mail*, 16 February 83).

The first confrontation over the GLC policy came in November 1981 when the Appeal Court ruled that reducing public transport fares by 25% was illegal. In upholding the appeal of the Conservative-controlled Borough of Bromley, the Court decided that the Transport (London) Act 1969 required services to 'break even' and that the GLC had acted in an arbitrary and unreasonable manner. A High Court ruling in February 1982 that this did not apply to metropolitan councils, who could subsidise fares from the rates, was to little avail as government grant penalties forced the abandonment of these manifesto promises.

In January 1983 it was revealed that a Cabinet Committee, MISC 79, had recommended the abolition of the GLC and metropolitan county councils. The Conservative manifesto 1983 described them as 'a wasteful and unnecessary tier of government' and briefly stated that their functions would either be given to districts and boroughs or administered over a wider area by boards of representatives.

The case for   The government's case, in a nutshell, is that the councils did too little and cost too much. It was set out in detail in the White Paper 'Streamlining the Cities' of October 1983.

(*a*) Lack of responsibilities: their three main functions were fire services, police and public transport. In the case of public transport day-to-day management was vested with separate executives, and London Transport was scheduled to obtain autonomy in 1983/4. Residual oversight was also the case with police matters in metropolitan counties and in London responsibility was direct to the Home Secretary. Conflicts between the chief constables of Greater Manchester and Merseyside and their police committees in the aftermath of the 1981 riots led to conflicting claims of political interference and public accountability. The attempt of the GLC to establish its own police committee similarly fuelled the controversy about the role of the councils.

(*b*) Overlapping functions: the failure of the counties to find a strategic role or develop a working relationship with districts in areas such as planning is deemed to have led to confusion, duplicating of work and waste.

(*c*) Overspending: by straying into peripheral or politically mischievous areas, government control of spending has been cast into doubt. The example is cited of the GLC whose current expenditure rose by 185% between 1978–9 to 1983–4 and a 111% rise by the metropolitan counties (against an average of 80%). Between 1981–2 and 1983–4 the GLC's precept rose 118% and the metropolitan counties 29% while the rest managed 20% against 14% inflation. (*Politics Today*, p. 30) Not surprisingly these councils appeared regularly in the DOE's 'hit lists'.

(*d*) Savings: the government refused to specify the size of expected savings, as this would depend on the management abilities of successor bodies. Eight Conservative-controlled councils in Greater Manchester, Merseyside and West Midlands reported in May 1984 that Price Waterhouse believed £20 million would be saved by rationalisation alone. By early 1986 the NALGO union was predicting 5,000 redundancies, over 1,000 being in Merseyside.

The case against

(*a*) Cost: in February 1984 the six metropolitan countries paid £40,000 to another group of consultants, Coopers and Lybrands, who reported that no savings would accrue from abolition, though by 1985 they were estimating that abolition of the GLC would cost £150 million, but save £30 million a year in operating costs (half what the government had hoped).

In response to the White paper the GLC produced its report 'The future of the Greater London Council' which began by criticising the absence of testable financial and expenditure analysis, and pointing out the new costs that would result from more managements, and the impact on the Inner London Education Authority and joint services. In addition 40% of the GLC budget is for debt charges – some £300 million.

The transfer to boroughs and districts of twenty-one responsibilities could result in increased staffing there, and the creation of what Labour believed would be at least fifty new bodies, would cause a massive increase in bureaucracy: new premises, staff and expense. Council finance chiefs concurred with this analysis in October 1983. Most embarrassingly for the government, the GLC Conservatives presented proposals in January 1984 for a restructuring costing £200 million less than abolition.

By 1986 the costs argument had been relegated. It was clear, for example, that only 1% of the GLC staff of 23,000 and work-force of 180,000 had not found another post and would be made redundant, and that the successor joint boards would be the largest local authority overspenders (at 15% over, they were 5 times worse than Labour-controlled London boroughs).

(*b*) Complexity: while the White Paper saw abolition as stream-lining, enabling the public to understand the system, critics described the web of thirty-nine joint boards and forty-eight committees as a confusing mess. The Labour Environment spokesman condemned the conversion of a two-tier system into a twenty-seven-tier system in London and twenty-two tier system in the provinces. The GLC's functions split 58 ways to 7 quangos, 15 joint boards, one joint committee, one housing trust, one directly elected education authority, 32 borough councils and the City of London.

(*c*) Weakening accountability: the joint boards and committees were to be made up of indirectly elected members, drawn from district and borough councils. This was condemned as a weakening of local democracy and Mr Jenkin's own criticism of the ILEA in 1977 as a 'constitutional monstrosity' free to be extravagant and irresponsible was recalled. More than 70% of the GLC's responsibilities went to non-elected or indirectly nominated quangos. Many Conservatives who favoured abolition of the metropolitan councils doubted the wisdom of leaving the capital, alone among great cities, without directly elected representatives. To answer critics, in September 1984 Mr Jenkin offered a mini-parliament for London.

(*d*) Quality of services: concern was expressed that devolved services, such as tourism, support for the arts, green belt land, housing, historic buildings, planning and traffic management, would not fare so well in the hands of all districts and boroughs. And it was warned that far from assisting industrial development, authorities would compete and duplicate efforts. Leeds University's Institute of Transport Studies thought that the best elements of city transport services would be destroyed. The Bishop of Rochester voiced concern for voluntary work and the fate of London's homeless. The West Midlands lost its consumer protection service, said to be the best in Britain. In London, £200 million was transferred from the shires to soften the rates blow, but elsewhere ratepayers suffered rises up to 37.4% (Calderdale) while the bus-users of South Yorkshire saw a cut in services and a 230% increase in fares.

(e) Public opinion: opinion polls have consistently shown the public supporting retention of the councils. A Harris Research Centre Poll in April 1985 shoed 74% opposed to abolition with 80% wanting an elected body for London. Polls in the metropolitan counties have shown similar opposition, and by July 1984 they were showing 66% against and 18% in favour (*Guardian*, 23 July 1984). Reflecting this, two-thirds of MPs and a majority of Conservative MPs thought abolition a vote-loser (MORI poll, *Guardian*, 29 August 1984).

The process of abolition
(a) *Opposition pressure*   The campaign against abolition began immediately, with the GLC coordinating a formidable publicity campaign which by July 1984 had cost £10.6 million, despite Conservative protests. In addition to its campaign unit, the councils employed a professional lobbying company. Conservatives in West Yorkshire took exception to some advertisements but these were cleared by the Newspaper Society.

The local government union NALGO instructed members not to cooperate with government in 1983 and in July 1984 the Methodist Church called for withdrawal of abolition legislation. The Labour Party pledged restoration of the GLC in September 1984.

(b) *Timetable*   A major difficulty for the government was the scheduled elections of May 1985. There were two options:

(1) *Deferral*: to allow councillors to stay in office until abolition in 1986. This was Mrs Thatcher's preference but Conservative MPs feared the obstructive damage the councils could do and protested at the idea of legislation to keep Ken Livingstone in power.

(2) *Substitution*: councillors nominated from the district and

borough councils would take over the running of the abolished
authorities in 1985. The problem here was that the government would
be accused of engineering a change of political control without elections.
This was the course of action advocated by Patrick Jenkin and the
government moved the proposed abolition forward a year to 1985. They
were determined that the local elections, which would turn into a
referendum while the Commons had voted for a second reading of the
abolition bill, would not take place.

The Paving Bill
To facilitate substitution, a Local Government (Interim Provisions)
Bill was brought forward in March 1984 to pave the way for abolition
(it thus became known as the Paving Bill). It sought to control events
by giving powers to stop abortive work and obstruction. In the
Commons, senior Conservatives, Edward Heath, Francis Pym and
Geoffrey Rippon, joined Labour in attacking the Bill as squalid, hasty
and not part of the manifesto.

Parliament
The government's real problems came in the House of Lords, which
not only disliked the measure but its arrival before the abolition bill
itself. The combination of a bill that seemed unconstitutional, was not
covered by the manifesto and tested the *raison d'être* of the Lords was
irresistible. After mustering their inbuilt Conservative majority on a
three-line whip for its second reading, the Lords defeated the bill by
a majority of forty-eight on an amendment, despite Mr Jenkin's offers
to accept changes and his leaks of it being a resigning issue. It was hailed
as the most serious defeat for the government in five years. In fact,
the government quickly switched to deferral of elections and added
more restrictions on disposal of land and signing contracts, and this
was passed by the Lords. Suggestions that leaders would be disqualified
for obstructive acts were not carried through – Conservatives were
now worried that Ken Livingstone was no longer an asset for them as
they seemed to be taking increasingly heavy-handed action.

Conservative back-benchers, led by Edward Heath, Ian Gilmour
and Geoffrey Rippon, continued to oppose parts of the Abolition Bill,
on the grounds that too much power was being transferred up to central
government, that there had been no Royal Commission, that it was
an enabling hybrid measure with vague powers, and that London would
be left with no elected authority. Tories worried too about the loss of

power in marginal boroughs and some argued for a London authority (opposed by the Prime Minister) while the Home Office doubted fire brigade savings. There were even reports that the minister, Kenneth Baker, was unconvinced but committed to abolition.

The House of Lords continued to cause problems, only failing by 4 votes to substitute an elected authority (May 1985) and imposing four defeats – making the government agree to a representative body for planning. The government tried to counter the counties' successful public relations with glossy pamphlets, but the campaign went on – pointing to the inadequacy of the parliamentary process, when only 16 of the 98 clauses were debated by MPs, and the ILEA's schools and colleges were 'dismissed in just 5½ hours. A fraction of the time it takes to sort out the average school timetable'.

The GLC had one last populist triumph in banning lorries from the roads at nights and weekends and won its case in the High Court. It was less successful in the courts, however, in its attempt at a deathbed spending spree – a £40 million grant to the ILEA and £77 million to umbrella organisations to pass on to voluntary groups were stopped, but £5.8 million left to 40 organisations on its last working day was released after a legal challenge.

Power politics

Beneath the constitutional and administrative debates ran the theme that a political vendetta was being waged. Ken Livingstone was convinced that Mrs Thatcher was attacking the GLC because 'she is appalled that we are an example of a Labour administration which gets elected and continues to fight for its policies' (The *Guardian*, 15 January 1983). The *Daily Telegraph* was equally convinced that abolition would see the end of 'many sinecures used as power bases from which to wage political warfare and subversion not only against this Government but against the British polity'. (8 October 1983). It is in the heat of this political debate that the models and conventions, described at the outset, have to be tested.

The future

The Opposition

Metropolitan abolition caused the Labour Party problems with Ken Livingstone arguing against the official policy of non-co-operation, believing in the inherent weaknesses of the process. In April 1986 the

NEC and MPs had drawn up a policy of re-creating the GLC, leaving abolished the metropolitan counties (always resented by Labour districts) and moving towards a single tier of local governments. This would entail the organic change favoured by Labour in 1977 whereby the 9 large city districts such as Bristol, Leicester and Southampton would regain wider powers, many shire districts would disappear, and a directly-elected regional tier would be created. The latter would control services such as water, transport, police and economic planning – a policy long favoured by the Liberal Party and the Alliance. Labour would also increase grants to enable councils to play a major part in combating unemployment. The Labour Party in Manchester moved towards another Liberal Policy in proposing co-ordination of services in neighbourhood offices.

The rates
Under attack for its control of local spending the Government announced a review of finance in October 1984 and quickly began to discuss the Whitehall collection of the £6.9 billion business rates. Despite reports such as that of the Cambridge University (DOE-sponsored) study of 1986 stating no connection between rates and private sector jobs, government and business saw an inevitable connection in that 'high spenders' such as the ILEA could raise 73% of their revenue from non-domestic rates.

This was accentuated in 1985 when rate revaluation in Scotland produced rises of up to 50% and an outcry from small businesses. A £40 million aid bill was speedily passed and the government resolved to promise reform in England and Wales. In January 1986 the green paper 'Paying for Local Government' proposed to replace the domestic rates over 10 years by a community charge (a 'poll tax' sounded like a penalty for voting). Business rates would be collected centrally and distributed with grants. Councils would keep only a light rate on industry, though the system of a needs equalisation grant would transfer £700 million from the shires of the south to London and the North. Nevertheless 75% of local spending would be disbursed centrally, as opposed to 44%, and the system was likely to produce large fluctations in rates. This sweeping change, including the new rating valuation for 4 million businesses, was postponed until after the next general election.

Reading

S. Bristow *et al* (eds.), *The Redundant Counties?*, Hesketh, 1984.

Politics Today, 13 February 1984, Conservative Research Department.

The Future of the Greater London Council, GLC, 1984.

J. Dearlove, *The Reorganisation of the British Local Government*, Cambridge University Press, 1979.

Reforming the electoral system

The results of recent elections have strengthened calls for reform of the British electoral system. This chapter considers the arguments in favour and against such reform together with the two most likely alternatives, the single transferable vote system and the additional member system.

Introduction

When Prime Minister, the Duke of Wellington declared that the British constitution required no further improvement: it was already perfect. Shortly afterwards in 1832 came the Great Reform Act and the subsequent transformation of the voting system from one involving a quarter of a million votes to the present day when forty million men and women aged over eighteen elect 650 members of parliament from single member constituencies on the basis of a simple majority vote. In the wake of the 1983 election not only Mrs Thatcher but the vanquished Michael Foot poured scorn on the idea of further electoral reform, but will history make their attitudes seem as shortsighted as Wellington's and if so, how long will it be before another Great Reform Act is passed? The fact is that a growing consensus has emerged across the political spectrum in favour of electoral reform. In the nineteenth century, the first past the post (FPTP) system was relatively advanced compared with the sundry authoritarian regimes in Europe, but many of those countries which went on to adopt the British system have since rejected it for proportional representation. Why should this be and what are the arguments against our present system?

The case against first past the post

The core idea behind representative government is that it enables all sections of society to have a say in the formation and conduct of government. This fulfils a basic right which all are held to have and, we have good reason to believe, makes it more likely that government will be carried out in the interests of, and with the general consent of, the governed. Critics maintain that because our present system is insufficiently representative it offends against basic human rights and delivers the wrong kind of government:

(1) *FPTP discriminates against smaller parties*

A party with thin national support might poll a substantial number of votes but win very few seats. Thus in 1983, despite the fact that 26% of votes cast went to the SDP–Liberal Alliance and that their candidates came second in 313 contests, they won only twenty-three contests outright: 3½% of the seats in the House of Commons. Over a quarter of the voting population therefore, received minimal representation. Under FPTP such parties struggle to win seats until they pass the threshold of about one third of the poll after which they begin to win seats in great numbers. Small parties face a virtually insuperable catch 22: they have to become big in order to stop being small!

(2) *FPTP favours the two big parties disproportionately*

This criticism is the corollary of the last. In 1979 Conservatives won 44% of the votes yet 53.4% of the seats: Labour 36.9% of the vote yet 42.4% of the seats. In 1983 the entry of the SDP helped split the non-Tory vote and the Conservatives were able to win 61% of the seats on 42.5% of the vote. Mrs Thatcher therefore gained some 100 seats compared with 1979 from a *reduced* vote.

(3) *FPTP elects on minority votes*

In 1979, 203 candidates were elected on less than 50% of the votes cast in their constituencies; in 1983 the figure rose to 334. Thus over half of the present MPs were elected in contests where the majority of voters did not support them. At the national level, as already shown, the same applies. In October 1974 Labour formed a government on 39.3% of votes cast. The *Hansard Commission on Electoral Reform* (1976) commented (p. 22) 'if fewer than 40% of voters (29% of electors) can impose their will on the other 60% or more, distortions are no longer a question of "fairness" but of elementary rights of citizens.'

(4) *FPTP favours parties with concentrated regional support*

It follows under FPTP that even small parties with highly localised support, e.g. nationalist parties, will do relatively well – as they did in 1974. But Labour has its support concentrated in the north where it duly wins the vast majority of its seats, and the Conservatives in the south where they do likewise. In 1983, excluding London, only three Labour MPs were elected south of a line from the Wash to Bristol, despite the fact that 17% of voters in this area voted Labour. Moreover, can it be good that few Labour MPs represent rural constituencies or towns and cities with expanding new industries, whilst few Conservative MPs have first hand experience, in their constituency surgeries, of decaying inner cities and the problems of obsolescent traditional industries? All this could change, say the reformers, if the system were changed.

(5) *FPTP creates artificially large majorities*

Over 70% of constituencies are 'safe' Labour or Conservative seats: their majorities are so large that defeat is unlikely. The reason for this is that the majority of Labour supporters are working class and are concentrated in the traditional industrial areas of south Wales, the north of England and central Scotland. In these areas the election of Labour candidates is virtually automatic. The Conservative Party gained over a third of working-class votes in 1983 but its main strength still lies in the middle classes, especially in the south. Elections are decided therefore by about 25% of constituencies mostly with mixed social composition which are 'marginal': where majorities are such that the contest will be decided by small shifts in the voting either way. Psephologists calculate that a swing of 1% from one of the large parties to the other will usually result, these days, in about ten marginal seats changing hands. A swing of only a few percentage points in voter preferences therefore can make the difference between defeat and victory, a small or a very large majority. Critics argue that such majorities, created by the vagaries of the voting system and the geography of class are not true reflections of public opinion and provide a false mandate for the winning party's programme. When combined with a strong showing by a third party the results can be freakish, as in 1983.

(6) *FPTP produces 'wasted' votes*

Those votes which do not contribute directly to the election of a candidate are said by some to be 'wasted' because they are not reflected in the House of Commons. Where the seat is safe these might comprise a substantial minority but, as we have seen, they might easily comprise the majority of voters in a constituency. It is also argued that the huge majorities piled up for some candidates are wasted votes which might be better used to reflect different and important shades of opinion. Small wonder, say reformers, that over 20% of the electorate regularly fail to vote. By contrast, voters in marginal seats exercise a disproportionate influence over the outcome of elections: their votes can be infinitely 'morel equal' than those in other constituences.

(7) *FPTP perpetuates the two party system*
Because only the governing and opposition parties appear to have viable chances of gaining majorities in general elections voters tend to withhold their support for smaller parties which more accurately reflect their beliefs, and cast their vote for the party they dislike least. For reformers this produces a number of evils. Firstly voter choice is limited to two rival philosophies which can be bitterly and irreconcilably antithetical when, as now, radical voices have won the internal party arguments. Secondly it encourages the maintenance of unwieldy political coalitions, like the Labour Party which endeavours for electoral benefit to pretend it is united. Thirdly – and perhaps most importantly – it sustains adversary politics whereby real issues are lost in the unseemly ritual rhetoric of the party debate and winning parties immediately set about undoing the work of their predecessors. The end result is that millions of voters occupying the centre ground go unrepresented, the political process falls into disrepute and the uncertainty surrounding our political future deters proper economic planning and investment for both the private and public sectors.

(8) *FPTP discriminates against women and ethnic minorities*
Women have never comprised even 5% of the House of Commons and the present percentage, Mrs Thatcher notwithstanding, is a mere 3½%. Coloured ethnic minorities fare even worse: there is no West Indian or Asian in the House of Commons (though the Lords have one of each, and, several black candidates in safe Labour seats will change the situation after the next election). The simple reason for this is that candidates are chosen by local party selection committees who 'tend to choose a "safe" candidate who will be as near to an identikit model of an MP as it is possible to find. The candidate will be white, middle aged and male' (Bogdanor, p. 113). Reformers believe therefore that

FPTP is inadequate when two parties dominate, farcical when a third party challenges strongly and inferior to certain of the proportional representation systems used by other countries. Unsurprisingly, defenders of the present system will have none of this.

The case for the first past the post system

Understandably, proponents of FPTP are found within the ranks of those parties which benefit from it: Labour and Conservative. As they are defending the status quo — always the high ground in British politics — they do not need to elaborate their views with the enthusiasm and detail of their opponents but they do, in any case, have a substantial case to put forward. They maintain:

(1) It is not the chief aim of government to be *representative* but to be *effective*. By creating administrations with healthy majorities, FPTP, with occasional exceptions, has provided strong stable governments which have been able to fulfil most of their election promises.

(2) The close personal relationship between MP and constituent is a valuable (and much admired) aspect of the present system.

(3) By-elections enable sections of the public to register their views on the progress of a government between elections.

(4) Adversary politics is as much a reflection of a new volatile mood amongst the electorate as it is of the FPTP system.

(5) Parties *do* have a chance to win seats once they pass a certain threshold; if smaller parties were to keep working instead of pursuing a sour grapes reformist campaign they might be able one day to enjoy the system's benefits.

(6) In 1979 the Liberals asked the European Court of Human Rights in Strasbourg to judge whether FPTP was a violation of their democratic rights — the Court ruled that such rights had not been violated.

(7) FPTP is well known and understood and has been in existence for some time. The disruption which a shift to another system would cause could scarcely be justified in terms of the movement for change which is not widespread and intense but is confined to: those parties with a vested interest in change, sundry pressure groups and individuals. As Angus Maude and John Szemerey point out in *Why Electoral Change?*

It is not enough to assert that it (electoral change) *might* be better, or even that it *must* be better than what we have. It is necessary to show pretty conclusively that it *would* be better and could *not* in any circumstances make things worse.

(8) It is a mistake to think, as is often argued, that economic success is closely related to voting systems. It is the skill, energy and character of its people which make a country prosperous, not the way it elects its legislature.

(9) FPTP may have disadvantages but they are not as grievous as those of its alternatives.

Proposals for electoral reform in Britain

What are the alternatives on offer? The human mind seems particularly fecund in this respect: there are literally hundreds, but only a few have been seriously considered in the British context. Having said this it sometimes comes as a surprise to British people that their government came close to changing our electoral system on two occasions. In 1910 the Royal Commission on Electoral Reform suggested that the alternative vote (AV) be adopted for parliamentary elections, with some experimental use of proportional representation – the single transferable vote (STV) – at the local level. The alternative vote is based upon the numbering by voters of candidates according to preference in single member constituencies. Any candidate who receives over 50% of first preferences is elected. If no one manages this, the candidate with the least votes is eliminated and second preferences distributed accordingly to the other candidates. This process is repeated until one candidate receives a majority and is declared the winner. The system is not strictly proportional but gives more voter choice and reduces wasted votes.

In 1917 a Speaker's Conference on Electoral Reform unanimously recommended a combination of both systems for parliamentary elections but the resultant Representation of the People Bill (1917) foundered on the Commons' preference for AV on its own and the Lords' for STV. The bill lapsed but, writes David Butler 'the survival of the existing system plainly expressed not so much an endorsement of its merits as a failure to agree upon the remedy for its faults' (Butler, 1964, p. 39).

The industrious Proportional Representation Society maintained the pressure, winning the support of several leading politicians. Following the hung parliament of 1929, MacDonald's minority government – partly to appease their Liberal allies – set up another Speaker's Conference. This time AV was favoured, but not without fierce opposition from advocates of PR and opponents of all electoral change.

The Commons endorsed the reform by fifty votes but the Lords rejected it and the government fell before the upper chamber could be overruled (Butler, 1963, pp. 58–83). Since then no serious legislative attempt has been made to reform the basis of the voting system. Indeed, during the period of two party hegemony after the war the issue became the virtual preserve of small pressure groups and the Liberal Party. The 1974 election results however – which in February gave the Liberals only fourteen seats from six million votes – put new and indignant fire into the reformers' cause. Their case had been already strengthened by the 1972 decision of the British government to introduce PR into non-parliamentary elections in Northern Ireland: if it was thought PR could help heal the divisions over there then why not use it to counteract the increasingly intractable polarities on the mainland? PR now became part of the political atmosphere of the decade, and the most favoured type of alternative system for Britain. It was recommended by many bodies and study groups for a reformed House of Lords, was used increasingly by professional bodies and, in its 'list' form was the dominant electoral system used by Britain's new EEC partners. In 1979 Britain was conspicuous in refusing to use PR in elections to the European Assembly and in 1981 electoral reform received the support of a whole new political party of converts in the shape of the SDP. Minority support also grew in the two big parties, but the results of the 1983 election elevated the issue into one of constant underlying importance. Table 1 illustrates the distortions. The right-hand column shows the way seats would have been distributed according to a strictly proportional system. Obviously the political complexion of any

Table 1   *1983 election results for England, Scotland and Wales*

	Votes (in 000's)	% of poll	Seats won	% of seats	Theoretical seat allocation in proportion to votes won
Conservatives	13,012	43·5	397	63	277
Labour	8,457	28·3	209	33	180
Lib-SDP	7,794	26·1	23	3·5	166
Nationalist (SNP & Plaid Cymru)	458	1·5	4	0·5	9
Others	189	0·6	0	0	1 (Ecology)

Adapted from Michael Steed, lecture to a conference, 27 April 1984.

resultant government would have been very different to Mrs Thatcher's, not to mention the policies pursued. Supporters of FPTP accuse the reformers of having centrist, moderate axes to grind and claim that PR's dubious advantages are won at too great a cost. PR supporters maintain that such criticisms are either biased, ill informed, exaggerated or based on selective use of evidence. The major elements in the debate are explained below.

The case for and against PR

(1) *Representativeness*

Against: opponents of PR, such as Enoch Powell, argue that it is not the purpose of parliament to offer a perfect reflection of society: the existing system is held to give adequate representation of most important interests, regions and ideas.

For: advocates of PR do not claim it will give a perfect reflection, merely a better one, which will give better representation to women, ethnic minorities and those views at present stifled by the simple majority system.

(2) *Complexity*

Against: the system is too complex for voters to understand.

For: a small number of votes will always be spoiled or filled in unthinkingly but whilst some of the mathematics behind PR systems might be complex, filling in the ballot paper is invariably straight-forward. Are we to assume that British voters are less able to cope than Irish, Italian or Belgian voters or the hundreds of thousands who fill in complicated football pools or bingo cards each week?

(3) *THE MP–constituent connection*

Against: PR would destroy the traditionally close link which exists between MP and constituent and for the recognisable, single MP would substitute a group of members, none of whom would have the same feeling of responsibility for their vastly enlarged constituencies.

For: the single member seat is no sacred British institution: multi-member constituencies functioned right into the present century and local government district council wards are usually represented by three members. Moreover, the Irish STV system arguably strengthens the connection (see below) and some PR systems (e.g. West Germany) retain single member seats.

(4) *By-elections*

Against: PR systems do not allow for this traditional means of testing public opinion between elections.

For: this argument is exaggerated in that local elections and regular opinion polls provide barometers of public opinion and, again, under certain forms of PR, by-elections can be fought.

(5) *Extremism and proliferation of parties*

Against: PR lets small extremist parties into the legislature, e.g. the Nazis under the Weimar Republic constitution, and causes the proliferation of small parties e.g. Denmark and Finland which have nine each.

For: where – as in Israel – the whole country is one multi-member constituency, this can and does certainly happen but by stating a specific threshold below which parties will not be awarded seats this problem can be minimised or eliminated: Sweden's 4% limit has limited party numbers to five and only four parties currently operate under West Germany's 5% limit.

(6) *Party power and selection of candidates*

Against: under PR political parties, not voters determine the names which appear on the candidate lists meaning that they are often of low calibre.

For: even under FPTP it is a small minority of the party faithful who choose candidates. Moreover the German and Irish systems allow equal or more voter choice in candidate selection (see below).

(7) *Coalitions*

Against: PR increases the number of parties and hence the chances of an indecisive result making coalition politics the order of the day. This in turn produces:

(*a*) indecisive government and political immobilism;

(*b*) long delays whilst coalitions are being constructed e.g. anything up to six months in Holland;

(*c*) regular crises when they break down and frequent changes in government;

(*d*) flagrant unfairness in that politicians in smoke-filled rooms decide the colour of governments, not the voter.

For:

(*a*) Indecisive results do occasionally happen under PR but it must be remembered that eight out of the past twenty-three elections in

Britain have been indecisive. Moreover coalitions under PR *have* produced stable governments in a number of countries including Sweden, Germany and Austria, and in Greece and Spain majority single party governments.

(*b*) Delays and crises and changes of government are exaggerated: between 1945 and 1975 Britain had more general elections, changed finance and foreign ministers to a greater degree than many PR countries including Belgium, Austria, Ireland, Israel, Sweden, Switzerland and West Germany (Finer, p. 24).

(*c*) Some PR systems, like those in Ireland and West Germany, give the voter a chance to express an opinion on proposed coalitions (see below).

(*d*) Coalitions which reflect consensus might reduce the potential role of conviction politicians like Mrs Thatcher or Tony Benn but it can be powerfully argued that if the majority of voters desire centrist or moderate policies then it is the function of a democracy to deliver them. Moreover governments which people want are more likely to be stable, and unifying and, if West Germany and Austria are anything to go by, encourage economic growth and development.

Criteria of acceptability

Clearly, defenders of PR are justified in complaining that their opponents seek to highlight those, of the many available examples of PR in practice, which display it to least possible advantage as a potential system for Britain. However, this alone does not rebut the charge that PR will be bad for Britain; most reformers recognise that a British PR system should retain – as far as possible – the valued features of the present system:

(1) simplicity,
(2) strong and stable, preferably one party government,
(3) good constituency–MP links,
(4) a manageable number of minor parties.

It might already have become apparent that the systems employed in West Germany and Ireland appear to go a long way towards meeting these criteria and indeed, the German additional member system (AMS) together with the Irish single transferable vote (STV) system are the two only serious candidates offered by the reform lobby. Both systems are explained below and their merits debated.

The additional member system

AMS seeks to marry the advantages of FPTP with those of PR. Half of the 496 seats in the West German lower house (*Bundestag*) are elected according to the British system from one member constituencies; the other 248 are elected proportionately through a regional list system of nominated party candidates. Voters make two crosses on their ballot papers: one for a constituency candidate and the other on an adjacent list of political parties. It is the *percentage of the vote gained by parties in the latter ballot which determines, usually within a few decimal points, the total number of seats finally allocated.* Seats gained from the constituency ballot are topped up to the requisite levels from the 248 regional list seats. For example, in 1983 the Social Democrats gained 68 constituency seats and 38.2% list votes. The latter figure meant an entitlement of 193 seats, so 125 list seats were added, these being taken from the top parts of the regional SPD candidate lists. The Christian Democrats (CDU) did better in the constituency section with 180 seats and therefore needed only sixty-four list seats to make up their entitlement earned by 48.2% of this ballot (244 seats in all). The Free Democrats (FDP) won no constituency seats but 7% of the list votes won it 37 seats and similarly the Greens gained twenty-seven seats on 5.6% of the vote. Seat allocations are nearly but not quite proportional with votes because parties must gain *at least 5% of list votes or three constituency seats* before they are allotted *any* list seats.

Most voters are politically consistent in their choice but some split their votes for a variety of reasons, for example:

(1) Knowing that their constituency candidate has no chance Green supporters might vote for the candidate disliked least, but cast their regional list votes for their own party.

(2) Knowing that their party plans a coalition with the Free Democrats, SDP voters might cast their regional list vote for the FDP.

Advantages of AMS

(1) From total collapse in 1945, AMS (introduced in 1949) has helped provide stable coalition government in Germany which has itself enabled old wounds to heal and the economy recover. Two parties have dominated the legislature and since 1961 only two small ones have been represented in addition; in 1969 the far right NPD just failed to reach the 5% limit.

(2) It enables voters to express an opinion on proposed coalitions (traditionally declared by parties before elections).

(3) It retains the constituency link yet delivers a proportional result.

(4) With only two crosses required on the ballot paper it is simple to understand.

Criticisms

(1) Coalition government has produced a very crowded political centre ground in Germany which discourages radical new initiatives.

(2) It has enabled a small party, the FDP, to play a disproportionately big part in every government except one since 1961.

(3) It creates two 'classes' of MP: those popularly elected and the list representatives (in practice though this does not seem to matter in Germany).

(4) Constituencies are relatively large by British standards.

(5) Political parties determine candidatures in the regional lists (though electoral law insists that democratic selection procedures be adhered to) and it often occurs that candidates who fail to be elected in constituencies, get into the Bundestag through their nomination in the regional list. Moreover the whole idea of party lists is attacked on the grounds that the voter is asked to choose not between individual candidates with personalities of their own but faceless political parties. This last characteristic in particular seems to go against the grain of the Anglo-Saxon political tradition.

Some reformers have concluded that to be suitable for British political conditions, AMS needs to be modified. In 1976 the *Hansard Society Commission on Electoral Reform* accordingly offered its well considered thoughts.

The Hansard Society Commission's (HSC) variation

The last mentioned criticism weighed particularly with the HSC which felt it was of overriding importance that all candidates should be elected directly by voters (HSC, paras 116–17). Their proposals were as follows:

(1) Of 640 House of Commons seats three-quarters (not half) should be directly elected by FPTP from constituencies which would be enlarged but not doubled as under the German system.

(2) 160 seats would be available to make up party strengths to accord with votes cast but they would not be allocated to party lists. Instead they would be taken up by parties on a regional basis according to the percentages gained by losing candidates. The 'top up' seats therefore

would go to the best losers and only one not two votes would be required.

(3) Parties gaining less than 5% of the votes cast in any region would not gain any additional seats.

This variation offers several advantages: it requires no change in existing voting procedure; it would give representation to parties with substantial but not majority support in certain regions of the country e.g. Labour in the south, Conservatives in the north; it would retain the constituency connection; it requires all MPs to submit themselves to the voters.

However the scheme has several disadvantages as Bogdanor notes (pp. 72–3): 'failed' candidates would be able to sit in the House; it could easily happen that some constituencies could gain an unfair two, or even three, MPs; 'best losers' will frequently be determined by the number of candidates fighting their constituencies; small parties will be encouraged to fight every constituency in order to make the 5% threshold; the lack of a second vote would remove the possibility of indicating a preference for a coalition partner − PR after all would make coalitions much more likely, and disproportionality would often result if only 25% of seats were available to add to constituency seats.

The single transferable vote (STV)

In Ireland voters are divided into multi-member constituencies and at elections register their preferences for candidates as 1, 2, 3, 4 or as far down as they wish or there are candidates. In a four-member constituency a quota is set of *one-fifth* of the votes cast plus one: a simple calculation will reveal that only four candidates can possibly reach this quota figure. The quota can be expressed thus:

$$\text{Quota} = \frac{\text{total valid votes cast}}{\text{total number of seats} + 1} + 1$$

Any candidate who receives the quota number of first preferences is elected. However, in the likely event that not all the seats will be filled so straightforwardly, the person with the least votes is eliminated and their second preferences redistributed to the other candidates, some of whom may now make the quota. The surplus votes gained by those who make the quota are also reallocated if necessary. This process continues until all the available quotas are reached.

Complexity

Against: even STV supporters allow that the sorting of preferences is highly complex: if voters cannot understand the principles which underlie their system this could lead to cynicism and distrust.

For: the voter is asked to think – but not to the extent where confusion takes over: it is relatively easy to mark preferences on a ballot paper. In 1968 moreover, a referendum on the voting system in Ireland resoundingly endorsed it 3–2.

Party control

Against: it is likely that parties could still control candidate selection even under STV.

For: it is possible, however, that voters would be able to choose between candidates from different wings of the same party; STV offers a virtual built in 'primary' in this respect. The ability of individuals to attract personal followings would also help reduce party domination of the political system.

Coalitions

Against: STV would almost certainly lead to coalition government with all the attendant disadvantages.

For: voters are enabled under STV to register an opinion on proposed coalitions between parties.

Small parties

Against: the smaller the number of seats per constituency the larger the quota required to become elected. By reducing the number of seats big parties can squeeze out or disadvantage smaller ones: both Fianna Fáil and Fine Gael have tried to do this in the past.

For: the quota system is a guarantee against small party proliferation and since 1977 an impartial boundary commission has been set up in Ireland which has removed political influence from the process and which increased the number of five-member constituencies from six to fifteen; four-member from ten to thirteen and reduced three-member constituencies – the minimum size allowed – from twenty-six to thirteen (Lakeman, pp. 91–2).

Proportionality

Against: STV is not truly proportional – some say that it is not a PR system at all e.g. in 1969 Fianna Fáil obtained 45.7% of first preference votes but ended up with 51.7% of the seats.

For: anomalies notwithstanding, the overall result in Irish elections is usually pretty proportional and *much* more so than recent British election results. Further, as the HSC pointed out, strict proportionality is not that important, 'because the whole purpose of STV is to allow later preferences to have an effect' and these do not of course, show up in first preference percentages. STV would, moreover, if adopted in Britain give reasonable representation to Labour in the south, Conservatives in the north, the Alliance all over the country and the Nationalists in their respective countries.

STV would also allow women and ethnic minority candidates to stand with a good chance of election especially where, in the latter case, the constituency included substantial numbers of immigrant voters.

MP–constituency link

Against: STV would produce cumbersome, unnatural constituencies of over 200,000 voters, where neither constituents nor their multiple members could develop a proper relationship.

For: many existing constituencies are unnatural creations, having been chopped and changed about with great regularity, and where the seat is safe, MPs have little incentive to be good constituency MPs. Under STV on the other hand there *are* no safe seats; a sitting MP can quite easily be defeated by a rival candidate from his own party. This would of course make it more desirable to be a local candidate but STV would in any case make it easier for candidates to stand in their locality rather than 'migrating' to areas where their parties had significant support. Moreover, under FPTP the majority of voters often have to seek the aid of an MP for whom they did not vote: under STV this would tend not to happen as a wider range of MPs would be available.

Both systems have their fervent advocates but STV seems to have won the argument, at least within the SPD–Liberal Alliance. Its 1983 election manifesto proposed that 'natural communities (e.g. Hull, Plymouth, Leeds, Edinburgh) and counties (e.g. Somerset, Northumberland) would be single multi-member constituencies of different size, represented by different numbers of MPs. Preferential voting by STV will enable the voter to distinguish between candidates of a particular party and thus affect the character of that party in Parliament.'

The barries to change

Which of the two favoured systems suits Britain best? It is obvious that each would gain us different things at differing costs, the balance of advantage depending upon the value one places upon these changes; indeed, what is a gain for one person might be a loss to another. It cannot be denied that reforming the system carries with it political risks. Those who think the present system, despite its fults, produces acceptably stable and effective government will be disinclined to take such risks. But those like Professor Finer who 'fear the discontinuities, the reversals, the extremisms of the existing system and its contribution to our national decline' believe 'The time for change is now' (Finer, p. 32). However, politics is the art of the possible and whilst PR might appear desirable from many points of view it faces a number of major obstacles.

(1) Clearly it is not in the interests of the big parties to change the system and, whilst both have minorities who support PR, the majority are opposed either out of self-interest, conviction or a combination of both.

(2) The 'conviction' wings of the two big parties – Labour left and Tory right – do not wish to lose the chance of winning substantial legislative power, even on a minority vote, to do the things they believe necessary and right. In other words, Tony Benn is prepared to put up with a system which gives us Mrs Thatcher because he too wants for the left the kind of power it has given her.

(3) A MORI poll commissioned by *The Economist* (5 July 1986) suggested that the British people have 'a remarkable aversion to "coalition politics"'. When asked if the next election produces a situation in which no party achieved an overall majority, 50% believed it would be a 'bad thing' whilst only 28% thought it would be a 'good thing for the country'.

(4) Constitutional change is almost always a long drawn out business with no guarantee of success, witness the abortive attempt to reform the Lords in the late sixties and the devolution saga which dominated the seventies and finally delivered the *coup de grâce* to the Callaghan government. Even when everyone agrees change is necessary – and this is rare indeed – no one can agree upon its precise nature and extended, bitter controversy is the invariable result. It will be a brave or overwhelmingly powerful government which re-enters an area so carefully avoided since 1931.

When will change come, if at all? Some reformers are optimistic and perceive a steady but inexorable process of conversion which will result in reform, possibly quite soon. Others are less sanguine and point out that foreign experience reveals 'that changes in the electoral system have all emerged from considerations of party advantage' (Finer, p. 31). This means that, despite winning the intellectual arguments — and in my view they have — reformers will at minimum have to await an election result which denies a majority to either Conservative or Labour but gives the balance of power to the Alliance. It is only then that the Alliance will have the opportunity to trade its support for a change in the electoral system.

Reading

D. E. Butler, *The Electoral System in Britain since 1918*, OUP, 1963.

S. E. Finer (ed.), *Adversary Politics and Electoral Reform*, Wigram, 1975.

Vernon Bogdanor, *What is Proportional Representation?*, Martin Robertson, 1984.

Angus Maude and John Szemerey, *Why Electoral Change?: The Case for PR Examined*, Conservative Political Centre, 1982.

The Report of the Hansard Society Commission on Electoral Reform, June 1976, Hansard Society, 12 Gower St, London.

Enid Lakeman, *Power to Elect: the Case for Proportional Representation*, Heinemann, 1982.

Peter Hain, *Proportional Misrepresentation*, Wildwood, 1986.

I am grateful to Geoffrey Roberts for some useful comments on this chapter, and to Michael Steed for some of the data.

Chapter Six   *John McIlroy*

Trade unions and the law

It is easy to state that the function of labour law is to regulate the power of management and trade unions. The problem is that there is no agreement as to how that power should be balanced, indeed, there is no more vexed political issue in Britain today. Trade unions — organisations of wage earners — exist to improve the terms and conditions of employment for their members. What should be done about the consequences of their activities on economy and society? There has long been agreement that politicians must have a policy on trade unions. *What* those policies should be provoked the sharpest controversy because there is no agreed conception of trade unionism in practice, of its role in society. A Conservative may hold the view that trade unions should no longer exist, that they have outlived their usefulness and are a drag on economic growth, a boiler room for inflation. A Labour supporter may believe that unions have never been more essential, that the power of trade unions at the workplace is inadequate and that they should be involved in partnership not only in boardrooms but in running the country in partnership with the government. We could find Labour or Tory supporters who believed none of these things. That is why this area is such a confused battlefield.

In this short chapter we cannot resolve any of these problems but by looking at how the law has developed historically in relation to unions and how the present position stands, we can perhaps encourage a more informed debate.

State paternalism

The earliest institutions which attempted to control the labour market were the feudal *guilds* which covered both the master craftsmen and their journey men. With their decline many of their functions passed to *the state* which attempted directly to control the employment relationship. From the Ordinance of Labourers, 1349, a succession of statutes gave power to the local magistrates in the quarter sessions to fix wages, the duration of employment, the hours of work, numbers of apprentices and the utilisation of machinery. From the Statute of Labourers, 1351, a series of laws totally outlawed associations of workers and laid down rules for the conduct of employees with criminal penalties for misconduct. State sponsored wage fixing was not finally abolished until Acts of 1813 and 1824 but long before then it had ceased to have any practical effect.

Laissez-faire

The rising capitalist class opposed state intervention in favour of the freedom of new industrialists to use their resources as they wished and to follow only the dictates of the market in relation to prices, wages and the utilisation of labour. The free pursuit by individuals of their own economic interests would provide the best allocation of resources in the overall interest of society. The acceptance of this doctrine of *laissez-faire* was reflected in the legal sphere by the doctrine of *freedom of contract*. Employers and employees should be left to control fully their own relationship by voluntarily coming to legally binding agreements.

The breakdown of paternal state regulation as industrial capitalism developed at first led groups of workers to petition the magistrates to maintain wages. Increasingly, it gave a fillip to trade union organisation already stimulated by workers recognising that in reality there was little equality between employer and individual employee and that in practice freedom of contract, because of the imbalance of bargaining power, often meant dictation of the terms of employment by the employer.

Trade union organisation was anathema to the supporters of *laissez-faire*. It distorted the operation of the market, impeded freedom of contract and competition and sought to replace the individual with the collective. Its growth produced two responses.

(1) *Parliament*, fearing the impact of the French revolution, introduced the *Combination* Acts, 1799 and 1800. These measures outlawed

unions and made all agreements for increasing wages or altering hours criminal.

(2) *The judiciary*, through the common law system which gives them the ability to make law, *developed criminal and civil liabilities*. Union organisation itself amounted to a 'criminal conspiracy', the judges decided. Unions were 'in restraint of trade', their activities involved crimes such as 'intimidation', 'molestation' and 'obstruction'. Industrial action involved also civil wrongs such as breach of contract.

Coming to terms with unions

If in 1806 unions were totally illegal, a hundred years later they had attained a fair measure of acceptance. The right of unions to exist, organise, bagain and take industrial action, was only recognised after a long process of struggle. The legal landmarks were:

(1) *1824–5 Repeal of the Combination Acts* legalised some union activities but set out a list of criminal offences which caused future problems.

(2) *1871 Trade Union Act* relieved unions from liability for 'restraint of trade' and gave them civil status and tax and administrative advantages.

(3) *1875 Conspiracy and Protection of Property Act* removed unions' liability for criminal conspiracy in trade disputes.

(4) *1906 Trade Disputes Act* protected unions against actions for civil conspiracy and for inducing breach of employment contracts and gave union funds protection against civil actions in trade disputes.

The change from total suppression to development of a legal framework giving some legitimacy to unions may be explained by:

(*a*) The already existing *tradition of co-opting* newly emerging groups witnessed by the inter-penetration in Britain of the old landed aristocracy and the new industrialists.

(*b*) The fact that it was *a gradual process*. For much of the century trade unionists faced strong disadvantages. In 1872 alone there were 17,000 prosecutions of workers under the Master and Servant Act repealed only in 1875.

(*c*) The fact that for most of the century *trade unionism remained weak*, limited to a small respectable elite of well under 20% of the working population.

(*d*) Concessions to labour could be made because of *the*

economic success of Britain, the first industrial nation to dominate the world market and create a lucrative colonial empire.

(*e*) The granting of citizenship rights in the political sphere via the *extension of suffrage* to most urban male workers in 1867 created political pressure for the extension of rights in the industrial arena.

Immunities

The *form* that the statutes legalising unions took is important. Because of the common law's built in bias against collective organisation, a problem exacerbated by the social background of the judiciary, the unions did not seek a *code of positive rights* such as exists in most other countries. They sought *immunity from* legal doctrines which would impede their activities. This was the response of a cautious and pragmatic union leadership of conservative bent, operating in a society which, lacking a written constitution, gave major play through the common law system to a narrowly class-based judiciary and which was soaked in *laissez-faire* values. It has been argued that the immunity form was the consequence of the fact that the working class lacked universal suffrage well beyond its formative period; and the failure of its own political party to frame a more specific and positive programme of rights for trade unions and trade unionists until the turn of the century. Britain was the first industrialised nation. Its working class, therefore, had little experience elsewhere to draw upon. In contra-distinction, unions in other countries, developing in later and different conditions, secured a *right* to organise, a *right* to bargain, a *right* to strike.

But in Britain the method of immunity still governs today's Labour legislation. Once the mould was set it was not ruptured. No major social upheaval provided the opportunity for rethinking and restructuring trade union law. This system of immunities to exclude the judiciary did not give unions 'privileges' or 'place them above the law'. The system of immunities was simply the *method* by which unions were given basic rights without which they would not have been able to fulfil their social and economic roles.

The judges v parliament

The system of immunities did not fully protect the unions. The common law system was still there and could be developed by the judges. Unions were, for example, given immunity from civil wrongs when they were acting 'in contemplation or furtherance of a trade dispute'. It was left to the courts to decide *exactly* what that phrase meant. If they felt that unions action did *not* come within the definition then there was no protection. The judges were able to limit union activities by interpreting existing legislation and thereby developing new liabilities.

British labour law became a battleground between the judiciary and a parliament reacting to pressures from labour. For example, the famous Taff Vale case (1901) which found that unions were responsible for the wrongs of their officers upset the protections the unions thought they had been finally given in the 1870s. Parliament then had to over-turn the judgement in the 1906 Trade Disputes Act. Similarly in the *Osborne* judgement (1909) the right of unions to use their funds to support the Labour Party was struck down by the courts and the position on political expenditure had to be redefined by parliament in the 1913 Trade Union Act. Judicial undermining of the unions often coincided with periods of sharp class conflict such as the Great Unrest of 1900–14. The courts reflected middle-class fears and public opinion.

Voluntarism

When in the 1950s the eminent Labour lawyer, Kahn-Freund com-mented, '... there is perhaps no major country in the world in which the law has played a less significant role in the shaping of relations than in Britain and in which today the law and the legal profession have less to do with labour relations', he was expressing the orthodox view: the 1906 settlement represented the final paragraphs in a concordat accepting that unions and employers should regulate their own affairs. The unions, given the freedom to organise and act by the system of immunities, also wanted parliament to set minimal rules on such issues as health, safety, welfare and social security. For the rest they preferred to rely on their own efforts through collective bagaining. They did not want laws on union recognition, let alone on unfair dismissal or the rights of shop stewards. The employers too saw collective bargaining as the optimal means of achieving equity and equilibrium. The state having guaranteed the conditions for such self-regulation and under-pinned it by the Conciliation Act, 1896, and the Industrial Court Act, 1919, was prepared to leave well alone.

The British system of state abstention and self-regulation was seen as representing maturity in industrial relations, the product of an explicit philosophy of voluntarism or collective *laissez-faire*. Whilst there can be no doubt that historically, legal control of industrial relations in Britain has been slight in comparison with the USA,

Germany, Japan, or France, and that primacy has been accorded to collective bargaining, not law, the orthodox view requires some qualification.

(1) In both world wars the state introduced a whole battery of measures to control unions and industrial action such as the *Munitions of War Act*, 1915, and *Order 1305*, 1940.

(2) *The Emergency Powers Act*, 1920, and the *Trade Disputes Act*, 1927, although used sparingly, gave the state extensive powers to intervene in industrial relations.

(3) For much of the inter-war depression, the weakness of the unions, particularly after the defeat of the General Strike, meant that they represented little challenge to management prerogative or state economic objectives. *There was little necessity for intervention*.

(4) The same was true while the post-war consensus on full employment, the welfare state and the role of union leaders in managing their members was underpinned by economic stability. When the beginning of the disintegration of Britain's post-war boom coincided with an escalation of aspirations by sections of the workforce, the fracturing of voluntarism and increased intervention of the law in industrial relations was on the agenda.

The 1964–70 Labour government

By the mid 1960s concern over inflation, strikes, labour efficiency and the inability of the state to plan (particularly through incomes policy) and increasing criticism of the overall impact of Britain's industrial relations on its economic performance in harsher international competition, led to attempts to change the voluntary system. All governments agreed on the necessity for change but there was disagreement on specific strategies of reform or repression.

The Donovan Report

The major justification of attempts to reconcile the continued existence of voluntarism with greater economic efficiency was the report of the Royal Commission on Trade Unions and Employers Associations published in 1968. Donovan saw the answer to what it analysed as the 'disorder' in industrial relations producing wage drift and unofficial strikes as *the voluntary reform* of industrial relations institutions. Industry wide collective agreements had been undermined by local, often informal, bargaining by shop stewards. They should be replaced by comprehensive formal plant and company agreements. Areas such as discipline, redundancy and change at work should be the subject of formal agreements not custom and practice. There should be new efficient procedures and wage payment systems. There was a need to integrate shop stewards into the unions and provide them with more facilities and training. The Commission did suggest some sanctions against unofficial strikers. But the law as *a major means* of stimulating change was rejected. Laws against strikes, for example, would not work, would not be used by employers and would stir up resentment. Instead a new Commission of Industrial Relations would conduct investigations and *recommend* changes.

In place of strife

The purpose of Donovan was *gradually and through persuasion* to integrate workplace bargaining into the process of national determination of industrial relations by government, employers and unions, in the interests of incomes policy, manpower planning and more effective management. But the Labour Party leadership, seeing legislation as electorally popular, produced a White Paper, *In Place of Strife*, which proposed measures to deal with inter-union disputes, compulsory suspension of unofficial strikes while conciliation took place, compulsory ballots before official strikes and a compulsory register of trade unions. In April 1969 a short bill was announced covering the 'penal clauses'. It was adamantly opposed both by the TUC and by a large group of Labour MPs. Informed by his whips that there was no majority for the Bill, Wilson withdrew it on the basis of 'solemn and binding' assurances from the TUC that it would take greater powers of intervention in strikes.

The Industrial Relations Act

From the late 1950s views very different from those propounded in Donovan had gained ground in the Tory Party. Inflated union power gnawed at management prerogatives, corroded efficiency and tyrannised individual employees. A new comprehensive framework of law was the main instrument in solving the problems. First enunciated by Tory barristers in *A Giant's Strength*, 1958, these views underpinned the Industrial Relations Act introduced in 1971 by the Health government. A most wide ranging and revolutionary piece of labour legislation, the Act covered:

(1) *Legally binding agreements:* written collective agreements were presumed to be legally binding unless they specifically stated otherwise. Strikes in breach of such agreements would be illegal. The Commission for Industrial Relations could impose legally binding procedure agreements where none existed.

(2) The Secretary of State for Employment could apply for an *order prohibiting industrial action harmful to the economy*. There could be a *cooling off period* of up to sixty days and a compulsory ballot.

(3) A series of *unfair industrial practices* limited union rights to take secondary industrial action.

(4) A *Registrar* was established with wide powers to examine and rewrite union rules. Those unions which failed to register lost tax concessions and immunities.

(5) Registered unions could utilise a new procedure to gain *recognition and bargaining rights*.

(6) The *closed shop* was attacked by making pre-entry closed shop agreements void and by giving rights to individuals not to belong to a union.

(7) There were *individual rights* introduced for the first time: there was a legal protection against *unfair dismissal* and a *right to belong to a union*.

(8) A new Labour court, the *National Industrial Relations Court* was established to hear cases and appeals from the industrial tribunals.

The Act was a singular failure. Its ambition, scale and new institutions focused opposition. Its objectives, seeking to pressure union leaders to discipline their members whilst at the same time attacking their institutifonal interests, for example, the closed shop, were to a degree contradictory. In a full employment situation union hostility was effective. There were one day stoppages of one and two million workers before the Act was on the statute book. Employers collaborated in neutering the Act, ignoring its provisions on legally binding agreements and the closed shop. The Acts stimulated rather than minimised conflict and each confrontation intensified opposition. The government's one use of the cooling-off period provoked a six to one vote by railway workers in favour of their claim.

The use of the Act's penal clauses led to the imprisonment of five dockers in Pentonville for contempt. A major political confrontation with thousands of workers on strike and the TUC calling a one day general strike, was only avoided by a hurried House of Lords judgement overturning the Court of Appeal. The government carried through a *volte face* in its economic policies. From then on the Act was largely inoperative. This episode led many to conclude that in Britain a programme of legislation to restrict the unions simply would not work. In reality the débâcle had specific explanations in the weaknesses of the Heath government and crucially in the existence of full employment and the social power it gave the trade unions.

The Social Contract

The legislation introduced by the incoming Labour administration from 1974 was an essential part of the Social Contract; an attempt, given the deteriorating economic position, to involve the trade union leaders more closely than ever before in state institutions and the operation of the economy and ensure their co-operation and that of their members through incorporation rather than confrontation. The philosophy was to strengthen the Donovan approach by embodying some of its prescriptions in law. Against this background Labour's legal programme:

(1) *Restored trade union immunities to the 1906 position* in the process overriding certain more modern judge-made liabilities.

(2) *Extended the legal rights of individuals*, for example, strengthening their position in relation to unfair dismissal; introducing guarantee payments when workers were laid off; introducing a system of maternity leave and maternity pay; and developing new rights in the areas of sex and race discrimination and health and safety.

(3) *Introduced a series of collective rights for trade unions and trade unionists*: a new recognition procedure was established; unions were given the right to advance notice and consultation when redundancies were declared. Employers were required to disclose information to trade unionists for collective bargaining purposes; compulsory arbitration awards could be made against employers not meeting the general level of terms and conditions in their trade or industry. And there were new rights to time off and facilities for union representatives and protections against dismissal or victimisation for union membership or activities.

This represented a dramatic change in union attitudes and an important qualification to trade union voluntarism. For the first time they had adopted a strategy of reliance on law and the state, starkly contrasting with the philosophy of independence they had outlined to the Donovan Commission. A point that should not be overlooked, however, is that many of the changes were required not simply by Congress House but by the need to meet EEC standards.

One reaction was to criticise the new 'corporatism' on the grounds that the unions were endangering their role of representing their members by becoming appendages of the state. Many of the rights, it was argued, were extremely limited, and difficult to enforce with inadequate remedies. Reliance on legal and quasi-legal procedures could undermine more direct and potentially successful action.

The restrictions the unions accepted set the price of the legislation very high. The new structures could be built on in an anti-union way by a future hostile government. Another response was to argue that trade unions were running the country in defiance of democratic processes. In reality the TUC accepted some of the sharpest real wage cuts this century, rises in unemployment and cutbacks in welfare provision, in return for what amounted to influence not power. Its policies on workers participation, import controls and planning agreements were not implemented despite tight controls over industrial action and support for restrictive codes on the closed shop, picketing and industrial action. Rank and file resistance to TUC policies erupted in the 1979 'winter of discontent', when voters went some way with the Conservative manifesto's judgement that between 1974 and 1976 Labour had enacted a 'militants' charter of trade union legislation. It tilted the balance of power in bargaining throughout industry away from responsible management and towards unions and sometimes towards unofficial groups acting in defiance of their official union leadership.'

Thatcherism and the unions

For many the 1974–9 Labour government represented the final failure of the reform—incorporation strategy. The post-war consensus, temporarily breached in 1970–2, must now, they argued, be laid to rest. The 1979 Conservative government was determined to succeed where Edward Heath had failed in establishing a detailed legal framework for trade unions. The repressive strategy – building on an attempt by the judiciary to circumscribe union immunities in a series of cases from 1977 – would be given a second chance.

This time it was part of a more rigorous economic perspective. The government declared themselves in favour of a monetarist strategy of removing artificial obstructions to the free play of market forces which involved increasing unemployment to interwar levels and cutting back the welfare state. Legal changes were essential to transform trade unionism, reduce wages to productivity-related levels and end restrictive practices, to renovate Britain's economic base. The legislation therefore lacked the integrationist conceptions of Heath's Industrial Relations Act. It was intended to weaken union organisation, undermine efficient union methods, limit solidarity and integrate unions into a 'joint interest with the employer' perspective, curtail unions' political involvement, and mobilise the passive rank and file against the union activists, at the same time as coercing union leaders to police those activists. The government's purpose was not simply the diminution of trade union bargaining power and the reduction of its coverage of the labour force through the development of union-free zones in the new high-tech industries. The intention was to transform the *nature* of trade unionism on the lines of the model offered by US non-political business unionism and to stimulate a restructuring of industrial relations through more direct employer–employee communications; the introduction of new technology; increased flexibility at work; the eradication of traditional union controls over production; the extension of the part-time labour force; and the development of long term 'no strike' collective agreements. In other words, legal policy was in-extricably intermeshed with other aspects of the administration's industrial relations policy.

The government's position was well thought out and well prepared. During the period of opposition, groups under Lord Carrington and Nicholas Ridley analysed past mistakes, future possibilities and the likely union response. The now famous Ridley Report was a model of forward thinking in contrast to the lack of foresight of the TUC.

The lessons learned from the 1971 experience dictated a cautious, step-by-step approach. These limited initiatives minimised opposition and allowed the legislation to develop in tandem with other aspects of government policies. When required, as in the 1981 confrontation with the miners over pit closures, Mrs Thatcher was willing to beat a tactical retreat rather than risk the consequences of a conflict she judged to be dangerously premature. The unions have been in a far worse position than in the early seventies with falling membership, dwindling finances, fears of redundancy, weakened workplace organisation and irresolute leadership limiting resistance. The three pieces of legislation, the Employment Act 1980 and 1982, and the Trade Union Act 1984, contain the following provisions:

(1) *Individual and union rights are limited:* it is harder to claim unfair dismissal or maternity leave, and the procedures for seeking

union recognition and extending the terms of collective agreements have been abolished. The Fair Wages Resolution has been rescinded.

(2) The *closed shop is weakened*. For employers to be protected against unfair dismissal proceedings the closed shop agreement must have been sanctioned by 80% of those covered by it in a secret ballot. Ballots must be held every five years. Existing employees are not bound by the ballot whilst even those employed later have a right not to be members if they can show genuine grounds of conscience. Compensation for those unfairly sacked in closed shop situations is dramatically increased and can total well over £20,000. Unions can be liable for damages if they seek dismissal of non-unionists.

(3) *Union members are given new rights* to claim unreasonable exclusion or expulsion from the union even if the rules are followed, if they work in a closed shop.

(4) *Industrial action is curtailed* by giving the courts new powers to strike down secondary boycotts and sympathy strikes, unless certain complicated and stringent conditions are met, and by removing immunities from those picketing at any workplace other than their own.

(5) *Union-labour-only contracts are made unlawful* by outlawing all agreements, tenders, lists of suppliers which require union membership as a condition of award.

(6) *Elections of union executives and executive officers must meet stringent balloting requirements* or they can be struck down by the courts.

(7) *Union immunities are removed if industrial action is called without a majority vote in a secret ballot*.

(8) *Ballot on whether a union can maintain a fund for political expenditure* must be held every ten years commencing in 1986. Unions will find it more difficult to use their ordinary funds for political campaigning.

(9) The *Taff Vale doctrine is re-enacted* so that unions as organisations are made responsible where members or officials commit civil wrongs unless the union denounces the action in question and polices the membership. Union funds are therefore at risk.

The union response

Throughout the late seventies and early eighties union leadership was unimaginative and marked by a lack of strategic thinking. It now seems clear that the union leaders miscalculated in their analysis of both the ambitious scale of conservative policy aspirations and the determination of Mrs Thatcher to see things through. They were initially disoriented by the limited nature of the 1980 legislation and the fact that Jim Prior, Norman Tebbit's predecessor as Employment Minister, was a politician of moderation. More basically, their view that the administration would turn back from the consequences of its policies, particularly as unemployment soared, and do a 'U-turn' like Edward Heath illustrated a lack of understanding of Thatcherism.

The limited 'Day of Action' against the Conservatives' first set of measures gave way to a more orchestrated strategy at a time when the unions were already significantly weaker than in 1979. At a special conference at Wembley in early 1982 the TUC agreed a programme of action to immobilise the Conservative measures. Power was given to the General Council to call industrial action if an affiliate was brought before the courts.

However, in a series of small cases during 1981 and 1982 major unions accepted injunctions. Unions generally were on the defensive and little help was afforded by the TUC to unions such as the rail union, ASLEF, which had asked for support in their own disputes. At the 1983 Congress a policy of 'new realism' of seeking an accommodation with the government was adopted by the unions. When in the autumn of 1983 the Post Office Engineering Union was restrained by the Court of Appeal under the 1980 Act from boycotting attempts at privatisation of telecommunications, Len Murray informed them that the TUC was not interested in urging unions to break the law.

This approach was taken a stage further in 1983. The National Graphical Association locked in a dispute over the closed shop with a small employer, Eddie Shah, refused to comply with an order to restrain unlawful picketing under the 1980 Act. It refused to pay fines eventually totalling £750,000 and had its total assets sequestrated. The TUC General Council, strongly influenced by Len Murray, failed to support the union. This appeared to represent a watershed in relation to the early '70s. The union rank and file no longer had the ability to take action independently of their leaders as had happened in 1972. And the leadership were not prepared to initiate it from above.

The insistence of the government on banning trade union membership at the communication centre, GCHQ, and its inability to proffer even the smallest concessions to the unions severely inhibited the 'new realism', whilst the alternative, the Wembley principles, had been undermined by the TUC leadership itself and were increasingly seen as self-protective rhetoric related to internal union political processes, rather than a serious programme of action to derail the legislation. The 1984–5 miners' strike was the most important industrial struggle in half a century. The defeat of the miners with their left-wing leadership removed a major obstacle from the path of Conservative policies. The new legislation was used only in the most limited fashion by the National Coal Board itself. Its use by companies which traded with the Board, however, led to sequestration of the assets of the South Wales NUM. But what marked the dispute and eventually produced a complete takeover of the national union's assets by the courts was a plethora of actions brought by working miners using long established common law rights. Nonetheless, the confrontation confirmed the lessons of the NGA-Shah dispute: under prevailing conditions unions were in no position to repeat the successful resistance of the early seventies. Its aftermath produced a new realism in practice as unions took steps to ensure that their activities stayed within the law and obeyed injunctions when they were issued. The Austin Rover strike in late 1984 involved all of the unions represented, except the Transport and General Workers Union, in accepting the court's edicts on ballots. The TGWU, fined £200,000, decided, in its turn, to modify its stance. When, in the 1986 Wapping dispute between the print unions and Rupert Murdoch, SOGAT's assets were taken over because of their failure to obey court orders, the union's behaviour contrasted with that of the mineworkers: they apologised and purged their contempt.

In a specific sense the introduction and operation of a new legal framework for industrial relations constituted a Conservative success story. From a broader perspective the verdict has to be a more qualified one: there can be little doubt that Mrs Thatcher's success with the unions owes far more to the disciplining impact of record unemployment levels than it does to a change of attitude on the part of union members and activists. And the continued dependence on sustained unemployment as her second term reaches completion is, in an important sense, a failure. The reforms on balloting within the unions have struck a certain resonance with members. But a majority of the ballots on the closed shop have shown impressive majorities for its maintenance. The provisions of the 1984 Act requiring unions to ballot on the maintenance of their political funds backfired badly: in union after union the members affirmed that they wished their organisations to be involved in politics rather than sticking to the industrial sphere. Indeed several unions successfully balloted their members on establishing a political fund for the first time. Trade unionists, if they limit their picketing, as the law demands, to the primary employer, do so not because they have been convinced by the government that secondary picketing is illegitimate but simply because they fear the consequences for their union funds if the law is utilised.

The unions have lost nearly 3 million members since 1979. Unionisation in the labour force is now well below 50%. Strikes and days lost through strikes are running at pre-war levels. The number of shop stewards in manufacturing is estimated at 40% below the figure a decade ago. The TUC's political influence is derisory. Unions such as the Electricians and the Engineers have eagerly embraced the new business model of trade unionism. But as long as these changes are fuelled by a deflated economy and underpinned by legal coercion the achievement in industrial relations generally and in trade union law specifically, remains a fragile one. Indeed, there has already been some reaction against present policies. Far from giving Mrs Thatcher a Falkland style fillip, her triumphalism during the miners' strike led to criticism and a faltering in the opinion polls. The Wapping dispute appeared to produce for the first time in many observers a realisation of the scope of the new legal edifice and its lopsided nature: whilst the employer was able to obtain a variety of remedies to restrain picketing and boycotting of his product, the unions had no rights to contest the mass dismissal of their members. It was pointed out that it was as if the Conservatives had legislated for half of the system that operates in countries which have a strong legal framework for their industrial relations. The legal restraints and responsibilities on unions were nearly all now present in the UK: what was missing were the correlative protections and rights given to unions in such systems. The *degree* to which union activities had been fettered, employment protection rights cut back, institutional stimuli to collective bargaining removed and greater freedom given to the judges to develop common law wrongs against the unions in the absence of immunities, was much remarked upon.

The future

If, as a nation, we are to remain in permanent recession, then the present restraint produced in the unions by economic fear and legal coercion may develop into an increasing if grudging acceptance of the recent legislation by the trade unions in the context of a further period of Conservative government. Alternatively, the real test of Britain's new trade union laws could come in a period of economic upturn when more employers feel the necessity to use the law. The degree to which the legal framework can actively change the behaviour of industrial relations actors and seriously influence the operation of the system is still unresolved.

For the Conservative leadership the present chapter is not yet closed. There is a new emphasis on legislation as an instrument of wages policy. A bill presently before Parliament will remove those under the age of 21 from the scope of Wages Councils which set basic minimum rates. Plans to abolish parts of legislation such as the Factories Acts, which restrict the hours of young people, are under active consideration. Legislation to circumscribe industrial action in essential services has been under review for some time. Any significant changes must now await a General election. Nonetheless, the Conservative Party's manifesto is likely to contain a crop of new legal measures aimed at trade unions. The SDP-Liberal Alliance supports the new framework in broad terms. In some cases (the political levy) it wants to go further but it emphasises the importance of complementing controls over trade unions with additional rights for workers, more participation and a background of profit sharing and incomes policy.

The policy of a future Labour government has been the subject of much contention: widely different approaches have been advocated. It now appears likely that Labour will cross the Rubicon and forsake the system of immunities for a charter of positive rights for trade unions to associate, bargain and take industrial action, whilst the employment protection rights would be restored to their 1979 position and developed beyond it. Part-time workers would be included in the protections. Legislation would guarantee workers an extended role in company decision-making. A national minimum wage also appears to be on the agenda. Of course, rights entail limitations and correlative responsibilities. Even though the immunity form will go, the right to take industrial action will be subject to specific exceptions. What appears still unresolved is the degree to which the courts will continue to be involved in industrial relations and the extent to which they will be replaced by specialist adjudicatory bodies. The Labour leadership has no wish to simply repeal the right to ballot on union elections and industrial action which are perceived as electorally popular. Despite opposition from the left the suggestion is that a Code of Practice would cover these matters. A union which violated its provisions could have its legal rights and its tax advantages withdrawn by a powerful new body tentatively termed the Industrial Democracy Commission.

What *is* clear is that the days of voluntarism have gone for ever. Whatever the immediate future holds it will leave Britain with an extended legal framework governing the relationships between union and employers and the ambit of union freedoms. It is the content of that framework which remains contentious and problematic.

Reading

G. S. Bain (ed.), *Industrial Relations in Britain*, Blackwell, 1983.

K. Coates and T. Topham, *Trade Unions and Politics*, Blackwell, 1986.

H. A. Clegg, *The Changing System of Industrial Relations in Great Britain*, Blackwell, 1979.

C. Crouch, *The Politics of Industrial Relations*, Fontana, 1979.

P. Fosh and C. R. Littler (eds.), *Industrial Relations and the Law in the 1980's: Issues and Future Trends*, Gower, 1985.

J. A. G. Griffith, *The Politics of the Judiciary*, Fontana, 1981.

R. Lewis (ed.), *Labour Law in Britain*, Blackwell, 1986.

G. Palmer, *British Industrial Relations*, George Allen & Unwin, 1983.

K. Wedderburn, *The Worker and the Law*, Penguin, 1986.

ECONOMIC ISSUES

Chapter Seven   *Geoffrey Lee*

Privatisation

This chapter considers the political and economic arguments for and against privatisation. It begins with an explanation of the rather complex terminology and a list of past, present and future candidates for transfer of economic organisations from the public (government-owned) to the private sector.

Terminology

'Privatisation' is used to cover several political initiatives.

(*a*) Denationalisation – this term was employed before 'privatisation' came into fashion. While some industries, such as British Rail and British Leyland, could be returned whence they came, most concerns in this process were never in the private sector.

(*b*) Sale of 100% of the shares of a newly-created (but still publicly owned) company; either on the stock market, e.g. Amersham International, Enterprise Oil and British Gas, or to management and workforce e.g. the National Freight Corporation.

(*c*) Issue of 51% i.e. a majority of shares in a newly-created public company e.g. British Aerospace, Britoil and British Telecom.

(*d*) Issue of 49% i.e. a minority of a public company's share, e.g. Associated British Ports.

(*e*) Placement of shares with investors, e.g. 24% of British Sugar.

(*f*) Hiving off and outright sale of profitable concerns – Sealink and Hotels (from BR), Jaguar (from BL), warship yards (from British Shipbuilders).

(*g*) Sale of shares and removal of custodianship/aid e.g. through National Enterprise Board (Ferranti, ICL).

(*h*) Joint ventures with private sector – Hoverlloyd and BR hover-crafts, Allied Steel and Wire (British Steel & GKN).

(*i*) Permitting competition in place of former monopoly – Mercury in telecommunications (25% government-owned), private generation and sale of electricity (only two companies studying feasibility by August 1984) and coach companies.

(*j*) Permitting and stimulating private contractors to tender for public services. Southend and Wandsworth Councils led the way on refuse collection. By September 1984 all but thirty-five of the 223 district health authorities had complied with the circulars requiring them to put catering, cleaning and laundry out to tender.

(*k*) Introduction of private finance into large projects e.g. road-building (Civil Engineering Economic Development Council).

Some of the categories above were interlinked: often the sale of a majority of shares was the first stage in selling off the whole; private sector take-overs occurred as worker–management buyouts failed (BR hotels) and government directed who could and could not own industries (RTZ's share of Enterprise Oil, and that Thorn-EMI and not AT&T should buy Inmos).

Main sales to date

1979/80	*£ millions*
BP (5%)	276
ICL (25%)	37
Suez Finance Co.	57
1980/1	
Ferranti (50%)	55
Fairey (100%)	22
British Aerospace (51%)	195
Automation & Technical Services etc.	91
Prestcold (100%)	9
1981/2	
British Sugar (24%)	44
Cable & Wireless (50%)	182
Amersham International (100%)	64
National Freight Corporation (100%)	5

1982/3

Britoil (51%)	225
Associated British Ports (49%)	46
British Transport Hotels (100%)	40
International Aeradio	60

1983/4

Britoil	293
BP (7%)	565
Cable & Wireless (25%)	260

1984/5

J.H. Sankey	12
Scott Lithgow	12
Lye Tinplate	16
Enterprise Oil (100%)	392
Wytch Farm Oil (50%)	215
Associated British Ports (48.5%)	51
Inmos	95
Jaguar Cars	295
Sealink	66
British Telecom (51%)	3,700
Total	7,380

1985/6

Britoil (48·8%)	450
RO Factory, Leeds	11
Hall Russell shipyard	–
Leyland Bus	12
Cable & Wireless (22·7%)	558
Unipart	50
Trustee Savings Bank	1,000
Warshipbuilding Yards	122
British Aerospace (48·4%)	400
BA Helicopters	27

Future Candidates

Short-term (pre-general election)

British Gas (100%)	8,000
National Bus Company (100%)	200
British Airports Authority	800
British Technology Group (ex-NEB)	–
Rolls Royce	(100)
BP (31·7%)	3,000
Leyland Trucks	–
British Telecom (49·8%)	6,000
Dockyard management	–
Short Bros	200
Ship repair yards	20
British Airways	1,000

Long-term (under consideration or advocated by pressure groups)

Water Authorities
British Airways
Rover (British Leyland)
British Nuclear Fuels
Electricity Industry
British Rail (main-line stations and routes)
London Regional Transport
BBC (Radios 1 and 2)
Civil Aviation Authority
National Girobank
Post Office
British Coal
British Steel
Royal Ordnance

In addition to any further sales, more NHS and local government services would be contracted out. In September 1985 it was reported that plans were being implemented to commercialise hospitals with restaurants, private health screening and shops, and in 1986 that the Prime Minister wanted to speed up tendering of cleaning, laundry and catering services to save more than the current £40 million – even if that meant using existing staff rather than improved methods. Social services departments were to make more use of voluntary agencies and charities and the DHSS sold 20 centres for homeless people. In July

1986 the DOE revived its plan to compel tendering for refuse collection, school meals, vehicle fleet maintenance and street cleansing. New Town asset sales had brought £317 million by 1985 and councils were even thinking of selling 480 playing fields to raise money. The radical Right were reported in March 1986 to have proposed tendering for packages of schools, urban and rural.

Meanwhile Central Government continued to hive off or contract out – Treasury computer operations, and army pay corps, dental and medical services (the last group being part of a reorganisation to free 4,000 soldiers for front-line duty).

The impetus for privatisation

The arguments for nationalisation had consisted of an intermeshed set of factors: economic ones such as economies of scale, coordinated investment and the public control of monopoly power; political-economic impulses to preserve key industries such as Rolls Royce and British Leyland; socio-political reasons such as the provision of uniform services and safeguarding regional economic development; and political determination to ensure the public ownership of key industries.

A similar mixture is to be found in the rationale for privatisation.

Political

(*a*) *Ideological underpinning*   It has long been a central tenet of Conservative political philosophy that the role of the state should be minimised, and the government which came into office in 1979 was clearly committed to rolling back the frontiers. In particular there was little liking for the nationalised industries; the eighteen largest employed 1.6 million workers, in protected or monopoly markets, with strong unionised workforces, and large debts. These 'dinosaurs' were said to increase the scale of public borrowing, increase taxation and cause unemployment. In the House of Lords Lord Beswick noted the 'sick language' used by the Prime Minister and her colleagues in describing them as 'horrific, poisonous, debilitating, voracious and a haemorrhage' (Hansard, 4 February 1981).

(*b*) *Policy formulation*   Yet while the political inclination may have been there, no radical programme of privatisation existed. In April 1977 John Biffen had called for the introduction of some private sector resources into nationalised industries but the Conservative policy study group had reported in 1978 that denationalisation 'must be pursued cautiously and flexibly, recognising that major changes may well be out of the question in some industries' (*Sunday Times*, 9 October 1983). The Conservatives were slow to reject completely the thirty-year Butskellite agreement on the boundaries of the public sector. For their 1979 manifesto they adhered to the so-called 'BP solution' of selling just under a half share in a few industries. Intellectual respectability and guidance began to be added — from the Institute of Economic Affairs, the Centre for Policy Studies, the Adam Smith Institute and Professors Beesley and Littlechild.

When the government had to channel hundreds of millions of pounds into loss-making industries such as British Steel and British Shipbuilders, and as some of their manifesto sales were thwarted by economic and technical problems, it seemed the process would falter. An article 'Whatever happened to the great sell-off?' in the *Observer* concluded of privatisation, 'The word hasn't yet made its way into any dictionary. Whether it will now do so is increasingly doubtful' (23 November 1980).

(*c*) *Policy commitment*   A radical change in policy was signalled, however, by Sir Geoffrey Howe in 1981 with the declaration that the postal services, British Telecom, BNOC and even gas and electricity were under consideration. Sir Keith Joseph has stated that in so attempting to deal with the problem and clear their desks, privatisation was a product of government, not opposition. It was very much in keeping with 'the resolute approach'. The 1983 manifesto promised to continue the process, and only as an afterthought were nationalised industries unsuitable for privatisation mentioned. It was said that ministers were competing to bring industries to market as proof of their political virility. Having sold off assets worth £3.6 billion since 1979, the Cabinet 'E' committee agreed to sell a further £10 billion over five years — it was clear that privatisation had become a central and distinguishing policy of the Thatcher government. Mr John Moore, Financial Secretary in the Treasury and in reality the minister for privatisation, attacked the failure of the concept of public corporations and warned that 'no state monopoly is sacrosanct' (*Financial Times*, 2 November 1983). By 1983/4 the scale of the shift in the debate was astonishing — groups were then calling for the privatisation of the railways, coal, gas, electricity, the universities, the BBC and more of the NHS. In response to the question what would be left at the end of a third Thatcher government, Mr Moore was said to have replied 'the Treasury'. Stockbrokers Grievson Grant identified a package of £28½ billion assets in 1984 and went on to suggest another available £55 billion which the Government could sell.

The proof of ideological commitment is the willingness to privatise for nil gain; the introduction of private management into the 2 royal dockyards would have cost as much as it would save over 3½ years and selling Rolls Royce would involve writing off debts of £372 million, injecting another £100 million and yet still giving state support. The latter has the symbolic political attraction of reversing the Heath Government's 1971 'lame-duck' takeover.

(*d*) *Public opinion*   Bolstering the government's case is a public opinion far from hostile to privatisation. A MORI poll in 1983 showed 39% favouring privatisation against 21% wanting more nationalisation (*Sunday Times*, 9 October 1983). £40 billion has been spent on nationalisation and write-offs since the war, but it has shown to be a vote-loser. An ORC poll in 1978 showed that 71% of respondents (against 19%) thought it to have failed, and 78% (against 13%) believed Labour should abandon the policy (*Times*, 10 July 1978). And in times of high unemployment, the unions' defence of jobs and index-linked pensions was muted.

(*e*) *A share-owning democracy*   Just as the Conservatives have sought to strengthen property-owning democracy (e.g. by council house sales), fostering a share-owning democracy is a political ambition. Share ownership in Britain has been rising − from 7% in 1979 to 14% or 6 million people in 1986, with large organisations such as pension funds owning 72% (*Financial Times*, 24 April 1986). By contrast, in the USA 42.5 million citizens own shares, with most of western countries ahead of the UK.

Small investors have been favoured in sales such as British Aerospace − of the 158,000 initial investors, 150,000 held less than 1,000 shares. In the Britoil sale small investors were offered a loyalty bonus whereby after three years they would receive a free share for every ten held.

The major effort came with the sale of British Telecom when a £7.6 million advertising campaign was launched by the government in the press and on television to persuade people to buy shares and so share in BT's future. The simplicity of the procedures was stressed, booklets on the city and shares and investment were provided, and incentives were offered in the form of £18 vouchers to offset rental payments and a 1 for 10 scrip issue. Application forms could be taken to banks and post offices. In offering free shares and other incentives to BT employees the government was dealing with nearly a ¼ million potential investors. The flotation of BT in November 1984 was hailed as a triumph for the government as two million people bought shares, many for the first time (small investors being favoured in the allocation of shares). Of BT's 233,000 employees, 96% ignored union advice and applied for free shares. The selling of TSB and British Gas are expected to widen ownership further. The government was not pleased by the executive director of the Bank of England scornfully dismissing the prospects of dispersal (November 1984).

(*f*) *Workers as shareholders*   The idea of workers becoming share-holders in their own company is not new – Sir Alfred Mond, the founder of ICI, advocated this. Unlike co-operatives, worker share-holding leaves control undisturbed and has been advocated as the answer to socialism, in making workers 'capitalists'.

During the process of privatisation, worker shareholding has obvious attractions – it weakens opposition, particularly if free shares are offered, and may impede renationalisation later. In the longer term, it may motivate staff and increase productivity – Keith Stuart, Chief Executive of Associated British Ports, was convinced that staff aware-ness of the business had increased since workers had taken 8% of the shareholding. Between 1979 and 1986 some 600,000 workers were transferred from the public to the private sector, over half had become shareholders and the proportion of state industry had fallen from $10 \cdot 5\%$ to $6 \cdot 5\%$. Besides weakening the trade unions, it has been argued that worker shareholding, in producing lower wage claims, will assist the economy. In November 1983 British Airways, as preparation for its privatisation, offered its 36,000 workers low wage rises for two years in return for a profit-sharing bonus plan, with money held in trust for share purchase. The frequently cited example of worker shareholding success is the National Freight Corporation, where management took the initiative in 1981 and organised the biggest buyout in British industry. 82% of the company is now owned by 13,000 of the employees, and after eighteen months their £1 shares were worth £4, with £2 million shared as dividends.

The management of the Vickers and Cammell Laird warship yards worked to persuade employees and local residents to invest to the extent that 80% of the work-force subscribed, with the whole oversubscribed twice.

Profit-sharing schemes have been encouraged by the 1978 and 1980 Finance Acts which conferred tax benefits on employees and companies. Nigel Lawson's 'Popular Capitalism' budget of 1986 was well received by 58% of people − it offered tax incentives to buy shares, employee share schemes (1·5 million workers now covered), and outlined a profit-sharing plan that would link 20% of wages to those profits.

(g) *Public borrowing* Between 1979 and 1983 privatisation revenue totalled £1·8 billion and the sale of council houses £4·55 billion. These sales of assets reduce the Public Sector Borrowing Requirement (PSBR − or the amount government has to borrow each year to balance income with expenditure). Additional expenditure is therefore possible by allowing a higher PSBR when these sales are added. In 1983/4 the asset sales brought £3·1 billion which was 30% over the intended PSBR target of £10 billion. For 1985−6, if the proposed sales were subtracted, the PSBR of £7 billion or 2% of GDP would have to be halved. Privatisation thus enables the government to cling to the monetarist claims of expenditure control and sound finance, while continuing to spend with a large deficit − keeping pressure off ministers.

By 1986 the central issue was whether the Chancellor could generate enough revenue for tax cuts and/or public spending to ensure a suitable approach to the election. Though the government minimised the fact, the £4·5 billion a year in 1986−8 from asset sales would be crucial.

(h) *Civil service interference* Nationalised industries have always had to submit their investment and borrowing plans to the Treasury and report to their 'sponsoring ministry'. But beyond the formal controls there have been the 'lunchtime directives' to chairmen and informal pressures − to set an example on pricing, wage settlements and to favour British manufacturers, e.g. of aircraft or computers. The chief executive of National Freight described privatisation as 'breaking out of a strait-jacket' and the chairman of Cable and Wireless of an end to the 'psychology of restraint' − C & W had seen the 'dead hand' of the Treasury delay its plans and veto a vital project. The idea of being free to make commercial decisions and being rid of constant meetings with officials has proved attractive to corporation boards, and serves the government's purpose of reducing the role and size of the 'bureaucracy'.

Commercial

(*i*) *Expansion*   In freeing the corporations the government believes they will be able to invest more, expand and meet international competition.

In 1981 BT lost customers as it raised prices to keep its £1 billion self-provided investment going. The Treasury had withdrawn the chance of raising a £360 m bond and BT had to be helped twice by raising its borrowing powers. Privatisation is intended to avoid this constraint and enable BT to compete with the privately-owned communications company, Mercury, and its backer Cable and Wireless (C&W), Standard Telephones and Cables and the formerly state-assisted ICL and with international competition. Once privatised, BT began to expand overseas, particularly in North America, through joint ventures (DuPont) and takeovers (Mitel, CTG and Dialcom). Similarly, British Gas intended to re-enter the spheres of oil exploration and production, and begin joint ventures, especially in the USA.

Similarly, the government believes it has no place in the dynamic, competitive environment of oil exploration and production – so hiving off Britoil from the regulatory functions of the British National Oil Corporation (BNOC). In August 1984 Jaguar Cars, hived off from BL, announced plans to expand production by 4,000 cars a year and employ 530 extra workers, to meet demand and German competition. Here was evidence, claimed government supporters, that privatisation works.

(*j*) *Efficiency*   Nationalised industries' accounts have been poor measures of their performance, for in addition to problems of inflation and depreciation, governments have altered prices or levied profits. Supporters contend that the threat of privatisation so concentrated the mind that efficiency improves dramatically. In 1983 British Steel's productivity was greater than West Germany's, BL's newest plants approach Japanese standards, and government spokesmen commented favourably as BT created and then reorganised its divisions, introduced profit centres, revolutionised its accountancy away from monopoly capitalisation, and generated an outward-looking, commercial perspective. Mercury launched a 12–25% cheaper service for some phone/calls, and both they and BT lost their exclusive rights to computer communication by phone network. Nor has OFTEL taken a low profile, as many has predicted, as it stopped BT linking with IBM, obtained interconnect terms favourable to Mercury, set up 3,000 'watchdogs' to monitor service and demanded more information to scrutinise prices.

(*k*) *Customer satisfaction*   By increasing efficiency and introducing new services the customer benefits: from British Rail's special offers; from BT's Advanced Business Systems or from a wider range of telephones and absence of a long waiting list; from lower rates bills where refuse services have been privatised; from a choice of airline services on UK routes; and in towns like Hereford, where competition on bus services was introduced − more frequent services and lower fares.

The promotion of efficiency and removal of 'take it or leave it' attitudes became central to the advocacy of privatisation.

The government could also claim to have taken steps to safeguard the public. In its Gas Bill it strengthened safety provisions − requiring a response to leaks within 12 hours (half the time required at present) and BGC will be responsible for leaks on the customer side. For Water privatisation they proposed an inspectorate to measure and enforce pollution controls, spending requirements on environmental protection, powers to set aside special protection zones and a statutory code of practice − this would only cost 3% of authorities' expenditure.

The case against privatisation

General

(*a*) *Confused objectives*   It was unlikely that the factors described above would weave together into a coherent strategy. The main inconsistency has proved to be between the ideological drive for liberalisation and competition and the Treasury-led demand for maximum sales revenue.

This was exposed most clearly in the privatisation of British Telecom and British Gas (BGC), monopolies capable of generating annual profits in excess of £1 billion. Having decided against breaking up BT on either a regional or product basis so as to maximise income upon flotation and create an international 'heavy weight' the Government had to institute a regulatory quango in the form of the Office of Telecommunications (OFTEL). Instead of creating bureaucratic controls which critics doubted would be effective, many Conservatives demanded competition. In this respect ministers were also faulted for safeguarding the fledgling Mercury at the expense of would-be leasers and resellers of BT lines.

When the BGC's oil assets were sold off as Enterprise Oil and only one-sixth of the shares were wanted by ordinary investors, the government were placed in the embarrassing position of blocking Rio Tinto Zinc's bid for 49%. While this was consistent with the aims of promoting competition (RTZ has oil interests) and safeguarding small investors in an independent company, it alienated free-market Conservatives and the City. The gas and electricity industries presented a similar dilemma – whether to break the production and distribution monopolies radically or simply sell the shares and apply regulation.

The Civil Aviation Authority's recommendation in 1984 that over thirty major routes can be taken from British Airways and given to competitors produced uproar. BA hotly opposed the plan as producing no competition or benefit to the customer, and retarding privatisation. In becoming efficient for flotation BA had become more of a threat to competitors.

When privatising Jaguar the government were accused by the all-party trade and industry committee of rendering BL and its privatisation less viable, and the government had to turn down a management–worker buyout of some of BR's hotels in order to try for a better price. A bitter dispute occurred over Britoil's capital structure, as the company tried to obtain government funds while the Treasury pressed for a sale of assets to save money. The result was a Britoil perceived to be weak with insufficient reserves while the government was still accused of wasting money.

Inevitably, others pressed the cause of privatisation to logical conclusions with demands for the break up of monopolies, buy-outs and decentralisation (CBI October 1983), and the widespread ownership of capital by giving away shares (Samuel Brittan, *Financial Times*, the SDP, and the Stock Exchange chairman). At times the government was trapped between its own inclinations towards market forces and political expediency. After secretly negotiating with Ford to take over Austin–Rover and having invited General Motors to discuss the Trucks and Land Rover parts of BL, it found itself assailed by angry Tory MPs led by Ted Heath and Michael Heseltine. Having followed orders to privatise BL, directors now began to bid for Land Rover and other offers, having been spurned, were welcomed. All negotiations were eventually dropped. Similarly, in deciding between state-owned Harland & Wolff and newly-privatised Swan Hunter for a £130 million order the government was squeezed between Harland's cheaper bid under 'competitive tendering' (and appeasing Loyalists), and yet not wishing to see a new company go bankrupt in the North-East (where there were marginal seats) after it was virtually promised the order before flotation. Both yards were given work.

(b) *The wrong problem*   Changes in ownership do not necessarily bring improved performance. Indeed, transferring ownership to pension funds and unit trusts, away from civil servants and politicians, may actually diminish accountability.

It has been argued that privatisation is desirable because all governments interfere with nationalised industries and only severance will provide a solution. This view discounts past proposed reforms such as the Select Committee on Nationalised Industries' 1968 report recommending a ministry for the corporations and the 1976 National Economic Development Council's advocacy of policy councils to direct them. Ironically a post-privatisation measure to rationalise controls over the public corporations was dropped in 1984 because of their opposition.

It overlooks too the major successes achieved in public ownership. BP thrived irrespective of majority or minority government shareholding, while Cable and Wireless have enjoyed steady success before and after privatisation. BL as a private sector company went bankrupt, while it improved dramatically in the public sector – against competition and, under Sir Michael Edwardes, it operated at a distance from government. Hiving Jaguar off may deprive it of BL's technological developments and public high risk investment money. Ironically, the government seemed to have been making a success of the corporations, in their terms, by their board appointments. A report by the Centre for Policy Studies in July 1984 showed that chairmen were increasingly sympathetic to government policies but prepared to challenge outside interference. It was the combination of uncompromising management under chairmen such as Lord King (BA) and Mr McGregor (BS), plus competition which produced major improvements in performance. Electricity prices are lower in the UK than most of France, and the main problem for energy corporations have been Treasury-demanded price rises as chancellors sought to levy revenue, fattened them for privatisation and provided a self-fulfilling prophecy of interference.

Ownership is less important than competition in terms of responding to customer needs. Cost reduction to avoid takeover or bankruptcy will not apply to huge companies like BT and BGC. In exposing these inconsistencies, left-wing critics and crusading privatisers found a common theme − if it is such a good idea, why only sell off profitable concerns?

Political factors

(*c*) *Mangement opposition*   Three board members of BT and BNOC resigned over the privatisation issue. Nevertheless, management has largely concentrated on obtaining the best terms − resisting attempts to break up the corporations (BT, BL, BGC) or minimising regulation (the degree of control allowed BT for pricing). The most open opposition came from Sir Denis Rooke, against selling BGC's showrooms, North Sea Oil and Wytch Farm oilfield in Dorset, and from Lord King and the BA board who mounted a powerful campaign against ceding routes. Critics argued that these supposedly sympathetic chairmen had not only delayed privatisation but impeded competition. The Institute of Directors also alluded darkly to key enemies in the civil service.

After the British Airways sale had foundered several times over Laker anti-trust lawsuits, Jumbo defects, arguments over restructuring its balance sheet and a downturn in business, Nicholas Ridley postponed the 1985/6 sale because of impeding renegotiation of transatlantic flights. In anger and frustration, Lord King organised a management buyout in March 1986, but this was blocked after a public row. It was speculated that Ridley had wanted to restructure BA into 3 or 4 airlines to promote competition and increase the sale price. BR has argued that its managers do not have the time to devote to privatisation schemes.

(*d*) *Union opposition*   Unions have good reason to oppose privatisation; over nine-tenths of workers in nationalised industries are union members, many in closed shops, while three-quarters of manual and one-third of white collar workers in private manufacturing are unionised. Whilst some workers in successful enterprises such as Amersham have been unaffected, others in hotels have seen their pay, working conditions and security suffer. Unions have taken a strong anti-privatisation stance − at the 1982 TUC ten motions were submitted with demands for renationalisation without compensation, except in cases of hardship. Action taken so far has included:

(i) Days of action: by the gas and other unions (e.g. NALGO) against the sale of showrooms, and by 180,000 BT employees in six unions against privatisation in October 1982.

(ii) Alliances – NALGO contributed £1 million to a fund and agreed to work with NUPE in the campaign.

(iii) Campaigns – NUPE and SCAT (Services to Community Action and Tenants) organised local campaigns against contracting-out services. The BT unions initiated a publicity and parliamentary campaign, the latter included a 11¼ hour filibustering speech by POEU-sponsored MP John Golding. NUPE produced education packs, and the unions turned from generalised defences to critical analysis of efficiency, costs and consequences.

(iv) Education of the membership against buying shares, e.g. TGWU in National Freight Corporation and POEU in BT.

(v) Prolonged industrial action. This has been most bitter against loss of jobs through contracting-out at several hospitals and councils. In BT the POEU escalated their action in 1983, refusing to connect the rival Mercury, targetting government departments and Mercury's backers (Barclays, BP and C&W). By October 2,500 engineers were suspended and £¼ m a week was being paid in strike pay. The High Court at first ruled in the POEU's favour as job security was at stake but the Appeal Court reversed this in Mercury's favour in November (controversy arose later when it was revealed that the Master of the Rolls held shares in C&W). Despite a TUC attempt to raise funds to help the POEU, the action was called off. Industrial action does not deter a determined government with a renewed mandate, but it airs countervailing arguments and may make contractors or investors hesitate. Public opinion may be open to argument too – a Gallup poll in May 1985 showed 45% favouring privatisation of British Gas, with 35% against and 20% 'don't knows'.

(e) *Labour renationalisation* Labour's original policy was one of renationalisation without compensation but this was modified for the 1983 manifesto. Given the sums of money involved, a future Labour government would have to resort to a combination of partial and selective reacquisition, co-operatives and employee involvement in decision-making. Roy Hattersley's 1984 paper on new forms of public and social ownership highlighted this. In 1986 Labour explained that 'social ownership' would entail a public sector able to work outside cash limits with corporations able to develop commercially beyond their standard roles. Employees would collectively hold shares and would have board representation. Shares in key privatised companies could be exchanged for the original price or kept as bonds with a rate of interest. They promised to give local control and more power to consumers. A holding company and an investment bank would co-ordinate. Health service contracts would be cancelled and private schools taken over. In spelling out in detail its plan to 'renationalise' BT, Labour surprised the government, BT's share price fell and doubts appeared over the sale of British Gas.

(*f*) *Public opinion*   Labour renationalisation could well be impeded by public opinion. But that same opinion can be cited against privatisation, which polls have shown to be a low priority. Indeed a CBI—British Institute of Management survey in October 1983 revealed that only 6% of managers agreed with the government policy — privatisation ranked seventeenth on their list of priorities. The anti-privatisation of BT campaign succeeded at least to the extent that 46% thought it a bad idea in October 1983, compared to 37% in December 1982 (those who favoured it fell from 43% to 39%) according to a Gallup Poll. An NOP poll in June 1985 showed that 67% of those questioned thought the electricity industry should remain in the public sector.

(*g*) *Dubious motives*   Initially it was said that government was diverting attention and right-wing criticism from aid to 'lame duck' industries such as BL and British Steel. The privatisation connections of Conservative MPs were condemned — twenty-one owned shares in cleaning, catering or laundry firms or were part-time directors or consultants. It was alleged in July 1984 that a DHSS enquiry on contracting took place after a minister was entertained by a bidding company. The City too came in for attack as the government paid over £50 million in fees, expenses and commissions between 1979 and 1983. It received more than £128 million for the sale of BT, and auditors subsequently found £1 million illegal multiple applications and irregular allocations to two top industrialists. The government found that the rules were too indefinite to take action against profiteers buying 'institutional' shares. The Public Accounts Committee in 1986 criticised this lack of control as well as changes in the BT accounts. In December 1985 Conservative Lord Teviot was found to be receiving £20 per hour for proposing amendments to the Transport Bill on behalf of commercial bus operators. It was noted that £15 million speculative profit was made on the first day of trading in C&W shares. At the TUC conference in 1984 Mr Bickerstaffe of NUPE concluded 'wherever public need is met by private greed, corruption is not far behind ... For privatisation read profiteering, expense account lunches and sweatshop wages' (*The Guardian*, 7 September 1984). (In fact there were complaints in the City that the government was using its influence to force down fees to an unrewarding level.) The TUC reported that privatisation led to top directors obtaining an average 85% pay rise over 2 years, plus special share options and bonuses.

(*h*) *Shareholding* The ideal of a wide shareholding seems not to have been realised, for after initial interest small investors sell for a profit. Of 65,000 Amersham buyers, only 7,717 were left by October 1983. 10% of BAe's workforce did not apply for their £50 of free shares. C&W shareholders reduced from 157,000 to 26,000 in a year, and BAe from 158,000 to 26,000 at the end of 1982. The number of BT shareholders fell from 2·3 million at the time of the flotation to 1·58 million in March 1986, with the big institutions controlling 62·5% of the non-government shares. To avoid setting fixed prices too low the government was increasingly turning to the tender, on which city institutions bid low, meaning that the temptation of big gains for individuals was missing. By offering low prices for monopoly shares, it was argued that a false impression of risk capitalism had been given, and these large institutions were unwilling to take necessary risks or bring accountability to companies.

Socio-political

(*i*) *Decline in service* In October 1983 the chairman of the publicly-funded National Consumer Council warned of the dangers to consumers in privatisation, that less information would be available and that loss-making parts of the business — rural telephone boxes and bus services — would wither. The Labour Party and the TUC thought their fears were justified when BT began to rebalance its tariffs to the advantage of long-distance and international callers and to charge for 999 repairs. Deregulation of bus services under the 1985 Transport Act left ⅕ of routes with no bidders, with 35% less rural mileage compared to an 8·5% cut in urban areas. Weekend, evening services and children's reduced fares all suffered and led to complaints from Tory MPs who thought the policy helped the Liberals win the Ryedale by-election. Studies also suggested that bus privatisation would cost £3 for every pound saved and raise rates by 22% (*The Guardian*, 3 December 1984). Fear for rural post offices also stymied Post Office privatisation before an election. The National Consumer Council warned that gas prices would rise because the regulatory OFGAS would be unble to prevent cross-subsidisation of industrial contract customers with profits from tied domestic householders. The BT − like price formula of Retail Price Index minus x%, plus 'y' to reflect additional costs in buying North Sea gas, was not deemed to be strong enough. Water privatisation raised social issues; metering would be to the disadvantage of those in dirty jobs or with large families, and would commercial pressure mean disconnections?

Councils and public complained that privatised refuse services were inefficient and poor performance penalties were imposed (*Sunday Times*, 31 July 1983). Similar complaints arose over NHS contracting − checks at a Cheltenham hospital revealed 73% to 85% rejection rates on sheets and pillows, against a NHS target of 5%. Trust House Forte withdrew from tendering in September 1984 claiming the conditions imposed were detrimental to patients and staff. The TUC sent out a report claiming that 70 contracts had gone wrong.

(j) *Job Losses*   Privatisation was said to be costing jobs; 3,000 in the NHS where contractors had been told they could abandon standard terms of employment and had cut members and used part-timers; 4,000 in BR's engineering division, and up to 9,000 bus jobs due to deregulation, abolition of metropolitan authorities and break-up of the National Bus Company into 70 units. The unions also complained that BT was threatening jobs by buying Swedish and American exchanges for the first time.

Legal−political

(k) *Ownership*   The right of the government to sell public assets has been challenged, beyond the basic political objection to 'giving away' public investment.

The Trustee Saving Bank's flotation in 1985 was postponed when Scottish depositors claimed it belonged to them and were upheld in the Court of Sessions. After acrimony with the Bank the Treasury pushed an act through Parliament in 1985 saying that the TSB belonged to no-one and established ownership with the successor companies.

The Law Lords, however, in August 1986, published their decision that these had been state assets and the Treasury had given away £1 billion from the sale and £800 million assets. The £5 million campaign to sell to a million shareholders had been started in July, and the Opposition called for the Minister to be sacked for 'gross incompetence'. The Treasury maintained its position that this was a normal flotation, not privatisation. When the proposals to privatise the water authorities were published, Conservative MP Robin Maxwell-Hyslop asked what compensation rate payers would receive given that they had paid most towards the assets. The union quickly promised a legal challenge as these had never been nationalised resources. It was partly this time-consuming and controversial prospect that led to postponement until after the general election.

The government also had to accept defeat and delay at the hands of Lord Denning and his colleagues in the Upper House. Dispensing legal advice to the unions, Denning blocked the Dockyard Services Bill to privatise management in Rosyth and Devonport because a trade union consultation process had not been observed.

Political—economic

(*l*) *National interest*   It is contended that economies of scale dictate that some industries are organised on a national scale, and that bringing competition into the telephone, gas or electricity systems simply produces duplication and waste.

Some industries were acquired for the public sector because of their strategic position, particularly the oil industry — beginning with BP before the first world war. Selling Britoil caused the loss of future profits and its cash flow into the Treasury. The imperative of control can also be claimed for British Nuclear Fuels and the Royal Ordnance Factories. There was political uproar when it seemed that the state-funded microchip company Inmos would be sold to American Telephone and Telegraph (AT&T) for a mere £50 m. Claims that the government had undervalued state concerns to ensure sales led to accusations that they were 'mortgaging the future' and 'selling the family silver' (Lord Stockton, 1985).

Some 18·6% of the BT shares went to foreigners and over £100 million was taken as immediate profit.

The greatest furore met the secret talks to break up and sell BL to American companies, especially in the wake of the Westland affair.

£2·4 billion had been put into recapitalising BL since 1975 and attempted explanations that BL could not thrive were rebutted by the charge that BL exported £1 billion a year, while GM and Ford had negative balances of trade of £656 million and £501 million respectively. Complaints of anti-Americanism were swept aside as critics accused the government of 'dogma and defeatism' (Ted Heath), of reducing Britain to an offshore assembly operation and jeopardising hundreds of thousands of jobs in motor and parts manufacturing. Opponents claimed the government was not acting in the national interest by reneging on its promise to keep 25% of BAe; being pushed by Vickers' managers into privatising before awarding the Trident order to its monopoly supplier; and by allowing gas and oil companies to deplete reserves without effective control.

Financial problems
The mechanics of selling state assets often proved to be difficult and politically embarrassing.

(*m*) *Capital structures and controls*   It often takes public industries time and money to bring their accounts into line with private companies. BT's treatment of fixed assets led to qualifications on its accounts, a long argument took place over Britoil's capital structure, and BNOC's agreements with other oil companies were difficult to untangle.

One particular problem is the cost of honouring pension arrangements. £49 million of the £52 million raised by selling National Freight was used in paying off the pension scheme deficit, and to do the same for the Royal Ordnance Factories would entail the government paying out £100 m more than the sale would raise. To cope with the problem BA closed its scheme to pay off the £1·25 deficit (but running the scheme will still be a charge on profits). While BAe did not present such problems and was attractive to the market, the huge writing off of debts in the case of industries such as BA and the Docks Board (ABP) opened the government to attack.

The government was in the difficult position of honouring commitments (down to concessionary travel for BR hotel staff), exercising control in the public interest (e.g. through OFTEL), and still trying to convince the market to buy − in BA's case this led to a government promise not to exercise their influence as shareholders.

(*n*) *Timing* The government found it very difficult to 'get it right'. The Amersham issue was twenty-four times oversubscribed, 75% of Britoil was left with the underwriters, Associated British Ports and Jaguar were thirty-five and four times oversubscribed respectively, and five-sixths of Enterprise Oil was unwanted. The all-party Public Accounts Committee twice looked at and criticised the government's record, recommending phased sales.

Analysis of the sales of NFC, BP, Amersham, ABP, BAe, C&W and Britoil showed that by June 1984 the shares had risen to the extent that £799 million had been lost – to speculative gains in a rising market. BAe's shares had risen 143%. Critics pointed out that this 'rip-off' or 'shambles' was an opportunity cost worth sixteen NHS hospitals. The *Daily Mirror* dubbed it 'jumble sale politics' (28 June 1984).

Problems in this respect worsened as the market, which doubled in Mrs Thatcher's first five years, went down – wrecking the Enterprise flotation.

After the sale of BT the Labour Opposition claimed that the five times oversubscription and the 45p (or 90%) premium when the market opened meant that the government had wasted £1·3 billion, in addition to spending £320 million on the sale and was guilty of 'criminal incompetence' (House of Commons, 4 December 1984).

(*o*) *Investment* Floating huge concerns like BT and BGC created fears that a 'crowding out' of other investment – in gilts, industry, and building societies – would take place. Experts warned that higher interest rates and an appreciation of sterling would follow, putting pressure on companies profit margins.

Summary

The Conservative government almost 'happened' upon the policy of selling public assets. Despite many obstacles, inconsistencies and embarrassments it persisted and enlarged the process until privatisation not only came to be one of its main claims to success and its distinguishing feature but also a primary means of survival.

Reading

S. Hastings & H. Levie (eds.), *Privatisation?*, Spokesman, 1983.

K. Newman, *The Selling of British Telecom*, Holt, Rinehart & Winston, 1986.

J. Tivey, *Nationalisation in British Industry*, Longman, 1971.

J. Vickers and G. Yarsow, *Privatisation and the Natural Monopolies*, Public Policy Centre, 1985.

CIS Report, *Private Line*, 1982.

Adam Smith Institute, *Omega Project* reports.

NUPE Education Pack, *Keep Your Services Public*, 1982.

Roger Hall, 'Privatisation and British politics 1979–86', *Teaching Politics*, September 1986, pp. 460–76.

Chapter Eight   *John McIlroy*

Unemployment and the economy

In a society whose citizens have been taught that there is both a right and a necessity to work, large-scale unemployment throws up a myriad of problems, from the role of the state to the nature of human dignity. Today, more people are out of work than in the depths of the depression of the 1930s. Despite evidence of increasing acceptance of the present position – witness the extent of abstention of unemployed voters in the 1983 election and attitude surveys of the *employed* who have remained relatively unscathed in economic terms – unemployment remains one of the major political issues of the 1980s.

The dimensions of the problem

Between 1974 and 1978 unemployment rose from 600,000 to just under 1·5 million. In the first three years of the 1979 Conservative government, it rose to over the 3 million mark (see figures 1 and 2). It first stayed at this post-war record level, and then, in Mrs Thatcher's second term, exceeded it, touching 3·4 million, or 14% of the working population, by January 1986. Official statistics underestimate the position: those, particularly women, who do not register would probably add well over half a million to the overall figures. Moreover, another half million are 'employed' in the limbo of job creation schemes. At the same time average length of unemployment has increased: by 1982 nearly 60% of unemployed men had been out of work for more than six months and the position has worsened (see table 2).

These figures represent, despite improved welfare provision, 'a return to the thirties'. During the inter-war years, unemployment was rarely under a million. For three years, it was over 2·5 million, 20%

Figure 1

Unemployment in the UK, 1920-86

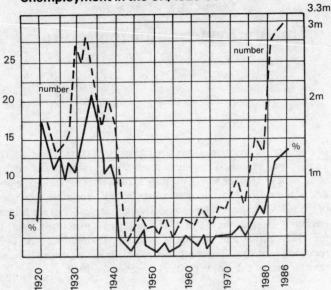

Source: Department of Employment *British Labour Statistics:
Historical Abstract;* Central Statistical Office *Annual Abstracts of
Statistics* (updated)

Figure 2

Unemployment and vacancies in the UK, 1972-86

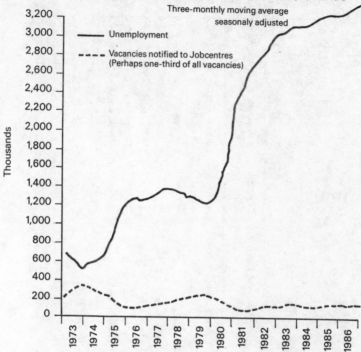

Three-monthly moving average
seasonaly adjusted

—— Unemployment

- - - - Vacancies notified to Jobcentres
(Perhaps one-third of all vacancies)

Thousands

* Figures affected by Budget provisions for men aged 60 and over

Table 2 *Unemployment – duration as of April 1986*

Male and female	Proportion of number unemployed	Male	Proportion of number unemployed	Female	Proportion of number unemployed
Up to 2 weeks	6·0	Up to 2 weeks	5·4	Up to 2 weeks	7·2
2–4 weeks	3·9	2–4 weeks	3·6	2–4 weeks	4·7
4–8 weeks	6·7	4–8 weeks	6·2	4–8 weeks	7·6
8–13 weeks	7·6	8–13 weeks	7·3	8–13 weeks	8·9
13–26 weeks	15·0	13–26 weeks	14·2	13–26 weeks	16·8
26–52 weeks	20·0	26–52 weeks	18·4	26–52 weeks	23·6
Over 52 weeks	40·8	Over 52 weeks	45·1	Over 52 weeks	31.3

Source: Department of Employment Gazette, July 1986.

of the workforce (see figure 1). The position is highlighted as during the twenty-five years after the war the problem was held to be solved. Between 1948 and 1968 unemployment averaged 1·7%. A prominent Labour economist, Michael Stewart, could comment in the sixties, 'Other economic problems may threaten; this one at least has passed into history'.

Unemployment is usually analysed in three categories. *Frictional* unemployment represents workers who spend a couple of months between jobs because of problems of interchange and can occur when there is full employment. *Cyclical* unemployment is directly created by the economic cycle of boom and recession. *Structural* unemployment is the product of decline in industries or processes. Britain's present crisis is the product of the last two categories.

As well as economic recession there has been a significant erosion of the country's manufacturing base, a process called *deindustrialisation*. In the mid-sixties nearly 50% of the workforce worked in manufacturing, mining, construction, gas and electricity. Ten years later it was only 40%. Today, it is heading for 30%; this decline has not been compensated for by job growth in other areas. But if Britain's recent employment has been cyclical and structural, these factors have been exacerbated by the policies of the present government.

Unemployment has a *regional* as well as an industrial dimension. A breakdown of the statistics shows that unemployment in mid-1986 is 9·9% in the south-east and 10·7% in East Anglia. But it affects 15% of the workforce in Scotland, 15·7% in the north-west and well over 20% in Northern Ireland. These factors mask *intra-regional* differences. In parts of Northern Ireland and, indeed, in parts of Liverpool or Manchester, unemployment is over 50%.

Unemployment also has an *international* dimension: the higher unemployment in Britain in the late seventies and early eighties was also experienced in the USA and most European countries. Today, there are 11 million unemployed in the EEC countries. However, the general tendency for unemployment to grow in the Western economies masks specific differences. In the USA and in Finland the graph is falling; in Switzerland unemployment is under 1% whilst in Spain it is almost 20%. In Britain, the problem is particularly severe because of the historical weaknesses of the British economy and the solutions government selected to deal with these.

The impact of unemployment

(1) *Cost to the state and the economy*

This is difficult to calculate with precision. Factors involved include the cost to the state in unemployment pay, supplementary benefit and redundancy payments; part of the expenditure on the special employment schemes; loss of income tax, national insurance payments, VAT and other indirect taxes on foregone spending, as well as tax refunds, and the overall losses in terms of spending and production.

In 1980, Showler estimated that total tax losses added to benefit payments represented £4,128 million in lost public expenditure, 7·6% of the government's total budget. Two other economists, Glyn and Harrison, estimated that unemployment lost 20% of potential production in nine different industries. In 1985, Glyn estimated that full employment would have permitted production of around £52 billion extra goods and services a year which he calculated, allowing for extra consumption, could represent a trebling of council house building, a doubling of manufacturing investment and a 50% increase in pensions and in government spending on health and education.

In the 1983 election, Labour argued that prevailing unemployment figures represented a loss of £17 billion in tax revenue and increased benefit payments and a cost in lost production of over £30 billion per annum. Mrs Thatcher claimed the loss was only £6 billion. There can be little doubt that unemployment on today's scale is economically wasteful.

(2) *The economic cost to the individual*

Unlike the thirties, we have a welfare state, but poverty and deprivation can be *relative*. Living on supplementary benefit long-term means living in officially defined poverty. In 1979, Townsend found that those out of work for ten weeks or more were two and a half times more likely to be living in poverty than those who had not been unemployed, and if they got jobs they were likely to be poorly paid.

For a married man previously on average earnings, with two children, life on supplementary benefit means a 45% cut in gross earnings, a position unchanged in the last fifteen years. If he is living on unemployment benefit he loses around a third of his average earnings and this cut has increased recently, particularly with the abolition of Earnings Related Supplement in 1982. The average redundancy payment of a little over £1,000 helps only marginally. A recent

Department of Employment study of 2,000 unemployed men found that for almost half those surveyed state benefits gave them less than half of their previous earnings.

(3) *The social cost*

A wealth of evidence shows unemployment breeds shame, guilt, frustration and a sense of worthlessness. A 1980 Manpower Services Commission study of the long-term jobless saw unemployment as producing depression, anxiety and illness.In 1984 a report for the government's Office of Population Censuses and Surveys by Professor John Cox showed death rates among unemployed men seeking work at least 21% higher than expected and death rates among their wives 20% higher. Unemployment was to blame for the death of more than 1,800 men and 1,000 wives *per annum*. The research showed that, by 1981, unemployed men, compared to others of the same age, were more than twice as likely to have committed suicide, 80% more likely to have had a fatal accident and 75% more likely to have died of lung cancer. The report may understate the problem.

Another survey from the Nuffield Centre at Leeds University commented that 'The evidence of an association between unemployment and suicide is overwhelming'. This accords with US research which shows that for every hundred thousand who lose their jobs, mental hospital admissions increase by 6,000, deaths increase by 5,000, and prison intake increases by 1,900. Some of the social consequences of mass unemployment were evident in the 1981 inner-city riots.

(4) *The inequality cost*

Unemployment hits the poorest hardest. Particularly vulnerable are the unskilled manual workers, the young, the old, the disabled, those in poor health, women and black workers. As we have seen, unemployment also hits certain regions' industries and communities harder than others. *Unemployment is socially and economically divisive* and creates a barrier between the workless and those in jobs. The 1984/5 miners' strike has highlighted how unemployment produces resistance in threatened communities which has implications for social stability and law and order. However, as the situation has deteriorated there has been a levelling effect in relation to regional unemployment. Although disparities remain, the rates are closer together than they were during the thirties.

Theories of unemployment

The market economy

The classical economists thought *laissez-faire* (freedom of the market to operate) would tend to produce full employment. J.B. Say (1767–1832) and David Ricardo (1772–1823), two of the few economists who referred to the issue, argued that supply would create its own demand: the production of commodities would generate adequate purchasing power. Over production could only ever be temporary as it would be solved automatically by a fall in the market price and a return to natural equilibrium and full employment.

Marx

In contrast, Karl Marx (1818–83) saw unemployment as inherent in the workings of capitalist economy. He attributed the cycle of boom and slump since the industrial revolution to the attempt of capitalists to *compete* to expand their share of production. Wage costs rise as unemployment decreases and the 'industrial reserve army of the unemployed' which exercises a downward pressure in wages, becomes depleted. To increase productivity and profitability and lower wage costs, capitalists reduce the number of workers employed relative to the machinery and raw materials they work.

The first contradiction Marx saw was that reducing wages and replacing labour by machinery meant a smaller market for the goods produced. He wrote of the periodic crises of overproduction, 'The final cause of all real crises always remain the poverty and restricted consumption of the masses'. Moreover, profits, in Marx's model, came only from the exploitation of workers. With relatively few workers and a greater amount of machinery over which to calculate the rate of profit, increases in productivity brought a decline in the rate of profit. The result was a failure to invest and an increase in unemployment. As the slump produced bankruptcies, prices would fall, purchasing power would recover, a new boom would be stimulated.

Marx did not suggest policies to control unemployment. The answer was to get rid of the anarchic, wasteful system that produced it and replace the market with a planned economy where it would disappear. His predictions that the crises would get progressively worse and provoke upheaval have not been fulfilled. Booms and slumps continued. So did capitalism. Marx took some account of countervailing tendencies. His theory underestimated the ability of the system to adapt and adjust but it has been developed and applied to today's society by economists such as Mandel and Kidron. Varieties of Marxist solutions are still advocated by some on the left of the Labour Party, the Communist Party and the small revolutionary groups.

Keynes

Looking at inter-war unemployment, John Maynard Keynes (1883–1945) realised the inadequacy of the classical view but, unlike Marx, he wanted to make the existing system work. He saw that the conventional cures to recession, cut backs on spending and reduction of imports, led to a contraction of world trade and a diminution in purchasing power and therefore made the patient worse. A vicious circle set in: falling demand created unemployment, that unemployment further diminished purchasing power and, in its turn, created further unemployment.

Keynes saw the central problem as 'an insufficiency of effective demand'. He argued that the free operation of the market might lead to an equilibrium between sales and purchases but all the evidence suggested that this might not be at a level which ensures full employment; the total sum of money available to spend on goods and services and the total sum available for investment might together fall below the level needed to provide jobs for everybody.

In this situation, the state should prime the pump. It should reverse its normal policies and, if the problem of the free market is the reluctance of the private investor to invest, the state should revive effective demand by spending money itself. *It could thus manage effective demand: expanding it in slump; curtailing it in boom.* Full employment and economic growth could be launched by governments resorting to deficit budgeting: spending more than they collected in taxes; directly investing in public works such as schools, roads and hospitals which would not compete with private commodities; generating purchasing power through increased welfare payments; and influencing interest rates downwards to encourage private investment through expanding the money supply.

Keynes also stressed the need for some form of international co-operation in an increasingly interlocked and interdependent world economy if problems like mass unemployment were to be controlled. His ideas were influential in the Bretton Woods agreements which established the International Monetary Fund, the World Bank and the US dollar as a world currency, and were vital in generating the long post-war boom. Though particularly attractive to social democrats who welcomed the elements of state management, they appealed to a wider spectrum and became the new conventional economic wisdom in the 40s and 50s. They increasingly came up against the problem of inflation and were complemented by some form of incomes control. However, the full employment they helped to generate meant that such policies were only of temporary efficacy. In Britain the increasing necessity to put up taxes, borrow more money and expand the public sector to maintain full employment as the industrial structure developed towards high productivity sectors with less demand for labour, led to pressure on profits and wages in a context of sluggish growth. Large monopolies were able, to a degree, to insulate pricing, investment and employment policies from central government strategies. In particular, the power that full employment gave shop stewards who were relatively independent of union leaders limited the success of state invervention on wage cuts. Intensified state involvement proved unpopular. The results – a drop in investment, increasing unemployment, declining profits, static real wages and inflation – led many to argue that, in the end, Keynesian remedies had failed.

Monetarism

The most influential proponent of monetarism has been Professor Milton Friedman. Monetarists argue that there is no painless or simple way out of the unemployment problem. Jobs will only be available when a nation's products are competitive in the world market. This means attacking not only inflation but union power. For monetarists, unemployment is caused by mismanagement of the money supply – the notes and coins in circulation as well as money in short term deposits, in transit, in deposit accounts and public sector deposits. This is called M3. Monetarists believe that if there is too much money in circulation bidding for relatively scarce goods and services – 'too much money chasing too few goods' – prices will go up. In response, wages will go up and ultimately industry will be uncompetitive.

If the *growth of the money supply is controlled* through higher interest rates credit becomes more expensive and more difficult to arrange. Fewer goods can be purchased on credit so sales fall and bankruptcies occur. The less competitive and efficient companies, fighting to avoid going to the wall, are forced to resist the demands of trade unions, impelled to push down wages to real economic levels and pressurised to reorganise work more efficiently. As the most inefficient go under, increasing unemployment makes workers more willing to accept change. Trade union controls are thus weakened and the unemployed are willing to take jobs for lower wages and on different terms.

Government spending must also be slashed as it has increasingly been financed by borrowing and printing money, speeding up M3. This involves cutting state employment, privatising some nationalised industries and placing the rest under tight monetary discipline. Subsidies to private industry must be removed, ending feather-bedding, stimulating productivity and removing artificial insulation against the market. As trade unions have become monopolies, able to interfere with the operation of the market, there may be need for legislation to limit many of the practices such as picketing and the closed shop on which their artificial power to interfere with the economy is based. Monetarists see their policies as *creating* unemployment. As it increases so wages, which they see as the main ingredient in inflation, will fall. As the inflation rate declines so will interest rates. Growth can now recommence. But this time it will be based on healthy 'slimmed-down' highly productive companies, freed from union power and reliance on the state and able to compete effectively in the world market. Whilst Friedman stresses the need to free the market from inefficient government bureaucracy and social welfare, a strong state is essential to guarantee the rules of competition, to defend society and to administer certain essential industries such as electricity.

Keynesian economists have questioned whether the increase in the money supply causes the increase in cash incomes. Kaldor has argued that it is in fact the other way round and has claimed − with some justification − that the money supply theories are simply cosmetics for classical deflation: reducing demand and attacking the unions. Other problems are the scale and planlessness of the monetarist experiment. Vast levels of unemployment may be required, confidence may collapse and push recession into depression. Both economic and social costs may be too great. Powerful business monopolies may be able to successfully circumvent attempts to stimulate greater market competition. Strong unions may be able to resist strategies to increase productivity. There is no guarantee of what kind of market you will be left with. There may be tension between economic liberty and political freedom so that the strong state required to guarantee the free market becomes a dictatorship. In Chile − advised by Friedman − monetarist policies increased both unemployment and inflation on an enormous scale. In Britain inflation has decreased but unemployment remains large-scale and is still slowly rising.

The political economy of jobs

(1) *Politicians become committed to full employment*
Sir William Beveridge's, White Paper, *Full Employment In A Free Society* (1944) was strongly influenced by Keynes' theories. It argued that the state should take responsibility for employment just as it did for defence or for internal policing. Beveridge defined full employment as a situation where 'those who lose jobs must be able to find new jobs at fair wages within their capacity without delay'. This break with the past and with the market was influenced by the following factors.

(a) A strong leftwards move in politicss which combined with a mood of national unity to create opposition to any return to the divisions, social turmoil and suffering of the inter-war period.

(b) War-time planning and controls showing what could be done if the state played a more active role; a role required for post-war reconstruction.

(c) The war had halted the UK economy's slide in the world market. Reversion to peace-time production created an acute shortage of labour. Not only Labour but the Tories were committed to a greater degree of intervention.

Initial expectations of full employment — Keynes thought it meant less than 6% jobless, Beveridge around 3% — were soon exceeded in practice: under the Attlee government it hardly rose above 2%. This created further pressure on the Conservatives. In the 1950 and 1951 elections both major parties were commited to full employment policies.

(2) *The politics of full employment dominate*
The boom was helped by Keynesian measures. But also important were technological advances made in wartime; the weakening of unions in many countries such as the USA, Germany and Japan; the need for reconstruction based on large reserves of labour. Britain was helped by the weakening of pre-war competitors and demand for manufactured goods from a devastated world.

The fifties saw the era of Butskellism; both parties committed to Keynesianism competed in the priority they accorded to the jobs issue. Before the 1959 election an increase in unemployment towards over half a million was widely seen as pressing a Labour victory and its eventual decline as a vital factor in the Tories' success. The prevailing orthodoxy was:

(*a*) it was possible to maintain full employment *and* control inflation;

(*b*) any party which questioned demand management to achieve this would lose votes as the opinion polls and attitude surveys showed the issue was crucial to the electorate;

(*c*) that unemployment involved hardship and stigma and only a tiny minority did not want to work;

(*d*) that incomes policies could be developed to handle the increasing problem of inflation.

(3) *The commitment to full employment begins to disintegrate*

As the 60s developed, the guarantee of full employment began to be seen as a problem in relation to inflation, international competition and pressure on profits. The boom began to fray at the edges as Japan and Germany challenged US dominance and the stability of the dollar; as US military spending, particularly in Vietnam, fuelled inflation; and as full unemployment shifted power to Labour movements. The historic weaknesses of the British economy once more became evident.

(*a*) The deflationary policies of the 1966 Labour government have been seen by some as a watershed. Unemployment not only increased from 1% to well over 2% and stayed there: but it was seen by Labour Chancellors, Callaghan and Jenkins as a weapon in curbing inflation.

(*b*) The 1970 Heath government, elected on a programme of a reduction in government intervention and planning, pushed up unemployment from 2·7% to 4% within eighteen months. Heath then did a 'U-turn' which provided a renewed test for Keynesian policies. He attempted to stimulate slow growth and curb rising unemployment by increased public spending and government aid to industry. The 'dash for growth' collapsed in the government defeat at the hands of the miners, a growing balance of payments deficit, and increasing inflation.

(4) *The commitment to full employment disappears*

The failure of the Heath government led many to conclude that attempts to increase production by simply increasing demand will not succeed. Rising unemployment seemed to be a symptom, not of deliberately weakened demand but of major firms being unwilling to alter long-term expectations of production and profitability in response to increased overall demand, so that the increases in public spending simply funded increased imports and diverted investment into property speculation. Whilst the price of property rose, industrial profits declined. This produced important changes in political policy.

(*a*) In September 1974 Milton Friedman delivered an important lecture in London. Tory economic expert, Sir Keith Joseph in his Preston speech, declared his conversion to monetarism and a new view of full employment *as a problem*. 'We are dominated by the fear of unemployment. It was this which made us turn back against our better judgement ...'.

(*b*) Sir Keith was soon supported by Margaret Thatcher. Her election as Tory leader in early 1975 was crucial for the monetarists. By 1977 other leading economic figures such as Sir Geoffrey Howe had been converted and former Heath supporters such as Prior were carried along with the tide. A year later Sir Keith was telling the Bow Group 'Full employment is not in the gift of government. It should not be promised and it cannot be provided.' The Tories went into the 1979 election committed to the new strategy.

(*c*) The new climate was strengthened by the policies of the 1974–9 Labour government. The Wilson and Callaghan administrations ditched the ambitious 1974 manifesto which had promised expansion, wealth redistribution and a move to a planned economy. Its practice can be described as 'moderate monetarism'. It attempted to control the money supply, cut public spending and the welfare state, transfer resources to private industry and boost profits. Callaghan stated that the Keynesian option of spending your way out of a recession no longer existed and announced the disappearance of 'the cosy world ... where full employment could be guaranteed by the stroke of the Chancellor's pen'. Unemployment, under 600,000 in 1974, was just under 1½ million in 1978. It was, ironically, Labour who had in practice broken the full employment consensus.

(*d*) The new climate produced diminishing public concern. Unemployment levels undreamed of in the '50s when half a million jobless occasioned horror, preceded not only the return of the Tories in 1979 and 1983 but to a reassertion of the myths of 'scroungers' and 'work-shy social security fiddlers'.

(5) *Mass unemployment becomes normal*
As Britain's monetarist experiment got under way, the abandonment of full employment as a major political objective was heralded by statements such as that of Treasury Minister Nicholas Ridley: 'The high

level of unemployment is evidence of the progress we are making.'
A balanced assessment of seven years of Thatcherism must record that
even in its own terms the experiment has not been successful.

(*a*) The one undoubted bright spot has been inflation. By mid-1986
the annual rate of price increases had fallen to under 3%, half the figure
12 months before, and the lowest since 1968. On the other hand, it must
be recalled that inflation was only 10% when Mrs Thatcher came to
power and more than doubled in the early days of her administration.
Moreover, the position was still unfavourable compared with key competitors – USA 1·6%, Japan 1·1% and West Germany nil. Another,
as yet limited, success for Conservative policy may be discerned in the
increasing level of profits in the last three years.

(*b*) The triumph was purchased at a high price. Unemployment had
passed the 3·3 million mark and the underlying trend was still upward.
Manufacturing output fell by 1% in the first quarter of 1986, whilst
average earnings were increasing at an underlying rate of almost 8%.
Labour costs per unit of output were 8·3% higher than a year earlier,
whilst for Britain's competitors, such as West Germany and Japan,
they were hardly rising at all. The productivity gains registered in
industry in the early eighties, as plants closed or cut labour, appeared
to have petered out, whilst balance of payments difficulties reemerged
as the economy sluggishly revived from the bottom of the slump in
1981.

(*c*) Continued large-scale unemployment inhibited other aspects of
government policy: for example, the increase in social security payments
impeded plans to cut public expenditure. Having initially cut more than
£170 million from the job creation and training programmes of the
Manpower Services Commission that it had inherited from Labour,
the Thatcher administration presided during the next six years over a
massive expansion of the schemes.

(*d*) As unemployment soared the pure milk of monetarism outlined
by Sir Keith Joseph in pamphlets such as *Why Britain needs a Social
Market Economy* was increasingly replaced by a resort to more
traditional deflationary policies. Between 1979 and the 1983 election,
M3 – the broadly defined money supply – rose significantly faster
than government targets allowed. The government increasingly turned
to fiscal means to limit inflation by control over the Public Sector
Borrowing Requirement. It was not monetarist controls pressurising
wages that produced the fall in inflation, for example, but the fall in
world commodity prices – 10% between 1985–6 and in particular the

fall in the oil market. Moreover, state expenditure on job creation was accompanied by continued financial and technical support for industry, again in defiance of monetarist tenets, whilst the rhetoric on cutting taxes was not realised in practice. The gap between the theorising of new Conservative ideologues and the practice of the government has led many to revise early estimates of 'Thatcherism' in terms of its coherency and it novelty. It has been argued that the continuities between this and previous administrations and the pragmatism with which the Cabinet has tempered principle must also be taken into account.

Britain, today, has a slimmed-down de-industrialised economy. But unemployment shows no signs of falling from its present record levels. And it is clear that what progress Thatcherism has achieved has been by means of unemployment. Given the limited nature of that progress, the cost in terms of intensified social conflict and the inability of most analysts to sight light at the end of the tunnel, many commentators conclude that the success of Thatcherism has, in reality, been minor, purchased at disproportionate cost and delivered in defiance of its own original theories. As we reach the end of the second Thatcher parliament Britain's underlying social and economic problems still seem to be there.

Political responses to unemployment

(1) *The Conservatives*

The Conservatives are standing firm on existing policies. To reflate now might be electorally popular but would increase union power and endanger reduced inflation and increased profitability. The Tory leadership is gambling on the minimal impact that unemployment had on its fortunes in 1983 and the fact that, with wage increases well ahead of price increases, those *in work* have had small but relatively important increases in living standards. In Mrs Thatcher's phrase, 'There is no alternative'. It is a time for gritting teeth and simply waiting until the medicine works and the figures fall. The party's 1983 election manifesto stated 'We shall maintain firm control of public spending and borrowing. We shall continue to set out a responsible financial strategy which will gradually reduce the growth of money in circulation.' The failure of government strategy has thrown up various opponents from Sir Ian Gilmour ('Almost all the tenets of monetarism have been destroyed') to Francis Pym who, in 1985, launched the anti-Thatcher grouping *Centre Forward* and who participated with other Tory MPs in the cross-party 'Charter For Jobs'. The Tory 'wets' would like to see moderate reflation. As yet, they have no strong organisational expression. Despite the significant downturn in the government's popularity in the opinion polls and in by-elections, an increasing number of débâcles, such as the Westland affair, the resignation of important cabinet ministers and the apparent exhaustion of the administration's radical impetus, no individual or grouping which could act as an important internal opposition to Mrs Thatcher has emerged. Any real challenge must, in all probability, now await the verdict of the electorate on her second term.

(2) *The Labour Party*

The Labour Party advocates a return to Keynesianism. Its 1983 programme, under the heading *Ending Mass Unemployment*, stated 'We will expand the economy by providing a strong and measured increase in spending. Spending money creates jobs ... we shall borrow to finance our programme of investment.' There were two striking points about this otherwise classical statement: it spoke of reducing unemployment to below a million *over five years* and there were few specific details with vague references to 'back up' import controls 'if these prove necessary', 'a radical extension of industrial democracy' and 'negotiation' of development plans with companies. Even an almost certain commitment to incomes policy was veiled as 'a national economic assessment'.

The problem was that the manifesto, which many voters found far too vague, represented a compromise between different viewpoints in the party. In the immediate aftermath of the electoral defeat, it was possible to distinguish different views within the party:

(*a*) *The Labour right* represented by Denis Healey, Roy Hattersley and, most articulately, Peter Shore, believed in a cautious Keynesianism. They opposed moves to protectionism as likely to isolate an export-dependent nation in a trade war and were concerned that too full-blooded an expansion would collapse in rampant inflation. Incomes policy, employers and unions working together in tripartite harness with government was, therefore, essential to this approach.

(*b*) *The 'soft' left* had a far firmer view of an 'alternative economic strategy'. This involved not only expansion but – and here there are different emphases – a firmer commitment to import controls; the introduction of a thirty-five-hour week; selective nationalisation; public control of the financial institutions; workers on the board and compulsory planning agreements. There were again different views on the central question of wage controls.

(*c*) *The 'hard' left* – these views were given public voice by the Campaign Group. They saw the various alternative economic strategies as no real alternative to Thatcherism: although left forms of Keynesianism, they still suffer from its central defects. Expansion would lead to higher pay and less profitability as full employment approached and stronger trade unions pressed for wage increases. Price controls tight enough to avoid evasion would squeeze profitability and lead to a collapse in investment. A thirty-five-hour week would put employers' costs through the roof. Channelling more funds to capitalists does not necessarily make them invest. Import controls would lead to higher prices and retaliation. Capitalism must be replaced by a move towards a planned socialist economy and involving the workers in democratic planning.

By 1985, as the miners' strike looked increasingly booked for defeat, important changes took place within the Labour Party. The 'soft' left and even important figures such as Ken Livingstone previously on the far left realigned themselves behind the leadership of Neil Kinnock. This, in its turn, produced new policy developments. A turn to the centre right has taken shape and the key word is 'realism'. A Labour administration, it is argued, would be unlikely to re-establish full employment in one term: the creation of a million new jobs is now seen as a major achievement. Even then, in the words of Neil Kinnock, it would not be, '… the full employment of the 1950s, 60s or even the early 70s – we know it's not coming back in that form'. Controlled reflation, primed by a National Investment Bank with money from pension funds and insurance companies assured by tax penalties on firms which did not deliver, would operate in tandem with wage restraint agreed with the TUC. Progress in counteracting unemployment would be contingent on restraining inflation. This strategy would be accompanied by repatriation of foreign assets, more worker participation, plans for extended employee shareholding in companies and tripartite agreement between employers', unions and the state on economic targets. Local authorities, in particular, would be given an enhanced role in job creation. Whilst the desire for electoral victory has united a majority behind the new alignment, problems encountered by Labour in government could easily lead to a strong re-emergence of the conflicting approaches outlined above.

(3) *The SDP–Liberal Alliance*

In many ways their 1983 manifesto gave voice and coherence to the inarticulated views of the Labour right. They argued for carefully selected increases in public spending and reductions in taxation. In classical Keynesian fashion investment would be concentrated on railways, roads, hospitals, housing and transport whilst tax reductions would focus on reducing prices by, for example, removing the National Insurance Surcharge. Job creation programmes would be expanded and particular attention would be paid to youth, with firms being given financial incentives to take on the long-term unemployed. The Alliance saw their proposals as realistic and having a limited impact, reducing unemployment by one million after two years in government. They would, it was acknowledged, stimulate some inflation. This would be avoided by a formal pay and prices policy. An Alliance government would set up a Pay and Prices Commission to monitor pay settlements in large companies, introduce a counter-inflation tax to penalise those who went beyond the range of settlements laid down after negotiations between employers, unions, consumer groups and government; similar arrangements would apply to nationalised industries whilst they would establish an independent Assessment Board for public service settlements.

Most recently, whilst the Liberals have tended to stay in this framework, the SDP have tended to emphasise 'social market', 'modified monetarist' positions. In essentials, there is now no great gulf between the present strategies of the Alliance and Labour although their concrete application by a coalition or minority government would undoubtedly produce controversy in the ranks of both groupings.

The future

Britain's unemployment problem has been related to the world economic picture but has had its own specific characteristics. The UK has had sluggish growth, low investment, poor productivity and a powerful labour movement compared with its competitors. These factors are in turn related to the UK's history as the first industrialised country, past failures to innovate and reconstruct its industrial base, the privileged position given to finance capital and relatively large defence expenditure. Neither Keynesianism or monetarism have solved these underlying problems. The years since 1979 have seen important changes in the employment picture: an intensification of the movement from manufacturing to service industries; the introduction of new technologies; a weakening of union power; a growth of peripheral part-time employees. They have also witnessed the emergence of apparently permanent mass unemployment. Certainly the maintenance of the policies of the present government yields little prospect of an increase in employment. And if the policies advocated by Labour and the Alliance did not work in 1964 and in 1974 – despite differences in nomenclature and emphasis they are in the same mould as those implemented by the Wilson and Callaghan administrations – why should they work in the 1980s when firmer versions such as those of the Mitterand government in France faltered? Whilst a future non-Conservative administration would inherit a weaker trade union movement they would also inherit a weaker economic situation. There must be severe doubts about a re-run of Keynesianism and indeed any return to full employment.

There are those, such as Gorz, who argue that we should abandon that goal and look beyond the Protestant ethic that we need paid labour to fulfil ourselves. Such an emphasis seems likely to find little resonance in the programmes of the major parties in the foreseeable future. That future appears likely to involve a continuation of Britain's economic decline and an acceptance that full employment is no longer an immediate political goal. The people may be willing to tolerate unemployment on today's scale on the basis that 85% are not affected. On the other hand, increased industrial decline and intensified social conflict may see a turn to as yet untested left strategies. Certainly, with giant strides in new technology, the whole question of the future of work urgently demands political discussion.

Reading

D. N. Ashton, *Unemployment Under Capitalism*, Wheatsheaf Books, 1986.

M. Barratt-Brown, *Models in Political Economy*, Penguin, 1984.

N. Branson & M. Heinemann, *Britain in the Nineteen Thirties*, Weidenfeld & Nicolson, 1971.

B. Crick (ed.), *Unemployment*, Methuen, 1981.

M. Friedman, *Free To Choose*, Penguin Books, 1980.

Sir I. Gilmour, *Britain Can Work*, Martin Robertson, 1983.

A. Glyn, *A Million Jobs A Year*, Verso, 1985.

A. Glyn & J. Harrison, *The British Economic Disaster*, Pluto Press, 1980.

A. Gorz, *Farewell to the Working Class*, Pluto Press, 1982.

K. Hawkins, *Unemployment*, Penguin, 1984.

M. Holmes, *The First Thatcher Government 1979–1983*, Wheatsheaf Books, 1985.

B. Jordan, *Mass Unemployment and the Future of Britain*, Basil Blackwell, 1982.

J. Keane & J. Owens, *After Full Employment*, Hutchinson, 1986.

F. Pym, *The Politics of Consent*, Hamish Hamilton, 1984.

P. Riddell, *The Thatcher Government*, Basil Blackwell, 1985.

B. Showler & A. Sinfield, *The Workless State*, Martin Robertson, 1981.

A. Sinfield, *What Unemployment Means*, Martin Robertson, 1981.

S. Williams, *A Job To Live*, Penguin, 1985.

Energy and the politics of nuclear power

The easy availability of energy is one of the important differences between developed and underdeveloped countries. It is still possible to find a close correlation between per capita energy consumption and various measures of a country's wealth: for example the average US citizen uses 100,000 kilowatt hours per annum while the average UK citizen requires 55,000 kWh. These figures include not only personal consumption but also the energy employed in various forms of manufacturing. By contrast the consumption of a third-world citizen is minimal.

The problem of securing a stable energy supply is therefore one which is vital to all governments with advanced economies, not only in order to maintain the normal life of the country but also because decisions on the nature of the future energy supply will, to a very large extent, influence the economic development of the country. Within this context the inquiry into the proposal of the CEGB to build a pressurised water reactor at Sizewell will prove decisive to the future course of many UK industries during this century. However, decisions on energy policy have political, military and environmental, as well as industrial consequences, which must be carefully investigated before irrevocable decisions are made.

Traditional forms of energy production

Coal, oil and natural gas have traditionally been the major energy sources for Britain. Because they are ultimately all derived from organic material they are termed *fossil* fuels. These organic materials originally obtained their energy from the sun and now therefore consist of stored energy. These fuels can be employed to drive various types of machinery and can be burnt on site to produce heat, light and power. This, however, frequently entails the use of bulky machines, large stockpiles of fuel, and can cause pollution problems to the consumer. Electricity, when used for these purposes, requires smaller machinery, no stockpiles, and causes no pollution at the point of use — hence its greater consumer popularity.

Electricity is generated from coal and oil when these fuels are burnt to produce steam to drive electrical generators at power stations. The problems of pollution and stockpiles are shifted from the consumer on to the producer. Other types of energy source, such as wind, wave and water power are termed *renewable* because their immediate consumption does not affect their future availability. They also originate in the effects of solar radiation upon the earth and therefore, like fossil fuels, they are ultimately derived from the heat of the sun's nuclear fusion process. The difference between the two types of fuels rests primarily in the time at which the energy of the sun was 'trapped' being, respectively, many thousands of years ago and the immediate present.

Only one renewable fuel resource makes a significant contribution to energy supply — and that is hydro-electric power (HEP). Rainwater is stored by means of dams at high level and energy is produced when this water is allowed to fall through turbines connected to electrical generators. HEP generation can be rapidly brought 'on stream', i.e. made available to the national grid. It is therefore less wasteful than fossil-fuelled power stations which must be kept running 'idle' at a high temperature until they are called upon to provide electricity at peak consumption periods. All electrical generation is inefficient, with less than half of the calorific value of the fuel burnt reaching the consumer in the form of usable energy.

Problems of fossil fuels

(1) *Limited supply* The supply of fossil fuels is finite and although new reserves are actively being sought and developed these reserves will eventually be exhausted. Oil and gas are expected to run out in the first quarter of the next century whereas coal will last several hundred years. As each of the fossil fuels, especially oil, can be used as a basic chemical resource, it seems wasteful to burn vast quantities of such fuels merely to generate heat and light.

(2) *Political*   Dependence on foreign suppliers of fossil fuels can have grave consequences as demonstrated at the time of the 1973 Yom Kippur war. A group of oil-producing countries acted in consort to limit the quantity of oil produced in order to bring pressure to bear on the West to reduce its military and political aid to Israel. The consequent rapid increase in the price of oil (nearly 400% by 1974) has been held responsible by many economists for precipitating the present economic recession although it is clear that its continuation is due to other factors. Having discovered their power, and realising that their supply of saleable oil was limited, the OPEC countries acted to keep up the price of oil during the seventies. However, despite its apparent power OPEC never actually controlled the oil supply as many producers, including Mexico and, later, Britain, never joined the producers' cartel.

Initially OPEC was virtually able to dictate the price of oil, but this inspired a move towards more sensible energy consumption levels by the industrialised countries. More efficient manufacturing processes were developed and conservation measures suddenly acquired an urgency that years of reasoned argument by 'ecologists' had failed to inspire. These effects were dramatically reinforced by the recession as heavy industry in the West declined, an effect ironically stimulated by the oil price increase.

Over the past few years the weakness of OPEC's position has become clear. It has no control over non-members' production and cannot even force members to abide by production quotas. Internal quarrels, especially between Iran and Iraq, have almost provided a *coup-de-grâce*. Together with the decline in western consumption this has resulted in a drop in the price of oil to a point where it is, in real terms, cheaper than it was before the initial oil price increase. As the evidence indicates that energy consumption is strongly price-dependent – for example, the fondness of Americans for huge automobiles compared with the average Briton's small car is clearly associated with the low petrol price in the USA – this could lead to a return to old energy profligate ways. This is not really expected as seemingly permanent changes in living styles, and more importantly in technology, have taken place. What is more likely is that interest in energy conservation improvements will decline. Such an effect is, however, under government control through taxes and its ability to artifically raise energy prices.

Despite appearances, the problem of finite supply, especially of oil, remains. Economically recoverable oil will, at current consumption rates and unless there are quite dramatic discoveries, run out within the lifetime of many reading this book. Unless an energy policy is formulated now for this eventuality the consequences will make the current depression appear an enviable period.

(3) *Price* Coal is in much more abundant supply than oil, with reserves to last Britain several centuries. Its production provides employment in areas which are amongst the most economically depressed in the UK and does not adversely affect the balance of payments. However, because of geological factors, UK-produced coal will always be more expensive than that produced by several other countries, including the USA. The use of British coal by the CEGB therefore pushes up electricity prices. British industry is consequently placed at a cost disadvantage with respect to competitor economies. It should be therefore possible for Britain to import coal more cheaply than it can be produced here. This, however, has been proved not to be the case, as British attempts to import coal during the recent strike pushed the market price up to the UK level.

This price differential has however narrowed considerably over the past year as the NCB, having for the present reduced the NUM to impotence, has been able to close down many of the high-cost pits and has shed huge numbers of workers, many to lifelong unemployment.

This price argument ignores the effect of UK government on energy prices. Despite the fall in the price of oil and coal to the CEGB electricity prices have recently increased. This was caused by the requirement that the CEGB met government targets rather than any economic requirement. Dependence upon imported coal would also both adversely effect national independence and be a permanent drain upon foreign currency reserves.

(4) *Pollution* Sulphur dioxide in the smoke from coal-fired power stations is alleged to contribute towards the production of acid rain which has damaged the lakes and forests of other European countries. Such pollution on a continental scale causes friction between neighbouring states. The modifications to power stations necessary to eliminate these emissions would require the investment of many millions of pounds by the CEGB in Britain, and it is unwilling to engage in such a level of expenditure until the connection between sulphur dioxide emissions and acid rain has been proven beyond question. Unless competitor nations are also willing to meet similar bills for the reduction

of sulphur dioxide emissions by their plants, British industry would be placed at a significant cost disadvantage with respect to other European producers. However, other countries, such as Germany and Sweden, are convinced of the connection and are modifying their power stations now. To many of their politicians the CEGB's requirement that the connection be proved beyond question is akin to a demand that a given case of lung cancer be traced to a particular cigarette.

(5) *Diversity of sources*   The coal strike of 1974 followed by the conservative government's defeat at a general election convinced many politicians that an energy supply policy based mainly on coal would court continual economic blackmail by the miners' union. A policy was adopted of increasing the number of basic energy sources so that no one group of industrial workers in the country would have a stranglehold on the economy and the nations life. Pursuit of this policy requires an increase in the proportion of electricity – currently fifteen per cent – generated by nuclear means. At the present time the CEGB is attempting to obtain permission both to expand the number of reactors it operates and to introduce new types of reactors.

Nuclear power and how it is produced

In essence, nuclear and fossil-fuelled generation of electricity are similar in concept. An energy source generates steam which drives an electrical generator via a turbine. In a nuclear power station the energy source is the nuclear reactor. However, this reactor is a much more intricate and potentially dangerous mechanism than is found with fossil fuel burning stations where the energies involved are of a much lower order of magnitude. Nuclear fission generates dangerous radiation which must be contained. The heat generated must be carried away to the steam generators efficiently or damage may result to the reactor core. In the case of the major damage at Three Mile Island the reactor was rendered useless and presented several difficulties to engineers called in to render it safe and dismantle it. The reactor coolant must also be isolated as it itself becomes radioactive. In pressurised water reactors the primary coolant is sealed and transfers heat to a secondary cooling circuit which in turn drives the generators, thus preventing the radioactive primary heat transfer medium from coming into contact with the external environment. Provision must be made in all reactor types in case of failure of any part of the system, for example if the primary coolant circuit develops a leak not only must there be emergency core cooling backup systems but the leaking coolant must be safely collected and stored. Because of these safeguards and the need for total security the technical complexity of the reactor operating system is very high and the margin for error correspondingly low, hence the need for highly-trained personnel to operate the system in what is, apart from emergencies, a mundane job.

One a small proportion of natural uranium can be burnt in a reactor, although the non-fissile portion can be converted into plutanium. If the fissile proportion is even slightly increased, the power levels reached can be markedly improved. This process is termed *enrichment* and is extremely expensive in terms of capital expenditure and energy consumption. The sinking of the Mount Saint Louis in the English Channel in September 1984, whilst carrying uranium to the USSR for enrichment, has revealed that, dispite the military implications, an international trade has developed in the enrichment process. The Eastern bloc earns hard currency by enriching nuclear material which, after use in the civil nuclear power programme, may find its way into the western nuclear arsenal.

Nuclear power stations also require a 'moderator' to permit the nuclear reaction to occur and various mechanisms to stop the reaction when necessary. The various permutations of these factors have ensured that several reactor types are available, with differing costs, power levels and safety records associated with each type. The decision as to which design the CEGB should use in this country is therefore, irrespective of technical merits, essentially a political decision because of the potential dangers involved. In the UK most people seem content to accept whatever decision is reached by the government. In other European countries, all questions relating to nuclear power have become mass political issues, with some governments being obliged by electoral pressure to halt their programmes. It is often argued that the electorate and even the politicians are poorly informed of the technical issues surrounding nuclear energy.

Reactor types

Many countries attempted to produce their own reactor designs but because of high costs as well as design failures power-generating reactors have now standardised on to a few basic models. Those of importance to the UK debare are:

Magnox type

Gas-cooled with a graphite moderator, the Magnox was the world's first effective design for a civil nuclear power programme. The world's first civil nuclear power plant at Calder Hall on the Sellafield site in Cumbria is of this type; it forms the backbone of nuclear power generation in the UK but is now obsolete and several plants will be shortly reaching the end of their designed operating life-span. The costs of dismantling and making the sites safe is unknown.

Advanced gas-cooled reactor (AGR)

Intended as the successor to the Magnox stations, this design has higher power ratings. Unfortunately, the engineering and design problems were not fully appreciated at the time of development. The result has been long delays in construction, contractor bankruptcy and vast cost overruns. Despite all setbacks this design still has many influential supporters on both technical and safety grounds. It has been claimed that regardless of any or all systems failure it would be impossible to get this reactor to melt down.

Pressurised water reactors (PWR)

An American design using water under pressure as both moderator and coolant. These reactors have been built by many companies in the USA and have been sold world-wide. The French nuclear power programme, which supplies 50% of the country's electricity, has switched to this design. The French programme has been described as the biggest experiment ever undertaken into the safety of a given design. There have been many problems with PWRs owing both to lax operation and faulty construction. As a result of this and public anxiety PWR orders in the USA have ceased. In order for the nuclear construction companies to continue in existence, exports of PWR systems must be expanded. A commitment by the CEGB to build a series of PWRs would represent a lifeline not only to the reactor construction companies in the UK but also many in the USA.

Despite the dominant position established by this design doubts have existed since it inception regarding its safety, particularly its emergency safety procedures. These doubts have been heightened by the many 'incidents' which PWRs have suffered. The most notorious of these was the Three Mile Island accident in which a combination of operator incompetence, willful disregard of written procedures, malfunctioning monitors and sheer bad luck resulted in the partial melt-down of the core. That this incident did not result in the escape of very large quantities of radioactive material seems entirely fortuitous. The report of the Kemeny Commission on the incident highlighted the complexity of the safe operation of this particular design.

Whilst the CEGB accepts that the USA's generating industry has suffered unfortunate experiences, the CEGB claims that its version of the PWR includes an increased number of safety features which will provide enhanced reliability and make an accident much less likely.

CANDU (Canada Can Do)
A Canadian design utilising unenriched uranium as fuel and heavy water as moderator and coolant. Compared to other designs it has proven exceptionally reliable in meeting and maintaining its designed power output levels. It has had a much lower 'incident' level than the PWR. This design also produces a better yield of plutonium than other commercial designs, an important feature if plutonium is in turn to be used as a fuel.

The Canadians have proven very reluctant to export this design since the Indian government, despite assurances, employed as *CANDU* system to provide the plutonium for a 'peaceful' nuclear bomb.

Because of its record this design has attracted support from members of the scientific community. It does not, however, appear to be a serious contender as far as the CEGB is concerned.

Fast breeder reactors (FBR)
These can be designed to 'breed' more fuel than they consume. This is a feature of no other generating system. The tiny core, fuelled by a mixture of plutonium and enriched uranium, reaches such a power density that liquid sodium has to be used to remove heat effectively. The core is surrounded by a blanket of material such as Uranium 238 which under neutron bombardment is converted to a fissile material, Plutonium 239. Considerations of efficient fuel usage alone would require that FBRs, which are still experimental, eventually form an essential part of the power-generating network. However, FBRs are even more technically demanding than uranium fuel designs. In the event of a coolant failure, resulting in a meltdown, a FBR could actually explode in the same way as a nuclear bomb. Current commercial designs cannot explode in this particular manner, although non-nuclear chemical explosions resulting from design failures are conceivable and could generate considerable

fall-out. For a period it was feared that this could happen during the Three Mile Island incident.

In 1966 the Enrico Fermi One plant near Detroit suffered a partial melt-down when a piece of metal, part of a design feature to ensure that molten fuel could never flow into an explosive configuration, came adrift and obstructed the core cooling. This had potentially disastrous consequences in that a nuclear explosion could have occurred within a few miles of a major population centre. Since then those objectors to such plants who argue that they pose potentially massive dangers to the public have been provided with a much enhanced case. An experimental FBR has been in operation, however, at Dounreay in Scotland for several years without major incident.

Soviet models

The USSR is committed to a large nuclear power programme, especially in its European region. Owing to the closed nature of its society, design criticism has never reached western levels. This had disastrous results when one of the reactors at Chernobyl exploded following a fire. The design used appears to have been inherently unstable and, as far as can be surmised at present, the explosion happened because of this instability and operator error. It appears at the moment that the USSR authorities are attempting to place most of the blame for the accident upon their operators and are intent upon keeping this design in operation.

It must be stressed that there was no nuclear explosion but rather a chemical reaction between the graphite moderator and the water coolant, resulting in a fire and a subsequent explosion. The result of this was that a substantial fraction of the radioactive core was pulverised or vapourised and carried high into the atmosphere from which it was deposited over large areas of Western Europe.

The immediate response of the western nuclear industry was to protest that no reactor of this design existed in the West and that such a design would never have been permitted to operate. Sir Walter Marshall, the head of the CEGB, went as far as to claim that the accident held no lessons for the West. He appears to have missed the point that for many years he, amongst others, has claimed that no such accident could happen. For much of the public this is a simple demonstration that the experts are wrong rather than that Russian experts can be wrong. The realisation that an accident in a distant country could have effects here may have finally killed the hopes of the nuclear industry in much of Western Europe. However, despite many vocal groups, the experience of British politicians appears to be that this is still not an active issue on the doorstep.

There have been report in the scientific press that many of the control monitoring instruments were of western manufacture and that the Russians may claim that a malfunction of these instruments contributed to the disaster. These instruments are also employed in western reactors. Should the USSR actually attempt to claim compensation for these failures the resultant publicity could lead to more active concern amongst the electorate.

Inherently safe designs

All the designs mentioned above rely upon external intervention by various mechanisms in the event of a control problem to forestall accidents. Such mechanisms have a history of failure although in the West, so far, no civil reactor has suffered an accident which has led to major public contamination. It is claimed that so many safety systems are in place that the simultaneous failures of all systems is inconceivable. Yet many of the 'incidents' which have been reported have involved multiple failures. This has led to increased consideration of so-called 'inherently safe designs'. Such designs, of which there are several, instead of relying upon mechanical devices to prevent major accidents, rely upon the ingenious use of natural physical laws. For example, one design rests in a tank of boronated water, which will, in the event of coolant failure, be sucked into the reactor core, halting the nuclear reaction. Another deisgn, actually in operation in North Germany, contains fuel encapsulated in small balls. If the gas-cooling system fails the surface to volume ratio of the balls ensures that they can never heat up enough to melt. Such designs, although technically simpler and safer than conventional 'proven' designs, cannot eliminate all possible accidents. This was demonstrated recently at Hamm in northern Germany, when a small quantity of radioactivity was released after one of the fuel balls became jammed in a pipe. However, these reactors seem to be safe from the most feared nuclear accident – the melt-down.

Radiation risks and radioactive waste

Radiation can have two separate effects upon humans: mutations of individual cells increasing the probability of cancer, and damage to eggs or sperm increasing the rate mutation in subsequent generations.

Any release of radioactivity into the environment is undesirable, and a major release from a reactor accident or an escape of high-level waste must be avoided. Radioactive material has been released both accidentally and deliberately, as a result of both atmospheric testing of atomic bombs and the operation of nuclear reactors.

High-level waste, which is extremely radioactive, is produced by the reprocessing industry but exist only in small quantities. A much larger volume of low-level waste, such as contaminated clothing or medical isotopes, is generated each year. Much of this waste has been dropped in sealed containers in international waters. There is concern that if these containers were breached radioactive material would concentrate up the food chain, just as mercury does with tuna fish, and eventually contaminate part of our food supply. Given the small amount of radioactivity involved compared to the volume of the ocean this appears somewhat unlikely, but such dumping has produced anti-British feeling in Spain. The seamen's union in the UK is calling for a moratorium on dumping pending international agreement.

There is nothing sinister or unusual about the manner in which radiation affects the body; all that happens is that energy is deposited. It is the energy deposited which makes a punch or a rifle shot dangerous. Thus the measure of the amount of radioactivity received, i.e. the amount of energy (joules) deposited in 1 kg of a body, is the 'radiation-absorbed dose' which is measured in grays (Gy). However, the measure of energy absorbed is not everything, as may be seen by considering the effect of being punched with and without a piece of steel concealed in your assailant's fist. The energy in the punch is the same but the damage done is much greater. So it is with radiation, some forms of which cause more damage than others for the same energy deposited. Thus in order to be able to compare the effects of different exposures it is necessary to look as 'dose equivalents' measured in sieverts (Sv) rather than at the number of grays involved.

Just how radioactive a particular item is may be measured by its activity, i.e. the number of nuclear disintegrations which take place in the material every second. This is measured in becquerels (Bq). Because of the laws of quantum physics it is impossible to fix just how much energy a given disintegration will actually release, although averaged energy distributions may be found. Thus an important part of the research work currently taking place on radiation effects is the attempt to relate given levels of activity in the environment to the dose that people actually receive.

Uncertainties as to this relationship, as well as uncertainties as to the effects of given doses on the body, and no doubt different standards of public safety, account for the widely differing milk radiation levels set after Chernobyl.

The average expose as a result of man-made radiation is only about 1% of the natural background radiation to which the UK population is exposed. The average exposure per annum to radiation per person as a result of medical X-rays is about 80% of the background. Current dangers as a result of nuclear power seem therefore to be minimal. However, if the same radioactivity is delivered to a particular site in the body the effects are much greater. Such a 'hot spot' could occur, for example, by the breathing in of radioactive dust and its trapping in such areas as the lung walls. Radioactive material ingested in food may, and only may, be stored in a particular organ of the body such as the liver. It is possible that this may be the explanation for the apparent increase in cancer levels in Cumbria.

Chernobyl

Since the Chernobyl disaster the background against which the nuclear debate is conducted has sharpened markedly in many of the European countries worst affected by the fall-out. Battles between anti-nuclear demonstrators and police have become a weekly event in Lower Bavaria at the site of a proposed reprocessing plant. These demonstrators, including groups labelled by the authorities as terrorist supporters, have gained strong support amongst the traditionally conservative local communities. This is despite repeated assurances that the plant will be run to proper safety standards using the latest technology, and will not cause pollution − 'it will not be at all like Windscale/Sellafield' (*sic*). Terrorist organisations have recently murdered a senior member of the German nuclear industry, seemingly attempting to gain public sympathy after Chernobyl.

The German opposition party, the SPD, is now committed to a review of future nuclear policy, although many doubt that there is any serious prospect of the closure of German nuclear facilities under the SPD, seeing this promised review merely as a vote-catching exercise. The position of the Conservative CSU/CDU/FDP government in this matter seems increasingly weak. In Sweden, which voted by referendum to phase out nuclear power, the hopes of the nuclear industry of reversing this decision seem increasingly forlorn. Holland also is reviewing its position. Even in France, following the revelation of various incidents, doubts are being expressed. Yet Chernobyl demonstrated that no nation on its own can opt out of the nuclear world. Fallout knows no borders and the Soviet Union is determined to press ahead with its programme. Quite remarkably, despite public panic after the accident, nuclear power does not seem to have become a doorstep political issue within the UK, although it is being actively debated, within the parties.

Perhaps the most damaging effect of the disaster in the UK was the total undermining of faith in the authorities amongst informed members of the public. Keeping radioactive lamb on the market after it was known to be above recommended limits, remarkably little sampling of vegetable produce (one cauliflower, according to the *New Scientist*), and an extremely patchy monitoring net demonstrate a poor level of preparation to say the least.

The situation in some other countries was the reverse. In West Germany each state produced its own radiation limits. In the case of milk these limits varied from the federally recommended limit of 500Bq per litre to 20Bq per litre in the state of Hesse. These limits are to be compared with the UK limit of 2,000Bq per litre. Spinach was withdrawn from the market in much of western Europe and outdoor activities by children were discouraged in the vicinity of Munich.

Yet all of this must be placed in context. The 'normal' background radiation to which we are exposed is $1 \cdot 87$mS per year, of which 87% comes from natural sources and 13% from fall-out and pollution. The limits set for a worker in the nuclear industry are $5 \cdot 0$mS per year. A typical chest X-ray provides a dose of round $0 \cdot 1$mS. The average UK citizen's exposure as a result of Chernobyl will be less than 1% of a year's background exposure.

When the lamb ban was introduced the limits of radioactivity were set at 1000Bq per kilo. The following comparisons were drawn by *The 'Economist'*: banned lamb was three times more radioactive than fish caught near Sellafield; in order to reach international radiation exposure limits it would be necessary to eat 10oz. of meat each day for a year; in order to be exposed to the same levels of radiation as a person living in a Cornish house it would be necessary to eat several pounds of lamb each day.

This is not to suggest that the risks are unreal, rather that they were grossly exaggerated in what the USSR has seen as a crude anti-Soviet propaganda exercise. However, internationally agreed radiation exposure levels are constantly being revised downwards. It is now being suggested by various US insurance figures that there is an element of risk associated with medically-approved X-rays. Living in a Cornish house is coming to be seen as quite a risky undertaking.

Recent American research suggests that radon in houses, coming from natural radioactivity in the building materials and in the earth under the house, is a very serious health hazard. Between 2,000 and 20,000 US citizens are now believed to die of lung cancer each year because of natural radon being concentrated in their houses. This places environmental radon as the second most serious cause of lung cancer after cigarrettes. Even cigarrette-induced lung cancer is now thought to have a strong connection with the trapping of natural radon on the surface of the tobacco leaf.

So some degree of public concern about the release of radiation from man-made sources, including Chernobyl and Sellafield, is justified in this country. However, far more concern has been expressed about this than has been given to the problem of road traffic accidents, which are one of the principal causes of death nowadays. To those within the nuclear industry it seems that the association of nuclear power with nuclear weapons causes the man in the street to have a grossly misconceived estimation of the risks involved.

Advantages of nuclear power

Although the mere prestige of operating a nuclear reactor system seems to have been the major factor in decision by several US utilities to build such plants, it is a decision many have come subsequently to regret. Due to lax operating standards, 'incidents' with the reactors have occurred. This has entailed the companies concerned purchasing electricity from other utility companies to make good the shortfall in the supply of electricity to customers whilst repairs were being carried out to damaged nuclear reactors. If these problems could be avoided then nuclear power has several advantages:

Diversification of energy sources
The past and present difficulties with the miners would appear to be a very major factor in favour of a large UK nuclear power programme. These stations can supply a constant base load of electricity and require little movement of material to and from sites compared with that required by conventional power stations. As the plant operators have, in the past, proved not to be sympathetic to the calls for joint industrial

action with the miners, it is to be expected that they will continue to operate nuclear power plants during any future such industrial dispute.

The removal of external constraints over a country's energy supply is also an important argument for diversification. France has adopted a large-scale nuclear power programme principally for this reason. The UK is self-sufficient in energy with both ample oil and coal reserves. The previously mentioned political problem of industrial action in the mines and the advantage to foreign currency earnings of exporting oil have tended to militate against total dependence upon what might otherwise be required as a natural abundance of energy sources in Britain.

Cost savings
Currently the CEGB wishes to build at least one PWR in the UK even though there is a surplus of electrical generation capacity at present due to the reduction in demand experienced as a result of the economic recession. It is argued by the CEGB that the removal of older and therefore less efficient generating capacity and its replacement by the PWR would, in spite of large capital costs, result in an overall saving in operating costs and thus help in maintaining price stability for electricity consumers. This assumes that the CEGB projected cost figure for the construction of PWRs is correct. Previous experience in the USA with PWRs has shown that many cases of runaway cost escalation have occurred, undermining the economic basis of some projects.

Trade and technological innovation
The sale and construction of nuclear plant is a major growth area in world trade. In order for a UK construction company to have a chance of obtaining a share of this market it is necessary that there be a home market to keep the industry in business between foreign orders. In addition it is necessary to prove to foreign buyers that Britain has confidence both in the technology employed and in the construction techniques used. Abandoning Britain's share of the nuclear industry would have major implications for Britain's capacity to remain at the forefront of the construction and manufacture of high-technology plant and equipment. This, it is argued, would have very serious implications for Britain's export earnings and future share of the expanding industrial and capital goods market throughout the world.

The environment

Traditional power systems pollute the environment as an inherent part of their operational design. Coal-fired stations, in addition to producing sulphur dioxide and other toxic gases also, according to the CEGB, release quantities of radioactive gases. However, the amount involved is so minimal in comparison with releases from nuclear plants, that this claim can only be described as very weak propaganda. In theory, a nuclear power station, though it is bound to produce both high and low-level radioactive waste, ought to be pollution-free. However, in the event of a serious accident, such as a reactor running out of control, melting down or releasing large quantities of radioactivity into the atmosphere, the pollution which would result would far exceed anything which can be expected, even in the worst incident, from a conventional power plant. What is therefore being balanced is a known and continuous amount of pollution associated with the operating of conventional power stations against the potential hazards of a nuclear station in a worst case analysis.

Military use

It is possible to produce weapons grade material in nuclear power stations although Britain claims that there is no link between its civil programme and the production of plutonium for military purposes. The fact that the first civil nuclear power plant in Britain was designed to produce plutonium at the cost of electricity production casts some doubt on the veracity of this claim. Irrespective of the actual UK experience there is a considerable military appeal to some non-nuclear countries to adopt a civil nuclear programme.

Future energy needs

The amount of Uranium 235, the reactor fuel, is finite. It is estimated that current reserves have a lifetime, at present scales of usage, equivalent to that of oil. However, Uranium 238, the major constituent of both natural and enriched uranium, is converted to plutonium in the reactor itself. The plutonium can then itself be used as fuel in other reactors. The amount of plutonium produced is influenced by the reactor type and operating condition. Nuclear power is the only power system capable of producing fuel as it consumes it. In order for more fuel to be produced than is consumed a past breeder reactor programme is necessary. However, it must be noted that it takes several years for a FBR to produce enough plutonium to fuel another FBR.

The disadvantages of nuclear power

Civil nuclear power had its origins in the nuclear weapons programme. Many people have an emotional reaction to civil nuclear power programmes precisely because of this fact. There are certainly grounds for concern in the military area. India has already used a Canadian-supplied plant to produce what she terms a 'peaceful' bomb. The export of such plant to unstable Third World countries makes any hope of halting the proliferation of nuclear weapons seem forlorn. Even if these countries do not produce weapons, given the incentive and will to do so, it would seem impossible to prevent them actually achieving nuclear weapons status, short of preventative military action by the present nuclear powers. This is clearly out of the question, although Israel has already taken military action against Iraq's single nuclear reactor because the Israelis believed it to be the basis of an attempt by Iraq to produce nuclear weapons.

In addition there are several technical, political and biological problems associated with nuclear power.

Operational problems
Many of the problems experienced in the USA have been caused by inadequately trained and disciplined staff. The staff employed by the CEGB have proven to be of a much higher calibre, but if the number of stations is considerably expanded staff quality may also become a problem in the UK.

Reprocessing
Reprocessing is necessary as only a small fraction of the fuel in a fuel element can be consumed within a reactor at any one time. Various by-products form, which prevent the fuel element making any further contribution to the nuclear reaction. Most of the valuable nuclear fuel is still unused in the fuel element; this fuel can be recovered by chemically treatment at a reprocessing plant. The recovered fuel can then be fashioned into a new fuel element and then used once again. Unfortunately this process of separating the original unconsumed fuel and the fission by-products results in the creation of waste, which could very loosely be described as the ashes that are left after the nuclear reaction takes place, and plutonium. Unlike a fossil-fuel reaction, where the waste products are of no further use, plutonium can in turn be used as fuel in a fast breeder reactor or in the manufacture of nuclear

explosives. The alternative is merely to store the used fuel elements pending a long-term solution to the waste disposal problem of reprocessing. This already happens at many nuclear utilities throughout the world as there is a shortage of reprocessing capacity. Given the problems which have been associated with the Windscale/Sellafield complex, which have included cancer clusters, accidental leaks, deliberate release of radioactive material and a failure to fully inform the Black inquiry of the level of actual releases (under-reported by a factor of 40), a policy of no reprocessing might seem attractive. However, even if all the nuclear power stations in the UK were to close tomorrow, it would still be necessary to continue reprocessing. This is because fuel elements from the Magnox reactors have been stored in pools of water until their intense radioactivity declines enough to ease handling problems. As a result the elements have corroded, and cannot be indefinitely stored without a danger of radioactive leaks. There is a large store of these corroded elements which, in the interests of public safety, must be reprocessed. An alternative storage method, using inert gas instead of water, might prevent corrosion in future fuel elements. The strangest aspect of the current situation is that reprocessed uranium actually costs more than the world uranium price, so it is argued that it would be cheaper merely to store used fuel elements and to buy new fuel. Such an argument ignores the fact that world uranium supplies are finite, just as world oil supplies, and seemingly on the same time-scale. It will eventually become economically advantageous to reprocess fuel just to recover its unused uranium, without any cost consideration being given to the plutonium which will also be recovered.

Waste disposal

Waste from reprocessing is highly radioactive and is termed high-level waste. It must be stored for many thousands of years in order to prevent pollution and no sure method has yet been developed to achieve this. It is hoped to 'fix' the waste into glass which will be stored underground in stable geological formations. However, no glass has yet been proven to be able to contain the waste materials safely impervious to underground water intrusions. Wherever there is any suggestion that there might be suitable geological formations for the safe long-term storage and disposal of waste, immense local opposition is generated. Currently, large and increasing quantities of high-level waste are being stored in temporary sites such as Seascale, pending a solution to this problem.

Plutonium

Plutonium is recovered in the reprocessing of spent nuclear fuel. If this is not to be used as fuel then a stockpile will grow which must not only be isolated because of its high degree of radioactivity but must also be secured against theft because of its nuclear weapons potential.

Security

Whilst it is technically feasible that a terrorist group which stole plutonium could make a small nuclear weapon from it, several more likely scenarios must be guarded against. The threat to contaminate an area with plutonium or hijacked nuclear waste would have almost as great an effect without such risks to the malefactors. Thus all highly radioactive material must be constantly guarded. An armed police force has already been established for this purpose in the UK. If the amount of such materials and their transportation increased markedly, the resultant necessary increased monitoring of discontented groups would represent a serious erosion of civil liberties. Ultimately the interest of the public would demand such serious extensions of police power that the British way of life would be markedly altered for the worse.

Military

In an all-out war nuclear installations may become prime nuclear weapons and conventional targets whose destruction would cause economic disruption. The fear of attacks would cause panic amongst the populace living in the vicinity. While the release of radioactivity resulting from such an attack would harm the defending nation, it would also make its conquest less of an advantage to an aggressor. Thus it seems likely that such installations would be subject to superpower attack only in the event of a war of total destruction.

Political

The various problems mentioned above have, both individually and in combination, at various times caused political difficulties for western governments which have espoused nuclear power. It has generally been possible for the authorities to dismiss the fears which have given rise to these problems as arising from public ignorance, and it has often been claimed that those who fan public fears are either political malcontents or unwitting agents of foreign powers (see Hoyle, *Energy or Extinction?*). Such attitudes can no longer be taken as soverign governments are now expressing concern about unsafe nuclear installations in neighbouring countries. Both the Southern Irish and Manx governments have recently called for the closure of Windscale because of its discharges into the Irish sea. Concern has also been expressed about the destination of plutonium recovered at Windscale. The reprocessing facility works both for the civil power and military plutonium programmes. Material from both programmes runs through the same machinery and may have become mixed in the past. Because of the military aspects, inspectors from the International Atomic Energy Agency were only allowed restricted access to parts of Windscale. If official comment is to be believed, this has not been a real problem. The plutonium produced, although of mixed civil and military origin, has been returned in the correct proportions to both programmes. However, it has recently been admitted that, contrary to earlier repeated denials, civil plutonium has actually been directed to military ends. Under these circumstances it is difficult for many members of the public to believe anything that the authorities say in defence of nuclear power.

The costs of nuclear power

The grounds upon which nuclear power is often justified are those of costs. Given the evidence of 20 years of operation it ought to be possible to produce a clear set of figures which would give a cost which could be balanced against the disadvantages. Such is not the case. Not only do economic arguments about the relative costs of various forms of energy production depend on many interconnected variables, CEBG assumptions about which have been seriously undermined, but it has been shown that CEGB figures for costs, produced in the past, are worthless. The House of Commons Select Committee on Energy reports (1981) that the CEGB's cost figures are 'highly misleading as a guide to past investment decisions and entirely useless for appraising future ones'. The Monopolies Commission (1981) commented upon CEGB demand forecasting as 'seriously inaccurate and has led to premature orders for new plant which have increased costs,' and found 'serious weaknesses in its investment appraisal. In particular, a large programme of investment in nuclear power stations, which would greatly increase new capital employed for a given level of output, is proposed on the basis of investment appraisals which are seriously defective and liable to mislead.'

Under these circumstances the Board's figures must be closely examined when it proposes a new programmes. This has happened at the Sizewell enquiry where the objectors, despite a paucity of funding relative to the CEGB, appear to have cast serious doubt upon the economics of the PWR programme. This appears a somewhat odd situation in view of the French experience, where 65% of electricity is generated by nuclear means and electricity is cheaper than in the UK. The source of this conundrum, as became clear during the Sizewell Enquiry, is that the way in which nuclear power plants are built here is extremely disorganised. New structures will, however, oversee the construction of the PWR at Sizewell in the event of consent being granted.

The future of nuclear power

After Chernobyl it is impossible to imagine that attitudes to nuclear power will ever be as uncritical as in the past. Yet there are still very strong arguments in its favour. Diversification of energy sources, the promise of a virtually endless fuel supply from FBRs, potential cost savings, the employment provided in the nuclear construction industry, export potential, the national prestige accruing from a successful and innovative programme, together with assurances from the scientists involved that the probability of a major accident is negligible − in this country at least − and that a solution will be found for the waste problem, make, for many, a very strong case. If one also supports the British nuclear deterrent then the case becomes unanswerable.

A considerable industrial lobby in favour of nuclear power also exists. The CEGB's excess generating capacity means that a large conventional power station building programme is hardly to be expected. However, the replacement of conventional by nuclear power stations would generate a great deal of business, and so provide employment, for the firms involved in the nuclear construction industry. It is noticeable that Windscale and Dounreay both attract considerable support locally, where they provide employment, but beyond the border of the positive employment effects, opposition starts. No such lobby exists for 'renewable' energy systems. Indeed Tony Benn has claimed that, while he was Minister for Energy, reports of accidents involving nuclear material were kept from him by civil servants because of their sympathy for the nuclear industry.

Opposition to the UK nuclear power programme comes from very disparate groups. Some technologists, who might see nuclear power as inevitable in the long term, oppose the immediate programme. Many actually argue that the UK nuclear industry has not learnt anything from the past and that we are about to repeat many of the mistakes of the AGR programme. Although PWR technology is well understood, the model built at Sizewell will not be an exact copy of any other existing reactor. Thus we are really attempting, once again, to build a full-size prototype. While it might have been a good idea to build a PWR in the 60s, they would argue that these reactors are already outdated and that the reactor of the future will be based on one of the inherently safe designs. Thus instead of providing a new export product we will end up needlessly importing new design technology from other countries.

Some point to a more basic problem. Until a proven solution to the waste disposal problem is found, proceeding with a nuclear power programme in the hope that such a solution will be found, is not only potentially dangerous, but also seems to show some confusion between the role of scientist and magician. Yet others question the basic need to replace outdated conventional power stations, claiming that if energy conservation was accorded its propery priority the CEGB could retire many obsolete coal-fired stations.

Popular opposition comes from such 'issue' groups as Greenpeace and Friends of the Earth. These see the environment as in need of protection from human greed and question the need for continuous growth. In doing so they question the common basis of the mainstream political parties. Such groups advocate an alternative view of the future development of our society, in which people are valued above material progress. Owing to the UK electoral system, which discriminates against dispersed political minorities, their political party, the Ecology Party, has never won a place in the British parliament. Indeed, the UK electoral system, together with the desire of individuals not to waste their vote, probably makes it impossible for the Ecology Party ever to generate the bandwagon that carried the German 'Greens' to prominence under a different electoral system.

In other European countries the 'anti-nuclear' movement has broadened to include sections of the peace movement and groups concerned with the implication for civil liberties of a nuclear-powered state. Together such groups have had a great impact. Thus far this has not happened in the UK, although there are indications that this process may also be taking place here. With the opening of the Labour Party to control by party members recently, conference motions passed against nuclear power, reprocessing and the nuclear deterrent should be part of the party's manifesto at the next election. In the event of a Labour victory these should then become the policy of the UK government. This may well not turn out to be the case. While arguments within the Labour leadership about the future of the nuclear deterrent have been widely reported it does not seem to be as widely known that there are strains over nuclear power policy as well. The Labour Party Spokesman on the Environment has made it clear that if Labour were to win power there would be a strong group within the party who would fight against the Party's policy. His attitude is hardly surprising as he is MP for the area which includes the Windscale complex, itself the major source of local employment. Should it come to be believed that Labour would actually act against nuclear power the Conservatives, who are committed to nuclear power, would be well-placed to win the seat. In the traditionally Labour mining areas, regardless of its nuclear power policy, there is really no alternative to the Labour Party in terms of sympathy for the problems of the mining industry.

The Conservative Party's leadership seems to harbour not the slightest doubt about the desirability of a large nuclear programme. Doubts amongst party members are well suppressed owing to the party structure, where power rests with the leadership rather than the membership. Thus Conservative MPs, on the whole, tend to support the nuclear industry. It is only fair to point out that this support never seems to extend as far as supporting any suggestion that waste, even low-level waste such as soiled rags, be disposed of in their constituency. Without the possibility of such disposal, expansion of the nuclear industry is not only hampered, but may be dangerous.

The Alliance parties appear to have decided not to make a commitment on their attitudes until after the next election. The Liberal component tends to be anti-nuclear whereas Dr Owen tends to be aggressively 'realistic'.

It seems, in fact, highly unlikely that anything short of a Chernobyl-type accident in the UK could cause a reduction in the current level of nuclear electricity generation. What is actually at stake at Sizewell and in the associated debate is the size and nature of the nuclear contribution to future UK electricity production. Although the protestors have made a good showing at the inquiry, given the past history of such inquiries, it is highly unlikely that the inspector will reject the totality of the CEGB's case. What might however happen, and surprisingly it seems that the CEGB also sees this as a possibility, is that the case for PWRs will be rejected. That the CEGB fears this eventuality has been shown by their action in starting new AGR feasibility studies during the inquiry while, at the same time, placing PWR-related orders before the inspector reports. The report, due but still not out at the time of writing, must have been largely decided by the time of the Chernobyl disaster.

Postscript

Since this article was revised the CEGB has suddenly announced that the scientific evidence now shows that acid rain is linked to power station emissions. Over the coming years a large investment is to be made in clearing the UK of such emissions.

The report of the Sizewell inquiry is still awaited. As each day passes it becomes more likely that, in the event of a positive report, PWRs will become an issue in the next general election. The sceptical might wonder whether the CEGB might yet suffer an 'overnight' conversion on the issue of PWRs as it seems to have on acid rain.

Reading

Michael Grenon, *The Nuclear Apple and the Solar Orange*, Pergamon, 1981.

Tony Hall, *Nuclear Politics*, Penguin, 1986.

Fred Hoyle, *Energy or Extinction?*, Heinemann, 1978.

Martin Ince, *Sizewell Report*, Pluto Press, 1984.

Walter C. Patterson, *Nuclear Power*, Pelican, 1977.

Colin Sweet, *The Costs of Nuclear Power*, Anti-Nuclear Campaign, 1982.

Various booklets are available, free upon request, from the CEGB.

austerity —
Severe in
self discipline

SOCIAL POLICY

Chapter Ten   *Paul Wilding*

The debate about the welfare state

Until the mid-1970s there was no real debate about the welfare state. Certainly, there had been sharp questions about it from the 1950s – for example from the Institute of Economic Affairs in its many publications – but there was little debate. Critics were seen as eccentrics, people who had failed to come to terms with the post-war world. Supporters of the welfare state felt sufficiently confident and assured not to engage in debate.

In fact, supporters of the welfare state were its strongest critics through the 1950s, 1960s and 1970s – for example Richard Titmuss and Peter Townsend – but their criticisms were about the quantity and quality of provision. They wanted more, more quickly; they did not question the idea of the welfare state itself.

The consensus about the welfare state which existed from 1945–75 can easily be overemphasised. There were differences between the main political parties about what should be done and how quickly, but there was near universal acceptance of the major role of the state in welfare which had emerged in the years between 1945 and 1950. There was little questioning of that principle.

The collapse of consensus

What has become quite clear is that consensus about the desirability of a major role for the state in welfare has broken down for a variety of reasons. These are some of the reasons put forward:

(1) The consensus was never more than superficial. The welfare state in Britain has suffered from two damaging associations – with socialism and with austerity – and this has inhibited its wholehearted acceptance as a fact of late twentieth-century life.

(2) The era of painless financing out of economic growth ended in the mid-1970s. As long as the economy was expanding, private consumption and welfare spending could expand simultaneously. In the 1970s for the first time it was much more either one or the other.

(3) Paying for the welfare state has come to rest more heavily on those with average and below average incomes because the income at which people start paying tax has fallen. This gives greater credibility to politicians talking about 'the burden of taxation' caused by the welfare state and broadens concern about welfare expenditure.

(4) The welfare state has been blamed for Britain's economic difficulties. The high taxes which are required to sustain it have, it is alleged, fuelled inflation and reduced incentives, so weakening the economy. The welfare state is also charged with absorbing labour which would be better employed in productive enterprises rather than in the provision of social services.

(5) The welfare state has come under strong criticism for its ineffectiveness in achieving its aims. It has not, even its supporters agree, abolished poverty, achieved equality of opportunity in education, or equality of access to health services. In many services, e.g. higher education, the middle classes are clearly the main beneficiaries.

(6) Public confidence in welfare state services has been weakened by the continuous deafening chorus of complaint about lack of resources and standards of services which arises from those who work in them. An Enoch Powell pointed out many years ago, to secure more resources, those in the services feel they have to denigrate them and claim that they are worse than they should be. People therefore came to think that services were substandard – and therefore not worth paying for or supporting.

(7) Welfare state policies depend on faith in experts, the belief that there are people who know how to solve the problems of poverty, ill health, bad housing, urban redevelopment, juvenile delinquency and so on. The reputations of the key welfare professionals have gone down the skittles in the last few years – and the welfare state has suffered in consequence.

(8) The belief that public action is the appropriate way to deal with social problems was a basic building block in the consensus. This has been weakened by the emergence of new and more complex problems which no one is confident they know how to tackle – the problem of the inner city, the problem of order in society, the increasing numbers of very elderly, for example.

(9) From all sides, the welfare state is attacked for what it is alleged to do to *people* and to *society*. The New Right talk of 'the nanny state' destroying independence, initiative and self respect. Feminists accuse it of contributing to women's subordination. Marxists see it as propping up capitalism and disciplining the working class. The romantics talk of the 'schooled', 'medicalised' society.

(10) The essential underpinnings of the welfare state were provided by Keynesian economics. What Keynes did was to make legitimate high levels of government activity and spending. The eclipse (temporary or permanent) of Keynesianism means the removal of a basic philosophical prop to the welfare state.

Most of these points are contestable. They are clearly of varying degrees of importance but they make up the background to the debate about the welfare state.

Positions in the debate

It is difficult briefly to characterise the various positions in the debate on the welfare state without seeming to caricature them. The sketches which follow can do no more than indicate the broad lines of the different perspectives.

The New Right position

The New Right critique of the welfare state is the contemporary expression of anti-collectivism. It draws on the work of two distinguished academics − Milton Friedman and F. A. Hayek. It stresses certain values − freedom, individualism and inequality. It stresses the creative possibilities of the free market economy. It emphasises a range of doubts and anxieties about government action. It makes a number of general and particular criticisms of welfare state policies.

(1) The welfare state is a threat to freedom because

(*a*) it gives people little or no choice about the type or quality of service which is provided;

(b) services are not subject to effective democratic control.

(2) State provision of welfare is fundamentally inefficient because it is monopolistic. There is no competition between providing bodies and it is only through competition that efficiency is achieved.

(3) In a welfare state system what is provided is not what consumers want but what professionals and bureaucrats *think* they want. Public

provision is therefore inevitably unresponsive to individual needs and wishes.

(4) Although designed to help, in fact the welfare state damages people. It creates dependency and weakens individuals' sense of responsibility for themselves and their families.

(5) A welfare state leads to the view that the state is the main source and provider of welfare services. Other sources and systems of welfare – the family, the community, the voluntary sector, the market – are neglected and weakened and in time perish.

(6) Welfare state policies weaken the economy because they depend on debilitating rates of taxation which fuel inflation, destroy incentives and damage investment. The real sources of welfare – a healthy economy and economic growth – are therefore undermined.

(7) As well as weakening the economy, welfare state policies also weaken the authority of government. Governments become the focus of interest group activity as groups fight for the recognition and protection of their particular needs. Governments committed to particular welfare programmes all too easily become the creatures of particular groups.

Underlying the whole critique is one vital belief – *private provision is always better*:

(*a*) *economically* because it is not damaging to the economy and because it will be more efficient;

(*b*) *politically* because it does not make government the creature of particular interests; and

(*c*) *socially* because it does not make people dependent and because it offers choice and makes providers accountable to consumers.

The Marxist position

The Marxist critique has not become part of current political debate as has that of the New Right. The most obvious reason is that what Marxists say is of little or not immediate political importance. It is also difficult to talk about a Marxist critique because 'Marxist' is a loose category embracing a rich variety of opinions. It is, however, possible with this warning to sketch a Marxist position.

(1) Marxists see the welfare state as shaped by three forces

(*a*) the needs of capitalism

(*b*) class conflict

(*c*) the ideology generated by capitalism

Capitalism needs healthy, educated and contented workers. It needs systems which maintain workers in times when the onward march of economic progress is temporarily checked. It needs a state whose authority is seen as legitimate, and the provision of welfare can contribute to such legitimacy. The capitalist state is characterised by the conflict which Marxists see as the essential characteristic of the relationship between capital and labour. This conflict produced concessions by capital and/or victories for labour – and sometimes these take the form of welfare services.

Marxists are therefore ambivalent about the welfare state. It is both a source of support for capitalism and a symbol of victories won by the working class.

(2) Marxists lay much stress on the social control functions of the welfare state – i.e. its contributions to inculcating and reinforcing the values and patterns of behaviour required by the capitalist system.

(3) An important strand in the Marxist critique is the argument that many of the problems with which the welfare state seeks to deal are the direct product of the particular nature of the capitalist economy. They are not therefore amenable to solution by social services.

(4) Marxists also stress the limited possibilities of social services. They are not, they argue, a tool for changing society. The most that can be achieved through welfare state policies is, in Miliband's words, 'a certain humanisation' of the existing order.

(5) An anxiety which Marxists have is that, although providing tangible and immediate goals, welfare services will have a deradicalising effect on the working-class political movement. Workers will become content with the half loaf of the welfare state rather than striving for the whole loaf of socialism.

Marxists cannot, therefore, be optimistic about the possibilities of welfare provided by a capitalist state. On the other hand, they recognise the real benefits accruing to the working class from such provision. They contest the New Right arguments but they do not want to see welfare services become an alternative to radical social reconstruction.

The Fabian position

In many ways the welfare state represents a triumph of Fabianism – the belief that the amelioration or removal of social ills is possible by modest institutional change within a mixed economy. The group of thinkers has, from a fundamentally supportive position, produced a variety of criticisms of the welfare state which have been part of the raw material of the debate.

(1) This group supported the welfare state as a means of reducing social inequality. Their researches however, show that this has not happened. In health, housing and education, for example, there are still striking inequalities between class, sex, region and ethnic groups.

(2) They have come to accept that more resources are not necessarily always the best answer to unmet needs.

(3) They accept that state services can be bureaucratic, inefficient, inflexible and so complicated that people get lost in a welfare maze.

(4) They accept that the welfare state gives many professionals who work within it a degree of power which is problematic because they are directly answerable to no one for its exercise.

(5) They agree that the welfare state has made some pretty awful mistakes – e.g. some local authority housing developments.

(6) More and more supporters of the welfare state would agree that the concentration on services is bound to bring failure because the achievement of particular goals, for example, for health and education, cannot be achieved without taking account of factors which go way beyond the purview of the health or education service. What is needed, Fabians argue, is a broad health or education *policy*, not just health and education *services*.

The Fabian, welfare state supporter critique has contributed to the dissatisfaction with the welfare state. The group saw criticism as the way to improvement. The New Right, however, have used their work as ammunition in the struggle to destroy the credibility of welfare state policies and role back the state.

The feminist position

Feminists have developed a powerful critique of the welfare state based on an exposure of its assumptions, implicit and explicit, and their impact on the lives of women. They point out that:

(1) Social policies are based on certain unstated assumptions about sex roles. In the British welfare state those assumptions contribute directly and indirectly to the continuance of women's unequal position in society.

(2) Those assumptions – e.g. about women as carers – trap women, whether they like it or not in a traditional female role.

(3) The welfare state is a living witness to women's inequality. They are the main clients of many services, they staff many of the services.

But they have few of the top jobs, they contribute little to the decision-making and they are treated badly when they need help, for example when using ante-natal care or when suffering from depression.

Feminists are not (as a generalisation) hostile to the principle of the welfare state. They are, however, keen to point out how good (male) intentions can have unfortunate even if unintended implications for women.

The romantic position

This is the group for which it is most difficult to find a suitable title. The position is occupied both by genuine romantics like Ivan Illich and by people whose arguments are much more pragmatic and hard-headed. Essentially, it represents a reaction against the welfare system of the late 1960s and early 1970s and two of its salient characteristics — its size and its power.

(1) The romantics worry about the increasing size of organisations and systems because for them it spells remoteness and bureaucracy, and the inability to respond swiftly, sensitively and flexibly to individual needs.

(2) They are concerned about increasing professionalisation because they see this as involving costs as well as gains for clients — social distance, dependency, and a neglect of people's capacity for self-help on an individual or collective basis.

(3) The failure of the state welfare system to involve consumers of services in decisions about the shape and nature of current and future provision seems to the romantics both a reason why the welfare state has developed as it has and a result of such trends.

(4) Romantics worry, too, about the failure of the state services to take sufficient account of other systems and sources of welfare — family, neighbourhood and voluntary — and to work sensitively with them.

What romantics want is a small-scale, local, decentralised deprofessionalised, participative system of welfare. They see the welfare state as developing in the opposite direction, as becoming alienated from, and alienating, those who use its services.

IMPORTANT page

Warnings

(1) The debate about the welfare state is an ideological debate. Positions are not adopted on the basis of a scientific assessment of evidence and argument. Attitudes to the role of the state in welfare depend on social values, beliefs about society, beliefs about the role of government, and beliefs about the right ordering of economic and social relationships.

(2) Do not forget the achievements of the welfare state. Even its supporters spend more blood and ink on criticism than defence. Criticism is easy – so too is defence, but we are at a point when the welfare state looks a bit middle-aged and unappealing. Users had come – until the early 1980s at least – to take it for granted. The politicians and the media are only interested in its shortcomings. Stress is on costs and cuts – not on what is provided – and achieved. Since 1945 the real value of social security benefits has vastly increased, so have the number of seventeen and eighteen-year-olds continuing their education, so has the number of students in higher education. We have made an enormous improvement in the physical standards of our housing stock. We have a national health service which gives a better service at a cost of 6% of gross domestic product than the United States gets for an expenditure of 11% of a relatively larger GDP.

(3) The debate is also carried on at a level of generalisation which, while it may be satisfactory to politicians, is little help to the careful student. The welfare state, it is said, for example, is a threat to freedom. All kinds of questions have to be asked and answered before such a statement can be evaluated. What is meant by the welfare state? What freedom? Whose freedom? And so on.

(4) Certainly there are sharply distinct positions in the debate. There are those who believe that a market system with a modicum of residual state provision could provide all the welfare needed in our kind of society. On the other hand there are those who believe that only the state can provide what is required.

Between these extremes there is a considerable area of muddy middle ground inhabited by large numbers of people who would agree about a good number of things – that the pure doctrine of state welfare (i.e. the state does all) *has* collapsed, that there *is* a real role for a properly supported voluntary sector, that private provision *has* a role, that self help groups can make a valuable contribution, that decentralisation and more participation *must* be developed.

Conclusion

The debate about the welfare state is important because it is about the kind of society we want. It is real because it raises fundamental questions about individual and social responsibility. It is about economic and political issues, about the broad nature and pattern of social development, and about the more effective and efficient organisation, administration and financing of particular services in particular places.

The debate is confused. Therefore it can be unhelpful. But if policy makers listen attentively there is much to be learned.

Reading

M. and R. Friedman, *Free to Choose*, Penguin, 1980.

V. George and P. Wilding, *Ideology and Social Welfare*, Routledge & Kegan Paul, 1985.

R. Hadley and S. Hatch, *Social Welfare and the Failure of the State*, Allen & Unwin, 1981.

M. Loney, *The Politics of Greed*, Pluto, 1986.

R. Mishra, *The Welfare State in Crisis*, Harvester, 1984.

A. Seldon, *Whither the Welfare State*, Institute of Economic Affairs, 1981.

P. Wilding (ed.), *In Defence of the Welfare State*, Manchester University Press, 1986.

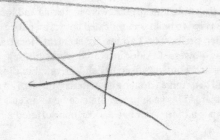

The politics of housing policy

It is inevitable that government should be closely involved in such a basic human concern as the availability and quality of the houses in which we live. This chapter examines the background and current issues in housing policy and places them in the context of the party political debate.

Development

(a) *Post-war activity*

During the second world war Britain had 200,000 houses destroyed and a further half million severely damaged. Demand was rising as demobilisation took place and marriage and birth rates rose. As in other policy sectors the solution was an extension of wartime state control and direction. 71,000 houses had been requisitioned and private sector rents had been held at the pre-war level. Procedures for compulsory purchase were streamlined, subsidies were increased and local authorities were empowered to build prefabricated houses on public open land. As during other periods of Labour government, local authorities assumed greater powers. Besides increased requisitioning, they built 80% of houses and controlled repairs and private building. Central government still determined design and materials through an increasing stream of circulars. This cash programme came to an end in 1947 as building materials and fuel ran low and Britain suffered a balance of payments crisis.

During this period, planning was revolutionised with the passage of the Distribution of Industry Act, New Towns Act, the National Parks and Access to the Countryside Act, the Town Development Act and, most significantly, the Town and Country Planning Act 1947 which gave local authorities the responsibility of producing development plans and the power to control the whole process.

At the same time the potentially damaging separation of housing staff and planners, who looked to different ministries and underwent different training and career paths, was consolidated.

(b) Conservative disengagement

Macmillan's promise during the election of 1951 to build 300,000 houses a year made a significant contribution to the Conservatives' success. An improvement in Britain's economic position, and a relaxation of council house building standards facilitated this — by 1954, 357,000 were being built. At the same time controls on their plans were lessened and councils could borrow funds on the open market.

Under the Conservatives, however, the private sector was actively encouraged. Licencing was abolished in 1954, rent control eased and the purchase of council houses forwarded. This was gradually formulated into a positive policy direction, heralded by the White Paper 'Housing: the next step'. As local authorities were guided from building towards slum clearance (a public health problem) the private sector was stimulated by legislation on rents, subsidies and improvement grants. From 15% of houses built in 1952, those for owner-occupation rose to 63% in 1963 (figures from Donnison and Ungerson).

Deliberately eschewing 'planning', the Conservatives appeared to be driving towards a residual role for the public sector which would look after only those in need. Planning concentrated on green belts and conservation, and any compulsory purchase had to be for a 'fair market price'.

(c) Intervention resumed

Demographic changes ensured that disengagement would not continue. A rise in the birth rate, more marriages and a reduction in family size all began to increase demand. At the same time slum clearance, emphasis on ownership and the steady decline of private rented accommodation created stresses at the poorer end of the market, and these began to surface as 'human interest' and scandal stories in the media. In 1963 the Milner Holland Committee was established to look at London's problems.

Labour   As a result, Labour could use housing policy to good effect in the 1964 election by concentrating on empty office blocks, tenants' rights, rents and building. Their National Plan of 1965 contained a proposal to build half a million houses a year and, following the Parker Morris Committees, council house size and standards were improved. Rent rebates were introduced and 'fair rents' established. Control was clearly re-established with the advent of the Land Commission which could buy land and encourage development.

Pressure groups   Forces on government to act on housing were increased by pressure groups at this time. The problems of the homeless were highlighted by the television programme *Cathy Come Home* and, in its wake, Shelter was founded in 1967. The Skeffington Committee had advocated public involvement in planning, and the middle class increasingly resisted road-building programmes and city-centre redevelopment, especially in 'gentrified' London boroughs.

Inner cities   Richard Crossman had turned the attention of the Labour government from large clearances to rehabilitation, and the Conservatives continued this 'total approach' to areas of special need by coordinating services. Labour attempted to press further in 1975 with the Community Land Act which enabled authorities to acquire land for development and draw revenue through a tax on transactions. But while some progress was made, Britain's economic problems impeded any real solution. Approximately 10% of inner-city land was unused and the social deprivation was severe. Perhaps one of the last major interventions on behalf of the disadvantaged was the Housing (Homeless Persons) Act which was created and processed in 1977 by coalitions of Lib-Lab leaders, allied pressure groups, back-bench MPs and DOE civil servants.

Finance   Two major attempts were made to reorganise housing finance during the 1970s:

(1) The Housing Finance Act 1972 sought to rationalise debts, rents and subsidies to best advantage. It caused disruption and opposition, notably at Clay Cross, Derbyshire where councillors were surcharged and barred from office, and it was repealed by the 1974 Labour government. It did, however, leave a system of allowances for private tenants.

(2) The Housing Policy Review of 1977 remained unimplemented

as the Labour government lost momentum and agreements on investment programmes were made instead with individual local authorities.

(d) *Thatcherism*

The Conservative government which came to power in 1979 was committed to free market principles. In seeking to 'roll back' the state and cut public expenditure, local authority housing programmes fared badly. The 1980 Housing Act also gave private landlords powers to raise rents and evict tenants, and provided a system whereby council and housing association tenants had the right to buy their homes. These and other current issues will be reviewed later.

Ideology and housing   Labour's extension of wartime controls and increased local authority powers were to turn into a ideological commitment. Such constraints were to prove increasingly unacceptable as Britain moved into the 1980s, and in the long term identified the party with bureaucratic restriction of tenants' freedoms, epitomised by the prohibitions on painting their own front doors. At the same time Labour exuded hostility to private landlords by retaining rent controls, and did little to encourage owner-occupiers.

As we have seen, the Conservatives adopted the contrary stance of relaxing controls and encouraging the private sector. In equating Labour policy with identity cards and food rationing they derived considerable benefit in the 1950s, and in a similar way seized the advantage in the 1980s by emphasising freedom of choice in line with publicly-expressed wants. In large cities, the Conservatives accused Labour administrations of 'social engineering' and bureaucratic incompetence while Labour warned its tenants of rent increases and deteriorating standards if they lost power. Here is to be found the bedrock of Labour support, for while 30% of the electorare are council tenants, over ninety constituencies have a majority of people living in council houses.

Deriding Labour's 'rearguard action' against council house sales the Conservative government made good use of their pursuit of a 'property-owning democracy' in the 1983 election. In her five-year anniversary statement in April 1984, Mrs Thatcher extolled the virtue of the wider spread of home ownership 'than at any time in our history; this is the way to become "One Nation" '. The opinion polls at that time gave the Conservatives a 6% lead over Labour, and significantly they had a 2 to 1 lead among homeowners while Labour led 2 to 1 among council tenants.

The Conservatives are on firm ground – the preference for home ownership is strong, particularly among young people, where 65% of 16 to 19-year-oilds want to buy. Britain has also seen an unparalleled rise in ownership – from 31% in 1951 to 64% in 1986, with the Building Societies Association predicting 75% by the year 2000. With this in mind, in May 1986 the Housing Minister, John Patten, could begin to suggest limiting the proportion of council ownership to force matters in areas such as Tower Hamlets (82% public-owned).

Labour response   Aware that they have been pushed on to the defensive, the Labour Party has had to re-examine its policies and beliefs. David Griffiths of the Labour Housing Group (LHG) took issue with the routine conference reaffirmations of 'the right of everyone to a decent home at a price they can afford' for its lack of egalitarian commitment and paternalistic omission of any reference to rights. What has been lacking in the past was any real equality of tenure and a new comprehensive approach was now required:

(1) The overall level of investment for both sectors should be determined by central government but thereafter Whitehall controls over local authorities should be removed.

(2) Local authorities could take responsibility for supply in both sectors, free to buy and sell.

(3) Standards should be raised to meet the expectations of tenants.

(4) Democratic rights should be extended to facilitate accountability and eliminate what Frank Field called 'serfdom'. Cooperatives and collective control would be encouraged, rather than ignored or discouraged (as in Riverside, Liverpool).

These policies, first seen in the 1977 report 'The assessment of housing requirements' of the Labour government's Housing Service Advisory Group, were seen as restoring some vision. The Labour Housing Group was scathing about the party's past 'hypocrisy' of restricting public sector investment and pretending that the huge concessions to owner-occupiers did not exist, or that they could be offset by the one-year rent freeze proposed in the 1982 Programme.

The ideological approach has its clearest expression in the Militant Tendency's policies in Liverpool, where even the national party's policy on housing co-operatives is rejected as being outside 'working-class organisation'.

The Alliance The nature of this debate is anathema to the Alliance. The SDP's 'A strategy for housing' begins with the words: 'The characteristics of British housing today reflect, with awesome accuracy, the failure of the two party system. The polarisation of tenure between owner-occupiers and council tenants is socially divisive and offers insufficient choice.' Both the SDP and the Liberals call for increased investment coupled with increased rights and devolved control. There have been some problems and dilemmas in their decentralisation and subsidy policies which will be reviewed later.

Current issues

(1) *Housing shortage*

In 1951 households exceeded dwellings by 800,000 but by the mid-1970s this deficit had turned into a surplus of 500,000. The Labour Housing Group delve beyond this figure, however, to discount empty properties, second homes and necessary vacancies. Even without concealed households they estimate an actual deficit of 421,000 in 1976, of 188,000 in 1981 rising to 362,000 in 1986.

The 1977 Housing Green Paper had outlined a requirement for 300,000 new homes every year until 1986 to meet problems and projected trends. In fact completions have fallen, as shown in Table 3.

Table 3   *Homes built*

Year	Council	Housing Association	Private
1975	140,000	19,600	153,000
1979	58,000	16,000	148,000
1981	26,000	12,000	120,000
1983	36,000	13,500	177,000
1985	22,600	12,000	168,400

Source: Sunday Times, 15 June 1986

(*a*) *Private sector revival* The Conservative government was able to take comfort in a 15% rise in private housing starts in 1986. They could also cite the Housebuilders' Federation's optimism for prospects that year, and link this upturn to public demand.

(*b*) *Public sector decline* The clear decline in public sector house-building, caused by public expenditure cuts which fell most heavily on capital spending and particularly on housing, is an obvious focus of political dispute. The Commons' Environment Select Committee, measuring against the 1977 Green Paper, foresaw a shortfall of 300–350,000 by the mid-1980s.

In November 1984 it was reported that Patrick Jenkin had reduced the Treasury's attempted £600 million cut in the public housing investment programme to £65 million. But the Treasury sought what were described as 'revenge' cuts of £1 billion by cutting from 40% to 20% the proportion of receipts from the sale of council houses which authorities were entitled to invest in new housing. The announcement in December sparked a major Conservative back-bench revolt from groups opposed to government policy on the economy and/or local government, and from those wanting some capital spending especially on housing and in the inner cities. – 30 MPs abstained and 3 voted against the government. In 1985 a cut of £185 million was imposed, though a creative accounting device on sales proceeds was used to turn this into an increase. Between 1979 and 1986 capital and current spending on housing fell by 60% (£6,870 million to £2,612 million). In this respect it fared worst (see Table 4).

Table 4   *Public spending = real change 1979/80 to 1984/85 (%)*

Law and order	+ 29·1
Social Security	+ 28·4
Defence	+ 22·8
Industry and employment	+ 17·8
Health	+ 16·7
Education and science	+ 1·0
Housing	− 54·6

Source: 1985 Report of the National Federation of Housing Associations.

In the 1986 debate on tax cuts versus public spending, housing was still not seen as a priority compared to education and the Health Service, and on becoming Environment Secretary Nicholas Ridley cut his predecessor's proposals by £250m.

(c) *Opposition criticism   The Labour Party* referred to this 'crisis' in their 1982 Programme caused by cuts at a time of accelerating demand as the 'baby boom' of twenty to thirty years ago created more new households. In England they claimed there were 500,000 households sharing a home and 300,000 married couples and single parents living 'concealed' in other households.

For the *Alliance*, the Liberal Party too criticised the failure to meet housebuilding targets, even during the Macmillan years, and the SDP have sought to puncture the complacency on housing. In their 'Strategy for Housing' they describe the structural changes in population:

decreasing household size as people live longer, more marriages end in divorce and young people leave home earlier. The increase in the number of households is running at about 165,000 *per annum*. Add to that annual number of houses demolished (around 35,000) and we can see the inadequacy of the country's new construction programme. (pp. 2–3)

(d) *Consequences*   The opposition pointed to resulting inadequate temporary accommodation, the worst problems being faced by single parents and women whose marriages had broken down, enforced entrapment in tower blocks for families, fewer transfers to sheltered flats for the elderly and tenants on older estates suffering inadequate amenities. Local authority waiting lists held 1–2 million people.

(2) *Decay*

According to the Department of the Environment's 'English house condition survey' of 1982 there were 1·1 million unfit homes, 390,000 more lacked amenities, and 574,000 needed repairs costing over £7,000. Another 2½ million were deemed to be fit but needed repairs that would cost between £2,300 and £7,000. While the government abolished the Housing Improvement Group, which produced survey data, the embarrassing information still appeared − a DOE inquiry in 1986 found that £19 billion was needed for repairs and improvement in the public sector (84% of the total and £4,000 per dwelling). A similar crisis exists in the private sector where £35 billion is needed. The problem particularly affects the elderly; 206,000 of the 480,000 in unfit homes, revealed in the last official survey, were pensioners.

As significant as these raw figures are the changing trends. By concentrating on the provision of amenities since the war, governments have rendered this problem less urgent. The rate of deterioration, however, has been exceeding renovations; 18% of the housing needed repairs of over £2,500 and those needing over £7,000 of repairs rose from 2·2% in 1971 to 3·4% in 1981.

This deterioration is a function of:

(*a*) *Age* In 1979 30% of the housing stock was built before 1919 and 22% between 1919 and 1944.

(*b*) *Public expenditure constraints* Grant-aided expenditure was restricted in the 1970s to prevent speculation and to save money. Slum clearance fell from 72,000 in 1971 to 20,000 in 1983. The imposition of VAT on building alterations in 1984 accelerated the decline as public sector spending was halved.

(*c*) *Building errors* Much post-war housing was substandard. 1·2 million council homes suffer from damp, a third from damp or condensation and 300,000 homes are 'difficult to let'. Some authorities, such as Liverpool and Manchester, have had to blow up flat blocks on which interest is still being paid, while Birmingham is contending with the colliery shale used in the foundations of defective system-built houses. In such overspill dwellings the kitchens and bathrooms are too small, heating systems outdated and expensive, constructional faults have been discovered and their environments have become vandalised. The Association of Metropolitan Authorities in 1985 estimated that it would cost £5 billion to repair the defects in system-built housing, particularly deck access, in the next 10–15 years.

Opposition proposals

The political response of the opposition parties is to deplore this state of affairs, the impact of government cuts and to demand action. The Labour Party believed a threefold increase in the level of building and renovation to be necessary, and given the failure of the private sector this would have to be public-sector-led investment. Standards would be reviewed and low energy housing provided to avoid past errors, and a rolling programme to improve problem areas begun. Local authorities would be allowed to improve for sale, the renovation grant would be simplified and extended and in action areas they would be given compulsory improvement powers. The Liberals also wished to simplify regulations on standards and the criteria for renovation grants, introducing Housing Renovation Areas. The SDP proposed an expansion of local authority and housing association building programmes, costing £500 m, creating 64,000 jobs and increasing capital expenditure by 15%. They would also encourage local authority intervention and abolish VAT on housing repairs.

Conservative response
Increasing public expenditure and more public sector control are not the panacea for the government elected in 1979. Instead, the remedies have included:

(*a*) *Improvement for sale*   The 1980 Housing Act made grants available to local authorities and housing associations to improve run-down dwellings for sale. By the end of 1982, 6,000 houses were being so improved by 100 authorities and ninety associations.

(*b*) *Homesteading*   By 1982 4,400 unimproved homes had been sold at low cost to would-be homeowners who would make them habitable.

(*c*) *Priority Estates Project*   Three 'difficult to let' estates in Bolton, Hackney and Lambeth were being systematically upgraded as an example, the process being reinforced by a report, film and seminars.

(*d*) *Housing Defects Prevention Unit*   Established in 1981 this unit analyses problems, disseminates technical information, and has produced sixteen Defect Action Sheets for public and private sectors.

(*e*) *New improvement grant system 1980*   Grants become available for pre-1919 properties, as well as phased payment, applicable to public and private sector, with higher rates for Greater London. In 1982 the rates were raised to 90%, and a special scheme was introduced to buy old prefabricated houses. Whole street improvement or 'enveloping' was extended. In producing a rise in spending from £200 million in 1979–80 to £900 million in 1983–4, the government claimed to be at last 'doing something' about the improvement problem. But by October 1981 officials were doubting the value of giving local authorities improvement grant funds which they would have otherwise found themselves, and in August 1984 the government was expected to halve available cash for the second year running. In 1985 the government declared that it was never intended to continue this indefinitely and moved to introduce loans and means-testing in order to reduce the expenditure to £250 million.

(*f*) *Right to repair*   The Housing and Building Control Act 1983 confers a statutory right on council, new town and housing association tenants to carry out their own repairs and claim reimbursement of at least 75% of the cost from their landlords.

(*g*) *Building control*   The 1983 Act attempted to remove bureaucratic controls. Supervision passed from local authorities to inspectors who issue certificates. Guidance through regulations can be provided by the ministry. These measures were attacked by the opposition as centralising at the expense of local authorities, likely to diminish quality and as being palliatives given the size of the problems. It was cited that the West Midlands had received only half the sum for 1984−5 that it needed to stem the deterioration of its housing. The Labour Party promised to reintroduce Parker Morris standards to increase room size.

(3) *Responsibility*

Conservatives   Withdrawing rapidly from housing project control and funding, the Conservatives have sought to reduce central government's role. This is evident with the housing benefit scheme which has been passed from the DHSS to local authorities. Unfortunately lack of preparation in the form of staffing, training and publicity led to chaos − at least 100 of the 500 councils in England and Wales were unable to cope, tenants suffered hardship and rent arrears among housing association tenants doubled to £10 million in August 1983. The confusion was criticised by the Public Accounts Committee in 1985. The system covers 7−8 million households, or one in three of the population, and led to a doubling of administrative staff to 9,700.

   The huge sums of money involved have ensured continuing government involvement. The DOE has tried to make councils tackle the problem of £200 million rent and £100 million rate arrears and considered cutting grants to force rent rises in 1985. Meanwhile the DHSS cut back on the initial 6-month benefit to pay mortgage interest, but in 1986 had to abandon proposals to make rate-payers find 20% of rent rebates. The most contentious subject is the cash from council house sales − local authorities are only allowed to spend 20%, with £6 billion frozen, to control inflation but also to avoid awkward questions of redistribution (the wealthier areas with 60% of the cash have only 30% of the need). Some councils, notably Liverpool, were turning to accounting devices to avoid such restrictions and were threatened with central government vetoes.

In 1986 the Audit Commission criticised both sides, calling on central government to give more cash to urban areas (as did the Church of England report 'Faith in the cities') and to allow councils to spend all their sales cash. At the same time local authorities were urged to double their rents from £15 and tackle arrears, and to streamline their reletting rules and use hostels. This clash is unlikely to disappear for one of central government's main solutions is to employ empty property – there are 120,000 empty council houses and flats, 20,000 of which have been empty for more than a year.

Housing associations and tenant co-operatives are important in this respect, as there are 500,000 to 700,000 empty private sector homes. Housing associations received more discretion to provide low-cost housing and, in 1982/3, more funds to do so (£690 million). Particularly attractive to the government was the example of Thamesmead, which voted to run its own affairs when the GLC was abolished.

One area where some spokesmen of the right, such as Sir Alfred Sherman, would have liked more control was over the building societies and what *The Times* called the 'mortgage magnet' (6 August). By competing in the money markets they were alleged to be keeping interest rates up and impeding economic recovery. These fears were in no way allayed when the Bank of England reported excess borrowing of £18·7 billion in 1982–84, i.e. mortgage lending 'leaking' as credit.

Labour The Labour Party regards it as an essential to reassert control – to stimulate investment, impede unrestricted council house sales, regulate private landlords and plan whole areas. There is, though, an ambivalence about the extent to which local authorities will determine their own investment and council house allocation under 'guidelines'. Housing associations are seen as useful to 'fill gaps' in Tory local authorities which are disinclined to build. Co-operatives would be likely to receive more encouragement, and a housing tribunal, rather than the courts, would deal with landlord/tenant disputes. As noted, Labour dislikes private tenancy where 80% is unsatisfactory accommodation and where harassment takes place (4% of London's 350,000 tenants).

Liberals The Liberals would direct to the extent of building 200,000 homes per year and acquiring land for building, if necessary by compulsory purchase. But on council house sales, the power would be taken from central government and given to local authorities. Disdaining bureaucracies, Liberals favour co-operatives, neighbourhood control through housing management committees and clearly defined charters of rights.

SDP   In some respects the SDP adopt a national approach – besides investment they favour a National Housing Bank to channel funds by offering index-linked investments. They accept that there is a dilemma for them in making national proposals about council house management, to remove 'crass political interference', given their belief in local autonomy. They go on to propose Neighbourhood Housing Trusts of tenants and officials, or at least a decentralised service with tenants being within 'pram-pushing' distance of offices. Also in favour are flexible joint systems of cooperatives, associations and building societies – widening the spectrum and moving away from 'rent or buy'.

(4) *Council house sales*
The Conservative government of 1979 gave council tenants, new town tenants and those of non-charitable housing associations the right to buy their houses or flats at discounts of between 33% and 50%. Over 700,000 or 11·5% of the housing stock were sold between 1979 and September 1984. The 1983 Housing and Building Control Act extended the scheme by:

(i) giving a discount of 60%, to 400,000 tenants of thirty years' standing

(ii) reducing the qualifying period from three to two years

(iii) giving 50,000 leasehold tenants the right to buy

(iv) giving new rights to buy or shared ownership to the elderly and least well-off.

By May 1984 the government was encountering opposition from councils who were terminating tenancies and from the House of Lords who exempted university land and homes for the elderly. In September, government launched a £1·4 million publicity campaign which was quickly condemned as 'political advertising'.

Aiming to sell the millionth council home in 1986 (20% of the 4·6 million English tenants) the government tried to sell council flats by giving an extra 10% discount and preventing councils imposing expensive repair clauses. The Housing and Planning Bill of 1986 goes further in giving councils the power to evict tenants so their homes can be sold and allowing councils to turn over management to private landlords.

The government found an obstacle to estate sales in that the required abolition of rent controls was unpopular and would have raised spending through rebates. To protect the 'right to buy' policy a Housing Defects Act was passed, obliging councils to repair defective pre-fabricated concrete dwellings (PRC's) or buy them back (16,500 of the 173,000 have been sold).

Labour opposition   Labour opposition is based on the premise that the best council housing is being lost, thus depriving authorities of revenue and flexibility. The first 'knee-jerk' reaction of the 1980 Conference was to pass a motion requiring resale to authorities at the same discount, i.e. below market price, despite NEC opposition. By 1982 the policy had changed to repurchase (when available) at market price, no statutory obligation to sell, outstanding options to be cancelled and future sales at market price. After the June 1983 election there were suggestions that Labour should simply abandon its opposition to 'right to buy'. The Labour Housing Group (LHG) vociferously opposed this as inegalitarian, divisive and socially damaging: right to buy should only exist if there was parity of treatment, if it was applied to private landlords, with no discounts and there was a 'right to rent' as well. The 1984 Conference agreed that controlled sales would be allowed, and in May 1985 a consultative document from the leadership was advocating the right to buy but with the reservations that inner city tenants might have to be given grants to buy elsewhere, that tenants could buy from absentee private landlords and that owner-occupiers could sell to councils and remain as tenants. Labour could point out that the ease of 'right to buy' schemes had led to council mortgage arrears of £14 million by April 1986, and repossessions up from 2,500 in 1979 to 12,000 in 1986.

The Liberals believe in sales, but with the power with local authorities and no sales of empty houses. The SDP were willing to let authorities claim a temporary waiver in areas of social need; they would reduce discounts and let councils buy back at market price.

(5) *Subsidies*
The *Conservatives*, as we have seen, have altered the pattern of subsidy distribution – cutting local authority expenditure in general, but providing funds for homesteading, discounts, for housing associations and for improvement grants. Life for homeowners was made easier by the changes to stamp duty and an end of conveyancing monopoly

but they had to circumnavigate the MIRAS changes on mortgage payments, 15% VAT was imposed on building alterations and in 1984 came the abolition of life insurance premium relief for endowment mortgages. Nevertheless owner-occupiers receive £3·5 billion in tax relief on mortgages (a 29% repayment subsidy) plus £2·5 billion in capital gains tax relief. The inquiry set up by the National Federation of Housing Associations and chaired by Prince Philip condemned this system in July 1985 as expensive, unjust in favouring those with larger mortgages and doing nothing for the elderly or first-time buyers. The report went on to advocate phased reduction (like Labour) with a new rent-fixing formula and means-tested housing allowances. Mrs Thatcher quickly moved in to assert that tax relief would stay as long as she did.

Labour believes that if the wealthy are to benefit from mortgage tax relief (MTR), it should be at the standard not the higher rate. In general Labour believe in subsidies as a means of freezing rents and dislike means testing. The LHG go further in demanding a housing wealth tax, parity of rent at the 1979 level, universal housing allowances based on cost and size, and mobility through 'housing on demand'.

A feature of *Liberal* policy in its local 'grass-roots' campaigning is to channel money into renovation and repair. They would buy land to direct it to co-operatives, the old, disabled and others with special needs, and they would build for sale to first-time buyers. Like Labour, they advocate equality of opportunity for women and racial minorities.

The *SDP* would:

(i) subsidise the cost of land in inner cities;

(ii) contribute to part of the capital cost of housing projects;

(iii) provide index-linked mortgages from a National Housing Bank.

Their 1984 Housing Green Paper reaffirms that they believe in subsidies based on need (using means testing) rather than type of housing and in greater equity between owner-occupation and rented housing. They would encourage investment, strengthen the Home Purchase Assistance scheme and shared ownership.

One policy proposal which surveys showed to be controversial among their own middle-class membership was the long-term intention to reform mortgage tax relief so it related to income rather than size of mortgage. The Alliance would introduce a standard rate restriction in the short-term and probably move towards a single annuity or income related assistance.

(6) *Green belt and planning policies*

In July 1983 the government issued two draft circulars. The first gave the minister power to override local authority plans and allow developers to build on green field sites. The second announced the relaxation of green belt cordons. It was quickly revealed that developers had five mini towns in mind, the first in Hook, Hampshire, where furious opposition grew. The announcements were made after the election and during a parliamentary recess. Nonetheless there quickly grew a mixed alliance of opponents — the Country Landowners' Association, National Farmers' Union and Conservative MPs oppose such development on grounds of self-interest and food imports; the council for the Protection of Rural England and Civic Trust bring environmental arguments to bear; and Labour councils and their associations see a loss of population from and forgone regeneration in the inner cities.

As a result the Secretary of State, Patrick Jenkin, backed down in December 1983, reaffirming green belt status and in February applied relaxations only to interim green belt land. Nevertheless the pressure was sustained and during 1985 there were moves to cut into the 4·5 million acres of English green belt and the 277,000 in Scotland. The major problems were always likely to be in London's 1−2 million acres where Hertfordshire county council intended to build 4,000 homes, and Consortium Development Limited (representing the major companies building 30% of UK homes) proposed a series of small, carefully landscaped minitowns of 15,000 people each. Developers claimed the lack of land had pushed up house prices (land forming 40% of the cost). In 1985 35 Conservative MPs framed a 'firm letter' to the Prime Minister and received in reply an 'extremely rotten letter' on economic growth and owner occupation. The government gradually developed its policy of not upholding a 'green belt museum' in which piecemeal development went on anyway, of deciding planning applications 'on merit', trying to resolve housing shortage problems, and easing the pressure on green belt land by forcing the release of unused land. Under the 1980 Local Government Planning and Land Act authorities are required to register such land and can be forced to auction it off — 110,000 acres were identified and 30,000 released by early 1986. They also claimed to be reclaiming 3,500 acres a year — the size of Bath.

(7) *The homeless*

It seems appropriate to conclude by looking at the other end of the social scale. Here in the housing sector we find teenagers, battered wives, ethnic minorities, groups unfamiliar with the social services, alcoholics and travelling people wanting only temporary resting places. While the numbers are uncertain, it is clear that the economic recession has worsened the problem. The DOE's 1981 report 'Single and Homeless' revealed that most homeless single people become so after marital or family conflict and that one quarter are women. Professor Greve, commissioned by the GLC, found that the official homeless total had risen by 700% in the capital since 1970 so that one in 10 people lacked a proper home. It was going up more rapidly in the suburbs and among black families. Claimants were being priced out of 90% of the cheapest bed and breakfast hotels and the £4 billion housing benefit bill increased as councils transferred families from the rates to Social Security. Meanwhile profiteering landlords were said to be charging double or triple rents at the taxpayers' expense in Liverpool. By 1986 203,000 households were presenting themselves to councils as homeless and the DOE estimated a further 330,000 'concealed' single homeless.

Here the subsystem of pressure groups is very different from that above, comprising Shelter, SHAC, Campaign for the Homeless and Rootless, the Gypsy Council and the Campaign for Civil Liberties. The process whereby they pursue their cause is difficult, as noted in the case of the 1977 Housing (Homeless Persons) Act. It usually consists of a study of the particular problem, mobilisation of change agents inside parliament and government and, crucially, exposure of the problem by the media.

As the 1977 Act showed, however, legislation does not secure implementation. Both the Labour and Alliance parties would seek to extend its provisions. *Labour* would

(1) increase the number of 'priority groups' for whom councils have to secure accommodation, so as to cover all homeless households during a parliament.

(2) They would close loopholes by closely defining 'intentional homelessness' and 'vulnerability' and not rely on authorities' interpretations of codes of guidance.

(3) The rights of homeless people in temporary accommodation would be strengthened and standards improved. During the 1980s considerable media exposure was given to deplorable conditions in hostels and bed and breakfast hotels.

(4) Criminal liability for giving false information would be removed.

(5) One place per 10,000 population for refuges for women.

The Alliance similarly deplore councils' evasions of their responsibilities. The *SDP* would

(1) extend the 1977 Act to cover single people under forty;
(2) give priority to young people aged 16–18;
(3) keep hostel places to thirty;
(4) provide extra lettings for the mentally handicapped.

Conclusions

Housing is not a policy area which attracts attention with the constancy of economic, education or defence matters. But nor is it sufficiently neutral that anyone could proclaim 'Keep politics [i.e. the politics of change] out of housing'. As we have seen, this is one of the most polarised, interest-based policy sectors in British politics.

Reading

D. Donnison and C. Ungerson, *Housing Policy*, Penguin, 1982.

Labour Housing Group, *Right to a Home*, Spokesman, 1984.

Labour Housing Group, Manifesto for Housing (43 Anson Road, London N7).

'A strategy for housing', SDP Green paper no. 12.

Politics today, 13 February 1984, Conservative Research Dept.

B. Pitt, 'Liberal Action on Housing'.

R. S. Forrest, 'The politics of housing', *Teaching Politics*, September 1986, pp. 426–45.

Issues in education

Education has developed into an extremely controversial political issue during the last twenty years. The optimism that stemmed from the passing of the 1944 Education Act which influenced thinking during the 1950s and 1960s has been replaced today by a sombre mood resulting from both pessimism and uncertainty. The political consensus on the aims and methods of education has crumbled under attacks from left, right and centre. Right-wing critics argued in the *Black Papers* that 'disastrous mistakes are being made in modern education' and the socialist and feminist left made its most articulate attack in *Unpopular Education*. But the most damning blow came in 1976 when the Prime Minister of the day, James Callaghan, delivered a much publicised speech in which he suggested that educational standards were falling and that schools were failing to serve Britain well.

The education system, which had enjoyed many years of public confidence, was now the subject of doubts and reservations in many minds. 'Scandals', such as the William Tyndale affair, did nothing to allay public fears that education was indeed in deep trouble. By the late 1970s it had become clear that in education too 'the party was over'. The years of post-war expansion had come to an end, to be replaced by stringency and educational cutbacks.

This chapter examines reasons why education has moved to the centre stage of party politics in Britain. This will involve considering the purposes which lay behind the growth of mass education and the role that education plays in shaping society. We shall see that different philosophies or ideologies about education come into conflict from time to time, and that these ideologies are particularly powerful when they are disguised as being 'scientific' in nature. The conclusion attempts to understand the significance of some recent educational issues by setting them in the context of the ideological struggle.

The growth of mass education

In his analysis of educational developments in the nineteenth century, David Glass revealed that two fairly distinct sets of considerations influenced schooling; one related to the middle class and the other to the mass of the population. The main concern regarding secondary education was that it should be effective in procuring wealth and maintaining or enhancing social status. The professions were raising their standards of entry and university education was acquiring new meanings for the old and new middle classes alike. Elementary education for the working class on the other hand was designed to elicit four major responses:

(1) to 'gentle' the masses;
(2) to instil discipline;
(3) to obtain respect for private property and the social order;
(4) to provide the kind of instruction which was necessary for an expanding industrial and commercial nation. Some argue that the objectives of the educational system remain basically unchanged towards the end of the twentieth century.

Before 1870, the provision of schools was left to private individuals and churches. The Elementary Education Act of 1870 empowered local authorities to 'fill the gap' and provide schools where voluntary church schools did not exist. The Act established school boards which were elected by rate-payers, and which could build and maintain elementary schools with money from rates, government grant and school fees. The expansion of schools was rapid and by 1876 it was realistic to make attendance compulsory for children who lived within two miles of a school. At this time it was felt that elementary schooling was sufficient for the majority of children, and the responsibility of school boards ended when a child was ten years old. Secondary education was the responsibility of parents and independent schools.

The Education Act of 1902 led to a major reorganisation with 2,559 school boards being replaced by 330 local education authorities. The new LEAs had power to provide not only elementary education but also secondary and technical education. The years that followed saw a great expansion in secondary education with a variety of schools being built. Some were purpose built and referred to as 'high schools', others were senior elementary schools which usually took the form of annexes built on to existing elementary schools. The special place examination (known later as the 'scholarship', then 'eleven plus') and free places at grammar schools became general after the 1907 Education (Administrative Provisions) Act. In large towns, junior technical, junior commercial and junior art schools took pupils from thirteen to sixteen.

The next major development was the 1918 Education Act, sometimes referred to as the 'Fisher Act', which raised the school leaving age to fourteen. It was intended that children over fourteen should attend part-time 'day continuation schools' but this reform was not compulsory and consequently not widely implemented.

Education for all

In 1926 the Hadow Report recommended that there should be a formal break in children's education at eleven. Elementary education should then be divided into primary and secondary stages. In 1938 the Spens Report considered the curriculum of grammar and technical high schools. The Norwood Report was published in 1943 and developed further the then current idea that children could be divided into three different types:

(1) those who loved learning for its own sake.

(2) those who delighted in applied science and applied art.

(3) those who dealt more easily in concrete things than ideas.

The report suggested, therefore, that there should be three kinds of secondary school:

(1) secondary grammar schools of the type that existed already for child type 1;

(2) secondary technical schools, to be developed from existing technical schools, for child type 2;

(3) secondary modern schools, to be developed from senior elementary schools, for child type 3.

The committees which produced these reports were impressed by recently developed intelligence testing, which could be used to identify the 'brightest' and 'dullest' pupils so that they could be educated separately from 'average' pupils. The majority of LEAs followed Norwood thinking and set up a *tripartite* system of grammar, technical and modern schools. In practice, however, a *bipartite* system emerged in most areas after 1944 since few technical schools were built.

The 1944 Education Act − referred to as the 'Butler Act' since R. A. Butler was president of the Board of Education − reorganised education into a national system based on three successive stages: primary, secondary and further. Elementary education was replaced by 'secondary education for all'. The Act reduced the number of LEAs to 146, made religious education compulsory, raised the school leaving age to fifteen, and established the first Minister for Education.

New directions

During the 1950s and 1960s there was a growing awareness that the new system of education was flawed. Criticisms were numerous:

(i) Secondary modern and grammar schools were never seen by parents, teachers or pupils as being equal. Grammar schools had acquired high prestige because of the strong links with higher education and the professions.

(ii) There were not enough grammer school places for all who wanted them. Only 20% of eleven year olds would go to a grammar school, leaving many parents disappointed.

(iii) An education system which 'fails' 80% of its pupils each year was seen as undesirable.

(iv) There was much geographical unfairness in the system since the number of grammar school places available varied from one authority to another. For example, in 1962 $11 \cdot 9\%$ of Bootle's eleven year olds went to a grammar school whereas the figure was $40 \cdot 3\%$ in Merthyr.

(v) The examination which pupils had to pass in order to go to a grammar school − the eleven plus − became a crucial, often emotionally charged event for pupils and parents. The exam had a bad effect on many primary schools which were geared to preparing children for the eleven plus rather than developing all aspects of ability and personality.

(vi) Free access to grammar schools had not benefited working-class pupils. Those working-class pupils who were selected for grammar schools tended to do less well, once there, than their middle-class peers.

(vii) Educational theorists began having doubts about the possibility of measuring intelligence in the way the eleven plus attempted. Some feared that intelligence tests could not identify the three types of Norwood child because they did not in fact exist. It was believed that the whole education system was based on a psychological fallacy.

The 'ideological comprehensivists', once seen as having radical ideas about common schools, began to win support as more and more people felt that graded schools were intolerable in a democratic society. It is hard to believe that in 1960 there were only 130 comprehensive schools given their preponderance today. Depending upon its political masters the DES has blown both hot and cool on this expansion. Circular 10/65 invited LEAs to submit plans for reorganising secondary schools into a comprehensive system. Circular 10/70 revoked this invitation but Circular 4/74 again applied pressure. Vacillation such as this created a climate of uncertainty in which local authorities could defy ministerial advice. The opposition of Tameside LEA to the policies of a pro-comprehensive Labour minister is the best documented of several cases.

Changes were not confined to the secondary stage of education. Innovations also took place in the establishment of middle schools which straddled the 1944 division between primary and secondary schools.

Education's internal struggle

As we have seen, the work of educational psychologists during the 1930s influenced the structure of postwar education. Intelligence testing was associated with pioneering psychologists such as Cyril Burt. Intelligence was seen as the ability to perform abstract thinking, and intelligence tests measured this ability. Psychologists felt that intelligence was an innate ability which led them to believe that *intelligence was inherited*. This was an assumption which had enormous social and political implications.

If dull parents produced dull children, bright parents produced bright children, and the social system rewarded people according to ability and merit then the existence of different social classes was based on genetic factors. Educationalists expected children from working-class homes to perform less well at school. Because they believed intelligence was inherited, educationalists thought it natural that schools should reflect and reproduce the stratifications which already existed in society.

Computer analysis has revealed that the data used in many of Cyril Burt's studies were fictious, and it is now generally agreed that any differences between social classes is not genetically determined. Some critics argued that IQ tests are not 'culture free' and this accounted for much of the difference between classes. In other words it should be of little wonder that working-class pupils did less well in tests the design of which favoured middle-class pupils. Indeed, it has been argued that IQ tests really measure social class membership and not intelligence.

Sociologists challenged psychologists' view of education and introduced new insights into how the education system might work. They rejected genetic arguments and stressed the *importance of the environment* on how well pupils would do at school. Educability depended on factors such as: (i) parental attitudes which could influence pupil's motivation; (ii) provision for general learning in the home – the availability of space, privacy, books etc.; (iii) language development. Since humans think in words, it was argued that the quality of thought depended heavily on the quality of language.

Social class categories seem a crude yet useful way to summarise many aspects of the home environment which influenced educability and attainment. Also studies revealed that an unconscious class bias often held by teachers influenced the way pupils were streamed at school. Well-clothed, clean pupils were often placed in higher streams than their ability would justify. Pupils of poorer appearance tended to be put in lower streams than their ability justified. And once there, these pupils deteriorated. Indeed, streaming in schools acted in the same way as a self-fulfilling prophecy. Pupils placed in the 'A' stream were expected to succeed and generally lived up to this expectation. In contrast 'D' stream pupils were expected to do poorly, and inevitably this proved to be the case. Sociologists argued that in many schools, streaming by presumed ability was reinforcing the process of social selection. Just as streaming *between* different types of school became discredited, so too did streaming *within* schools.

It was argued that the school was itself a micro-political system and the distribution of scarce resources within it reflected the inequalities found in society at large. In this context the school timetable could be viewed not as a neutral or technical document but as a bill of rights. Ken Shaw has argued:

If a smallish group of pupils gets regular contact with highly paid, experienced, high status teachers not overburdened with disciplinary problems or marking, in expensive specialised facilities, they are advantaged and they know it ... Other younger less successful children are taught in groups of more than 30, by newly qualified staff in overcrowded general purpose rooms. Most option systems present a real choice to able pupils; the less able are steered into what is left, so that choice for them is very restricted ... Who are the beneficiaries, who are the losers when the timetable is analysed from this point of view? And how does this match up with winning and losing in the world outside? There is plenty of evidence to show that the answer is: pretty closely.

Harold Lasswell once defined politics as 'who gets what, when and how'. Some sociologists were defining education in identical terms.

They felt that schools were bound to reflect the divisions that existed in wider society. In other words, education could not lead to change in society but could only reproduce and legitimate the sort of society that already existed. Within a free market economy schools were bound therefore to serve the interests of capitalism, namely the creation of profit and stability. The efforts of well-intentioned liberals to make schools the agents of social change were seen as having failed in the past and being bound to fail in the future. It was argued that schools will only change *after* the economic system that they serve has changed. Neither the introduction of comprehensive education nor innovations to humanise the conditions of schooling such as mixed ability teaching can alter the basic purpose of education, and that remains much the same as David Glass's analysis of education in the last century.

Education policy has therefore been shaped by 'scientific' arguments which have contained highly political ingredients. The arguments of traditional psychologists were attractive to right-wing individuals who saw the existence of social classes as natural and desirable. Sociological research lent support to liberal and left-wing individuals who wanted social change. Various studies identified much unfairness in the way some pupils were treated and encouraged measures leading to greater equality of opportunity which it was hoped would eventually lead to a less class-based society.

The deschoolers

The notion of deschooling has been with us since 1971 and is associated with Everett Reimer, Ivan Illich and John Holt. Their basic argument was that schools had failed and should therefore be abolished. In particular, schools had:

(i) failed to teach the basic skills, and had consumed more and more resources in order to achieve less and less in terms of knowledge and skills taught.

(ii) imposed a 'hidden curriculum' that indoctrinated pupils into accepting the status quo and the materialistic values of a technological society. Pupils were taught to conform in order to survive, to know their place, and to accept the judgements of others about what is worth doing and knowing. Schools, it was argued, actually damaged pupils.

(iii) employed many 'qualified' teachers who were poor teachers whilst failing to employ many gifted teachers who were not qualified.

According to the deschoolers, learning is in fact inhibited by schools. One solution proposed was that all members of society should receive 'edu-credit' cards. These would be spent following whatever courses people wished with whatever teachers (qualified or not) they chose whenever they liked. Ideas associated with deschooling have proved attractive to some on the political extremes. On the left, some were attracted by a form of education which promised to act as an ineffective instrument of social control. On the right there were those who favoured the idea of ending compulsory education. Also something akin to edu-credit cards, 'education vouchers', have been considered by Kent LEA in order to introduce market forces into education. Parents would be able to spend their vouchers on schools of their choice, private or maintained. Popular schools would prosper, with unpopular schools having to improve their reputations or face the prospect of withering away. The Conservative controlled Kent Authority failed to implement the scheme on the grounds of cost.

External political influences

The education system has also been shaped by the ideological struggle which takes place in wider society and which influences other institutions. The main ideologies are:

(i) *The aristocratic ideology* which produced schools giving a classical education to the children of the social elite. The emphasis was on character building and was deliberately non-vocational in character. This ideology is still associated with the traditions of a public school education.

(ii) *The bourgeois ideology* championed by the merchant and professional classes influenced the establishment of schools which provided specialist education for high status positions. One of the central concerns of grammar and independent schools has been the preparation of pupils for entry onto higher vocational and professional courses.

(iii) *The democratic ideology* of the early reformers was concerned with 'education for all'. It influenced the 1944 Education Act and the creation of the Open University in 1969. Within schools this ideology has resulted in mixed ability teaching and informal teaching methods.

(v) *The proletarian ideology* was held by those who felt that the children of the working class should be provided with a utilitarian education which was practical in nature. The proletarian education aimed at limiting the aspirations and political demands of the working class. The secondary modern school with its low prestige and non-academic curriculum is a manifestation of this ideology.

(v) *The manpower planning ideology* recognises pupils as 'human capital' who will eventually fill roles in the economy. Education is seen as the key to Britain's economic advance, and schools and colleges should supply the type of people needed by the labour market. The establishment of technical schools and colleges represented the presence of the 'economically useful' within education. In the past most universities have been suspicious of applied courses, and the CNAA was set up to validate vocational courses to prepare students for the world of work run by the new polytechnics created in the late 1960s.

There is a complex web of relationships between these ideologies with different ones dominating the minds of decision-makers at different times. The aristocratic and democratic ideologies are diametrically opposed to one another, with the former associated with an exclusive education and the latter with universal education. The aristocratic and proletarian ideologies are congruent with a society divided into 'well rounded gentlemen' and 'drawers of water and hewers of wood'. The eleven plus and the Assisted Places Scheme represent links between the bourgeois and proletarian ideologies with the most able pupils from working-class homes receiving an academic education on the basis of merit.

Educational developments in the early years of this century were influenced by a combination of the aristocratic and bourgeois ideologies. The democratic ideology was at its height during the 1960s with the expansion of comprehensive schooling. But it was not all out victory for the ideological comprehensivists since the private sector still exists and even within the maintained sector comprehensive provision is not universal. The 1970s and 1980s have seen the manpower planning ideology in the ascendancy, with education increasingly concerned with the provision of the technical skills required by industry.

Areas of controversy

(i) *The private sector*
The existence of a private sector in education has long been at the centre of party conflict. Most Conservatives agree wtih Sir Ian Gilmour's view that the egalitarianism which would result in everybody having to use the same school service would also mean that citizens would be increasingly regulated by state monopolies and be at their mercy. For Conservatives, freedom is associated with the absence of coercion (particularly by the state) and is best promoted by the expansion of the market.

In other words, competition maximises the freedom of the individual to satisfy his or her needs. It is argued that parental choice between the state and private sector, and within the private sector, ensures individual freedom within education.

This view is challenged by the Labour Party which is committed to the eventual abolition of the private sector. Labour also opposes the Assisted Places Scheme which strengthens private schools with public money at a time when many state schools cannot afford to buy sufficient text books. Labour also rejects the 'freedom of choice' argument and Roy Hattersley has argued that for ordinary parents there is no choice between Eton or the local secondary modern for their children's education. The private sector is seen as bolstering privilege and thus contributing to a divided society, and having little to do with protecting freedom and democracy.

(ii) *Teaching methods*

Arguments about which teaching methods are the most efficient inevitably develop into political disputes. This is because different methods are concerned not only with teaching particular subjects — geography, English, maths, — but also with moulding different types of pupils. Basically, traditional teaching methods tend to be authoritarian, associated with hierarchical social relations within the school with pupils playing a largely passive role and relying on the teacher as the expert. The 'closed' classroom encourages pupils to conform and not to expect to participate in decision-making within the classroom. In contrast, the 'open' classroom is characterised by a friendlier and more libertarian atmosphere in which there is not such a sharp distinction between teacher and pupil. Teaching will involve 'discovery' methods in which the teacher manages the learning process rather than expository methods in which the teacher directs the process. Teaching, then, can be an elitist or participatory affair and it should not be surprising that it is the subject of political conflict.

The progressive/traditional debate erupted in the mid-1970s over the very progressive methods used in the William Tyndale junior school. Inquiries and surveys into the efficiency of different forms of education are difficult to conduct because of all the other variables that have an influence in addition to that being measured. Publication of research findings are customarily accompanied by accusations of cheating, bias, muddled thinking, or distortion being directed at the authors. For example in *Teaching Styles and Pupil Progress* Neville Bennett suggested that progressive methods were less effective generally in teaching traditional skills. Other social scientists were highly critical of his research methods and one likened his conclusions to a zoologist on finding that all elephants are bigger than mice, except for one mouse which was bigger than all the elephants. In 1980 a survey published by the National Children's Bureau, *Progressive Secondary Schools*, claimed that pupils in comprehensive schools 'did as well and as badly as if selection had still operated and some had gone to grammars and the rest to secondary moderns'. Such a claim was predictably challenged in a Centre for Policy Studies report, *Real Concern*, which attacked the research for using dubious data and drawing the wrong conclusions.

(iii) *Control of the curriculum*

The 1944 Education Act said little about the content of the curriculum apart from the inclusion of religious education. The Act did, however, establish an informal partnership between central government, local authorities, teachers and the churches which would act as the decision-making structure. The working of this partnership has often been described as the 'mystique of English education'. Within it the DES played a rather limited role. Indeed, within Whitehall the DES was viewed as a very weak department with little direct control over the service it ran. For example, the curriculum was decided at school level. Teachers, together with the head and influenced by parents, examination boards etc., decided curriculum issues and could only be sanctioned if they performed below approved standards. However the publication of the Crowther and Newsom reports focused attention on the curriculum and the DES hinted that central (or state) control of the curriculum was worth considering. In his Ruskin speech James Callaghan hinted at teacher inefficiency in this area and gave further support to the idea of more centralised control of the curriculum.

The DES has flexed its muscles over the last decade and moved from its former position of weakness. Ted Tapper and Brian Salter observed that 'throughout the 1970s, the DES was engaged on a process of policy enclosure which effectively re-drew the old tripartite partnership of DES, LEAs and teachers' trades unions'. The department's increased power has been evident in the current debate on a core curriculum and subject criteria, making the emergence of national centralised curricula appear close at hand.

Opponents of state control point out that all authoritarian regimes control what is taught in schools. The national curriculum is, they argue, an Orwellian concept with possibilities of manipulation, indoc-trination and brain washing. Supporters dismiss this as a spurious argument since state control of the curriculum exists in most west European countries.

(iv) *Morale within the teaching profession*

A prolonged period of industrial action by teachers during 1985/6 which fell well short of an all-out strike nevertheless caused great disruption in schools. Teachers were bitter because their level of pay had fallen well behind those of comparable professionals as a result of the govern-ment's squeeze on the public sector. The Secretary of State for Education and Science, Sir Keith Joseph, was the target of much criticism from inside and outside the Conservative party for his handling of the dispute, and there was great public interest in his replacement when he announced that he would not be standing at the next general election. Sir Keith was replaced by the relatively 'wet' Kenneth Baker who distanced himself from his 'dry' predecessor by stating within hours of his appointment that he 'would want to ensure that the resources are available to ensure the success' of education.

One of Kenneth Baker's first tasks was to receive a report from HMI of Schools which was to add to the concern of the public and the embarrassment of the government over the state of education. The HMIs found that poor teaching adversely affected the standard of work in 30% of the lessons they saw but, almost as significant, poor teaching accommodation and lack of resources such as books badly affected 20% of the lessons they saw.

The public's perception of a demoralised profession working within dilapidated classrooms with insufficient books to go around put the government in a very defensive mood about education. In the past many Conservatives believed that 'there were no votes in education' but few felt that this applied any longer. Kenneth Baker has begun the uphill task of presenting education policy in a more positive manner, with many Conservatives hoping that he will be able to restore public confidence in the government's record before the next election.

(v) *The crisis in higher education*

During the 1960s higher education expanded in a period of optimism about the performance of the British economy. The 'Robbins' era saw high public spending on higher education become politically respectable with acceptance by all parties that there should be a rapid and comprehensive expansion of degree courses both inside and outside the universities. The experience of the 1980s has been very different, with resources devoted to higher education being cut back. University finance, for example, was cut by 15% in 1981 with a planned further reduction of 2% for each of the following five years. It has been calculated that by 1986 over 30,000 candidates who may have anticipated studying at university under normal circumstances will not have found a place. Some will have been absorbed into the polytechnics and colleges, but others will have failed to enter higher education at all.

Institutions of higher education have each been considering ways in which to cope with the financial cutbacks with those experiencing major economies, which have been as high as a 44% cut in funding, forced into making radical appraisals of their future roles. There is no one single organisation or system to plan and shape higher education, and as a consequence developments tend to be unco-ordinated and at times even haphazard. The discussion on the future of higher education illuminates this point. Based on their individual experience, some institutions argued that it was possible to survive cuts in public funding through developing links with the private sector and work towards becoming self-financing. Other institutions argued that this was not an option that was open to them given the nature of their courses. Another discussion focused on the distribution of the cuts: should all institutions accept their share of financial cutbacks or, rather than 'spreading the misery' amongst all institutions, would it be better if one or two universities were to close altogether? Others have argued that the root of the problem lies with the universities which spread their resources too thinly by doing both teaching and research: the financial problem could be solved if some universities specialised in research whilst the remainder became teaching specialists. Savings could also be made if ordinary degrees were awarded after two years of study, with only a proportion of students continuing on to a third honours year. And, of course, it has been argued that great savings could be made if students were financed by loans rather than by grants.

(vi) *The purpose of education*
In the past, schools have been criticised for lacking a sense of purpose regarding what they were trying to achieve with their pupils. Although schools operated efficiently on a routine day-to-day basis, there were no explicit goals concerning the development of pupils.

During the 1960s there was considerable clarification of the issue resulting from the national education debate on 'relevance'. Educationalists began asking in earnest what it was appropriate to teach pupils so that they should cope successfully as future citizens. The emphasis in education swung towards recognising and meeting each pupil's individual needs. There was an awareness that teaching was not only concerned with the subject matter of the various disciplines but also with the personality development of pupils. The curriculum had already expanded to include what were once viewed as purely leisure activities − such as drama, literature and art − since these helped to cultivate the senses.

A decade later the emphasis moved in another direction. As mentioned above, education was required to serve society's needs rather than the individual's needs. Schools were required to produce pupils suitable for the skilled manpower needed by industry. Consequently the 1980s have seen a rapid expansion of vocational and pre-vocational education, much of it controlled not by the DES nor by the LEAs but by the Manpower Services Commission which is controlled by the Department of Employment. Thus the issue of 'sex education' in the curriculum was relatively uncontroversial during the 1960s since the climate of opinion was in favour of developing the 'whole pupil' during his or her school years. In the more vocational climate of the 1980s however, opposition to teaching about the delicate issue of sexual relationships became more vocal. Some politicians, mostly on the right, wanted to see sex education banned in schools.

The proliferation of new vocational courses and qualifications is a strange response to Britain's long-term unemployment problem. The economy will continue to require educated and skilled manpower, but in much fewer numbers than ever before. Technological advance alone means that many companies are increasing output, raising profits and laying off workers at the same time. What the purpose of education should be in a de-industrialising economy is a problem still in search of a political solution.

Reading

D. V. Glass, 'Education and social change in England' in A. H. Halsey, J. Floud and C. A. Anderson (eds.), *Education, Economy and Society*, Free Press, New York, 1961, pp. 391−413.
Maurice Kogan, *The Politics of Educational Change*, Fontana, 1978.

Lynton Robins, 'Political socialisation in British Schools: some
    political and sociological approaches' in Lynton Robins (ed.),
    Topics in British Politics, London, 1982, pp. 221–43.

Brian Salter and Ted Tapper, *Education, Politics and the State*,
    London, 1981.

K.E. Shaw, 'The timetable: a Bill of Rights?', *Teaching Politics*,
    9, 1980, pp. 111–20.

Ted Tapper, 'Legitimating independent schooling: policy assumptions
    and educational realities' in Lynton Robins (ed.), *Updating British
    Politics*, London, 1984, pp. 234–43.

The politics of racism

A broad definition of *racism* would run: racism is a set of ideas and practices which asserts that:

(*a*) human beings can be divided into a series of distinct groups or races on the basis of identifiable physical features most obviously skin colour;

(*b*) these unalterable physical types are inherited;

(*c*) those who belong to the group or race also share a relationship between their inherited external appearance and other allegedly inherited characteristics such as intelligence; and that personality and culture are also the products of race;

(*d*) some groups or races are naturally inferior to other groups or races;

(*e*) argues that they require different and in practice less favourable treatment and as far as possible encourages action on this basis.

Whilst traditionally racists have argued in terms of biological inheritance, it has been pointed out that theories which use social, historical or cultural factors to distinguish between one group and another and to justify discrimination, operate in the same way as if they utilised biologically based arguments. Today we hear less about biology, more about 'culture' and 'nation'. Moreover, most racists do not have clear cut theories but a confused 'common sense' jumble of ideas which sees one group as more stupid, dirty, lazy, greedy than another, possessing strange, alien customs against which the habits of one's own superior group must be defended.

Some writers today distinguish between *racism* – the institutionalised practices in the social system which generate disadvantage for certain groups – and *racialism* – the specific acts of *discrimination* visited by one group upon another on the basis of the belief that the latter are racially distinct and consequently inferior. The attitude which can produce discrimination against particular groups is termed *prejudice*. Prejudice is seen as being based upon *stereotypes*, a broad mental view based on partial or distorted information: all Irish people are drunks, all Jews are mean.

The myth of race

Today racist ideas are generally accepted as possessing no scientific validity.

(1) It can be shown that the idea of race is a relatively recent one. The word first appears in English in 1508; it was only in the 1770s that it took on its present meaning. Moreover, it is only during the last three centuries that racism has developed its present political importance. In the more distant past differences between or within societies were not articulated in such terms. The culture and achievements of particular groups are not natural or pre-ordained but socially produced. Civilisation has not been the prerogative of the 'white race' but has arisen at different times in many different parts of the world.

(2) Physical differences do exist between human beings but they shade into each other on a spectrum. To decide which are important and which constitute dividing lines between different groups requires a selective value judgement. The way we are taught to look at the world, our political moulding and our material interests influence that judgement and may lead us to stress or exaggerate one difference above another. To divide or classify people in a racist way is to make a social, not a biological, judgement.

(3) There are still scientists today – Jensen and Eysenck and their followers – who defend the idea of inherited differences. The vast weight of scientific evidence however indicates that genetic differences between individuals within the same 'race' may be greater than the differences between one race and another. Scientists believe that over 90% of all the difference can be found within a given 'race' rather than between races so, biologically, a white Londoner is likely to be just as similar to or different from, his or her white neighbour as he or she is to a neighbour from Jamaica or Kuala Lumpur. Racism is scientifically discredited, but still grips people's minds and influences their behaviour. In the past Jews and Irish people were victims of racism in Britain. Today it is primarily black people.

(4) *There are not many races but one human race.* As the world's most prominent scientists gathered under the aegis of the United Nations Educational Scientific and Cultural Organisation, concluded

... all men everywhere belong to a single species. As is the case with other species all men share their essential hereditary characteristics in common having received them from common ancestors .... race is not so much a biological phenomenon as a social myth. The myth of race has created an enormous amount of human and social damage.

The black British

Blacks have lived in this country since the time of the Romans and were the object of immigration control as early as Elizabethan times. Our present black population, however, is largely the product of post-war immigration from the New Commonwealth – the West Indies, Bangladesh, India, Pakistan, Sri Lanka, parts of Africa, notably Kenya, Nigeria, Uganda and parts of Asia, such as Malaysia, Singapore and Hong Kong.

The heyday of immigration was the '50s and early '60s. In 1951 only 0.2 million people in the UK were from the New Commonwealth. Twenty years later the figure had increased to 1.2 million. Today Britain's black population is over 3 million and, though often still referred to as immigrants, half were in fact, born here. By the year 2000 it is estimated that there will be nearly 3.5 million black Britons, making up nearly 6% of our total population.

The largest single group is of West Indian origin; the other significant groups coming from the Indian sub-continent. The black population is concentrated in certain areas of the UK, following the immigration pattern. Blacks responded to the need for labour generally in the south-east; to the requirements of the metal manufacturing industries in the West Midlands; and the textile industries in Lancashire and Yorkshire. Outside the south-east, they are concentrated in Wolverhampton, Birmingham and Coventry, West Yorkshire, particularly Bradford and Greater Manchester. Different communities still live in distinct areas with, for example, a majority of Pakistanis compared with other groups in Bradford, and a majority of West Indians in Leeds.

Why they came

(1) *Shortage of labour* was a major economic problem for post-war Britain. A Royal Commission in 1949 estimated that 140,000

immigrants annually would be required. The black British came to answer shortages in transport, the hospitals, textiles, clothing and foundries. In the absence of an internal reserve army, Britain's 1950s boom was fuelled by immigration.

(2) *Citizens of the Commonwealth had the right to enter the UK and settle here.* This was confirmed by the British Nationality Act, 1948. Many, particularly the West Indians, looked to Britain as the 'mother country'. They had fought in the British armed services during the war, they spoke English and identified to some extent with British culture.

(3) *The black British came from areas of traditional emigration which were blighted by long-term underdevelopment.* Long before the first 400 came on the SS *Empire Windrush* in 1948, West Indians had migrated to the USA as cheap labour to build the Panama Canal, just as Indians had found it necessary to emigrate to South and East Africa to work on the railways. Unemployment and population growth constituted 'push' factors. From 1952, entry to the USA was controlled by the McCarren-Walter Act, whilst in the Punjab, for example, increasing agricultural competition was a factor.

(4) *The system seemed to suit everybody.* The British were getting labour for on the whole, low paid, socially undesirable jobs. The newcomers were leaving even worse jobs for better conditions and the possibility of saving for a return home. The mechanism of immigration was happily self-adjusting from the viewpoint of the UK: a fall in the number of advertised jobs led to a fall in the number of immigrants. However, few of the immigrants became self-sufficient enough to return home. Once here they encountered disadvantage and discrimination.

Blacks and disadvantage

(1) *Blacks are disadvantaged in housing*   In the 1970s more than 70% were concentrated in districts which contained nearly three times the national average of households, which had to share or altogether lacked basic amenities and were overcrowded. While, for example, only a quarter of white households lived at a density of over 1.5 persons per bedroom, and only 2% had 2.5 persons per bedroom, 54% of West Indian households and 65% of Asian households had more than 2.5 persons per bedroom.

(2) *Blacks are disadvantaged in employment*   A Department of Employment Survey in 1976 stated that blacks were

... concentrated in conurbations where the pressure of demand for labour has been relatively high and in some skilled and unskilled jobs to which it is difficult to attract other workers because of such features as low earnings, a need to work unsocial hours, and/or unpleasant working conditions.

Blacks are less likely to be in white collar jobs, and more likely to be in unskilled manual work and whilst 15% of white men worked shifts, this was true of 31% of black males. 79% of whites with degrees were in professional jobs but for blacks with the same qualifications the figure was only 31%. Earnings of non-manual workers were significantly higher among whites than among blacks. In the case of skilled manual workers, they were far higher. Only amongst semi-skilled and unskilled grades was there parity.

As unemployment generally increased between 1973 and 1980, total unemployment doubled: amongst blacks it is quadrupled. Between 1979 and 1980, registered unemployment rose by almost 12% amongst blacks, compared with 2·5% overall.

(3) *Blacks are disadvantaged in education* In 1972 West Indian children constituted 1·1% of all children in state schools but 4·9% of children in special schools. Black children are more likely to be perceived by teachers as inadequate and/or stupid.

The Rampton Report (1981) argued that racism and specifically the stereotyped attitudes of many educationalists played an important part in the underachievement of West Indian children. It also questioned research which found West Indian youths between twelve and sixteen surpassing their white counterparts. Other ethnic minority groups also underachieve. The 1985 Swann Report, 'Education For All' stressed that no single factor explained this situation. It recommended various changes – more black teachers, better teacher training, more English language programmes – but concluded that the best way to change the inadequate school performance of black children would be by improving the social and economic circumstances of their families.

(4) *Blacks are disadvantaged in society* Whilst certain of Britain's black citizens have achieved prominence in fields such as entertainment and sport, their exclusion from the centres of power is symbolised by the fact that there are no black Cabinet ministers, no black MPs, no black High Court judges and no black senior police officers. The appointment of Bill Morris as Deputy General Secretary of the Transport and General Workers Union in 1985 highlighted a similar

position in the trade unions. Blacks exist in what the Commons Home Affairs Select Committee termed 'a complete fabric of social and economic disadvantage'. The crudest index of this is illustrated by the densely detailed documentation of the physical violence blacks have to endure culminating in the Home Office Report of 1981. The 1984 report of the Policy Studies Institute (formerly PEP) argued that overall the difficulties of black citizens had intensified with the recession. There was a clear need it concluded for firm action by central government if further deterioration was to be avoided.

Racist discrimination

Racist discrimination played a significant role in blacks' continuing disadvantaged position. There were racist strikes and threatened strikes on the railways, buses and the hospitals in the '50s and '60s against the initial employment of black workers. Trade union bodies fearing undercutting of wages and conditions created colour bars. The Notting Hill riots of 1958 drew attention to the seriousness of the problem. As the first major research on the subject in the mid-sixties commented,

... after these three surveys all but those with closed minds must accept the fact that in Britain today discrimination against those coloured members of the population operates in many fields. In the sectors we studied, different aspects of employment, housing and provision of services, there is racial discrimination, varying in extent from the massive to the substantial. The experience of white immigrants such as Hungarians and Cypriots leaves us in no doubt that the major component is colour.

The 1976 PEP Survey found some improvement. Since 1967 discrimination in the field of housing had decreased although they still found, for example, discrimination against blacks in 27% of applications for rented accommodation. Discrimination against applicants for unskilled jobs still occurred in nearly 50% of cases, and for white collar jobs there was no improvement.

In the late seventies and early eighties a series of studies showed continuing discrimination in housing, education and all aspects of employment. The 1984 survey by the PSI documented a further worsening of unemployment rates for black workers. Surveys charted widespread racism within the police force and characterised black-police relationships as 'disastrous'. The Scarman Report on the Brixton riots saw the disturbances as most immediately an outburst against the police. At the same time as blacks were being portrayed in the media as 'muggers's there was, in reality, increasing violence *against* black citizens. In March–June 1981, for example, Coventry Community Relations offices logged sixty incidents of violence against blacks including what they regarded as two racially influenced murders. The deteriorating economic situation, mass unemployment and deindustrialisation exacerbated the position. In Liverpool, prior to the 1981 riots, black unemployment was estimated at 50%. Out of 1,738 people employed in Liverpool Environmental Health Department only eleven were black. The Social Services Department employed 3,840, but only thirty-five blacks. There were 30,000 blacks in the city but only 169 were numbered amongst the 22,000 council employees. As the 1984 PSI report stated:

We have moved over a period of 18 years from studying the circumstances of immigrants to studying the black population of Britain only to find we are looking at the same thing ... racialism and racial discrimination continue to have a powerful impact on black people ... the position of black people remains largely geographically and economically that allocated to them as immigrant workers in the 1950's and 1960's.

Britain's black citizens remained a specific grouping within the working class suffering double deprivation because they were workers and because they were black.

Explanations of racism

How do we explain the existence of racialist attitudes? A number of possible explanations are considered below.

(1) *The importance of ideas*, particularly the ideas of scientists who argued for the existence of races based on genetic inheritance. The problem with the explanation is that whilst these ideas may have had some influence, they were trying to explain and sometimes justify racist behaviour and structures that existed before the ideas were produced. The theories were developed in a particular social and economic context initially, for example, where slaveowners in the West Indies and southern states of the USA were being challenged and European powers bent on colonial conquest needed to justify themselves.

(2) *Racism is a problem of individual psychology*. But an individual's racial prejudice is learned within social structures in which racial discrimination already occurs. Such attitudes do not exist as part of an immutable human nature. There is no racial prejudice in some societies, while in South Africa racism is a mark of normal adjustment to society. This is not to argue that psychological attitudes, neuroses

and anxieties are not important in understanding the particular forms racism takes in particular situations.

(3) *To understand racism we need to look at the overall social, economic and political context in which it develops*. This kind of explanation provides us with the best means of coming to grips with the problem. We have to look for explanations to today's racism in terms of both the historical development of our society and the practical problems people face today. 'Slavery' and 'empire' are key words here. Britain's central involvement in the slave trade and its later accumulation of a vast empire of what were viewed as primitive inferior people took place at the same time as the equality of all men was being asserted in Europe. Racism usefully excluded 'savages' from the family of man, whilst the treatment meted out to blacks made them inferior in a very real way. Colonialism contributed to Britain's position as a great power and thus nourished chauvinist and racist ideas amongst all sections of the population. We also have to look at contemporary external factors such as the performance of former colonies since independence. But a crucial internal factor was the sudden appearance of a relatively large number of people of perceived inferior race within Britain, just as its role as a major power was ending and not very long before economic decline set in. The fact that immigrants not only had black skins but were brought here as cheap labour, worked in the worst jobs in the declining industries and lived in the worst housing, reinforced racist stereotypes amongst British workers. And the fact that they could be seen as competitors for jobs and increasingly scarce resources provided these hostile opinions with a cutting edge.

We now need to look at the reaction of politicians.

Immigration legislation

Breaking the ice

The initial response of British politicians to the post-war immigrants was cautious and contradictory. Both the Attlee and Churchill administrations explored but rejected restrictions on entry. Initial numbers were small, there were real manpower needs and there was a desire not to offend the Commonwealth. But neither government was prepared to will the resources and give the political leadership which might have minimised later problems. As the fifties developed the policy reaction was not to attack racism but to try to limit the problem and the consequent social disruption, by managing its victims and controlling the inflow into Britain of black workers. Pressure from right-wing constituencies and MPs to reduce black immigration in the wake of the Notting Hill riots led the Conservatives to introduce the 1962 Immigration Act. This measure was also prompted by a rise in the numbers entering Britain and the fact that the polls showed control was electorally popular. British citizens from the Commonwealth could now only enter if they were dependents of residents or students or possessed an employment voucher: Category A for those with a specific job, Category B for those with a scarce skill, Category C for other applicants. The Act was a temporary measure requiring periodic renewal. It was not *overtly* racist, applying to all Commonwealth citizens, but it did not apply to the 60–70,000 Irish citizens entering annually. 'The Bill's real purpose was to restrict the influx of coloured immigrants. We were reluctant to say as much openly' (Minister William Deedes in 1968).

Labour strongly opposed the Bill on the grounds that the government was succumbing to racist pressures. They promised the speedy repeal of an act they claimed was anti-Commonwealth and unjustified economically.

Establishing consensus

The two election defeats of Labour's chosen Foreign Secretary, Patrick Gordon Walker, apparently on the racist issue impressed the incoming 1964 Labour government. There was a desire not to appear 'soft' and consequently lose votes to the Tories, to create a bipartisan approach and 'take race out of politics'. Labour renewed the Act and in a White Paper in 1965 promised to strengthen it. The 1968 *Commonwealth Immigrants Act* was introduced in the wake of another right-wing campaign opposing the rights of Asians expelled from Kenya to enter a Britain 'bursting to the seams'. The Act removed the right of entry from all British citizens who did not have a parent or grandparent born in Britain. Instead, they could apply for special vouchers: 1,500 would be issued annually.

The ancillary 1969 *Immigration Appeal Act* allowed an appeal to those refused entry but required all intending immigrants to obtain an entry certificate following an interview and production of birth and marriage certificates. In many areas this led to obstruction and long delays for those with rights of entry.

Those from Australia, New Zealand and Canada who would, on the whole, have the *patrial* connection and who were overwhelmingly white, had the right to enter whilst British passport holders from the New Commonwealth who would, on the whole, not have the patrial connection and were overwhelmingly black did not. The Act, therefore, appeared to be not about numbers but about colour. Its passing was accompanied by a series of speeches from Tory Shadow Cabinet member, Enoch Powell, who spoke in terms of the destruction of 'nation' and 'culture' by black immigrants and eventual civil war. Given the mass media coverage, these speeches articulated, extended and made respectable racist attitudes: his widespread resonance was illustrated on 23 April 1968 when London dockers went on strike and marched to Westminster to support him.

Labour's patrial distinction was taken up by the Conservative *Immigration Act 1971*, designed to replace all existing legislation. The 'right of abode' was given to: patrials or those resident in the UK for five years or more; those born to or adopted by those born in the UK; and spouses. All aliens and all non-patrial commonwealth citizens needed permission and a work permit to enter Britain, although those already resident retained the right to bring in dependents. There continued to be no control over nationals of the Republic of Ireland and the EEC. Introduced to put an end to further large-scale immigration, the Act actually increased the numbers of those eligible for entry from the old Commonwealth. However, where Labour had succumbed to pressure not to admit the Kenyan Asians, the Tories in 1972 stood firm against pressure from the media and right wing politicians and allowed British citizens expelled from Uganda to enter the country.

Labour opposed the legislation although its opposition was undermined by the fact that it was based on its own 1968 Act. Labour spokesperson, Alex Lyon, promised its repeal, but this pledge was not redeemed. Labour did increase the number of special vouchers available for those with no rights of entry from 3,000 to 5,000 a year. It allowed entry to husbands and fiancés of women living in Britain, a right it had originally removed, but later tightened these provisions. It also halted the virginity tests on women seeking entry which had been openly carried out in the previous period.

Breaking the consensus
In 1977 Mrs Thatcher argued the necessity of 'holding out a clear prospect of an end to immigration'. A year later she claimed 'the British character has done so much for democracy, for law and done so much throughout the world that if there is a fear that it

might be swamped, people are going to react and be rather hostile to those coming in'.

This clear articulation of sentiments close to those expressed by Enoch Powell a decade earlier presaged a move to the right by the Conservatives. Mrs Thatcher was responding in 'authoritarian populist' fashion to what she saw as the real anxiety and concern of the majority. The Conservative new turn was accompanied by a significant improvement in the opinion polls; the fact that it was seen as stealing a march on Labour reinforced its momentum. Moreover, Britain was now in the years of surplus labour. The British Nationality Act, introduced in January 1981, (when primary immigration had slowed to a dribble), was intended to bring the law on nationality into line with the now consolidated system of immigration law based on patriality. There would now be three categories of citizenship: *British citizens*, broadly those with full rights of entry; *British overseas citizens* (New Commonwealth); and *Citizens of the British dependent territories* (e.g. Hong Kong, Bermuda). The latter two categories would now have restricted nationality as well as immigration rights.

Labour's stance was one of newly confident opposition. Their spokesperson, Roy Hattersley, claimed Labour was returning to its 1962 position and claimed that Labour's immigration policies had previously been based upon serious mistakes. The move to the left was accompanied by further demands from the Tory right. In October 1981 the Monday Club put forward a plan for the annual repatriation of 100,000 black citizens.

Anti-discrimination legislation

In 1965 Roy Hattersley argued 'Without integration limitation is inexcusable; without limitation integration is impossible'. To this end successive Labour governments have taken initiatives in the area of combatting racism. The position of the Conservatives has basically been one of grudging acquiescence, their hesitant acceptance of ameliorative measures contrasting with the vigour with which they have pursued the control side of the strategy.

The *Race Relations Act 1965* established conciliation machinery to deal with complaints of discrimination which was to be unlawful on grounds of 'race, colour, ethnic or national origin' in public places such as hotels, restaurants and transport. The Act was criticised on the grounds:

(1) It did not apply to crucial areas such as housing or employment.

(2) Enforcement methods were inadequate.

(3) Its impact was limited, judging by the small number of complaints.

Its successor, the *Race Relations Act 1968*, introduced in the same year as tighter immigration control, also covered housing, employment, the provision of goods, facilities and services and the publication or display of advertisements. The Race Relations Board was revamped and given a duty to investigate complaints of discrimination. It had to resolve disputes initially by conciliation and it had the power to take a case only if all else failed. It also established the Community Relations Commission to promote community relations and oversee the work of local community relations councils. By 1975 the Labour government argued the need for tighter legislation as:

(1) The 1968 Act had not succeeded in significantly improving the position.

(2) The definition of discrimination was too narrow and did not cover cases where *the impact* of rules and regulations, intended or not, was discriminatory.

(3) Enforcement methods were still inadequate. The Race Relations Board was inhibited by the need to examine every complaint, its powers were inadequate, individual cases were handled too slowly and the obligation to investigate denied more effective individual access to the courts.

(4) Compensation awards were very small and court orders difficult to obtain.

The *Race Relations Act 1976* built on this analysis. The definition of discrimination was extended to include indirect discrimination 'where unjustifiable practices and procedures which apply to everyone have the effect of putting people of a particular racial group at a disadvantage' (such as language requirements not necessary for a job). The individual can now proceed directly to an industrial tribunal or county court without awaiting a decision of the Commission for Racial Equality. This latter body replaced the Race Relations Board and the Community Relations Committee and was given new powers, for example, of serving non-discrimination notices and enforcing them by injunctions. There was also a new clause on racial incitement.

The Race Relations Acts have also been complemented by a series of measures to deal with urban deprivation with an anti-discrimination dimension. The Home Office has been responsible for the Urban

Programme (1968), the Community Development Project (1969), the Urban Deprivation Unit (1973) and the Comprehensive Community Programmes (1974).

Section 11 of the Local Government Act 1966 allowed local authorities to claim grant aid to employ extra staff in the event of substantial numbers of 'immigrants' in their area whose language and customs were different from the rest of the community. A local authority qualifies for assistance by showing that 2% of its school children have parents born in the New Commonwealth and resident in the UK for less than ten years. The Department of Education and Science has been responsible for Educational Priority Areas (1967), the Education Disadvantage Unit (1974) and the Centre for Information and Advice on Educational Disadvantage (1975). The Department of Environment has been responsible for the Housing Action Areas and the Inner Area Studies and since 1977 the Urban Aid Programme.

The politics of extremism

The National Front (NF), Britain's premier fascist organisation, was formed from a number of small racist sects in 1967. The Front projected an electoral strategy based on 'law and order', opposition to the EEC and, crucially, the compulsory repatriation of all black 'immigrants'. Their ten candidates in the 1970 election received only 3·6% of the vote. Their fortunes improved after the Conservative decision to admit the Ugandan Asians and as the economic pressures nurturing working-class racism intensified. A year later they were reported to have 14,000 members and received 16% of the vote in the West Bromwich by-election. However, despite growing publicity, their candidates polled only just over 3% of the vote in the two 1974 elections.

After a split (giving rise to the British National Party) in 1976, membership declined to around 9,000 and there appeared to be a move away from the respectable strategy of parliamentary democracy to street politics. The NF appeared to benefit from these tactics in 1976 and 1977, obtaining over 10% of the vote in twenty-five local elections. In two areas their vote was over 20%. Despite more publicity through running battles with the Anti-Nazi League, the NF met electoral disaster in 1979, their candidates collectively polling around 1·3% of the vote. Handicapped, perhaps crucially, by the tension between an inner circle embracing fully fledged Fascist philosophy and recruits won in the 1970s from conservatism who were right-wing nationalists pure and simple, the National Front declined into congeries of warring sects. Some observers explained this downturn in terms of the Conservative move to the right in the late seventies, itself possibly a response to the earlier vigour of the NF. The fascist groupings are today of minor political significance.

Black organisation and resistance

The black British have long established community organisations such as the Indian Workers Association with a strong left wing bias. The experience of racism has brought the different communities closer together. In 1980 there was an attempt to establish a National Co-ordinating Committee of Afro-Carribean and Asian Organisations. Asian youth movements have also been prominent in Southall and Bradford. The tendency amongst blacks has been to see the Labour Party as the vehicle for their aspirations and there is currently a debate about autonomous black sections within the party. However, some, particularly in the Asian community, have been attracted to the Conservatives, despite the judgement of many observers that Conservative policies involved writing off the black vote. Asians have stood as Tory candidates and Anglo-Asian and Anglo-West Indian Conservative societies have been established. The Alliance has also attempted to attract the black vote and, in the 1983 election, eight of their candidates were from the black communities. Prior to the 1979 election, a standing conference of Afro-Carribean and Asian councillors was set up and published a Black People's Manifesto for the campaign.

There are many examples of blacks organising self defence against white violence, but the most successful campaigns, those of the Anti-Nazi League and Rock Against Racism, were in fact inspired by the sectarian Socialist Workers Party, although they did involve wide support. It proved ephemeral and declined in tandem with the National Front. Official organisations have done little — witness the moribund TUC/Labour Party campaign against racism of 1976. But black workers have become more active in the trade unions and been involved in a continuing series of struggles of which Mansfield Hosiery, Imperial Typewriters, Grunwick and Chix are only the best known. Campaigns against deportation of individuals under the immigration legislation have also mobilised support. The future political trajectory of black citizens is to some degree contingent on wider political initiatives.

In the context of an overall turning towards activity in mainstream institutions, the three main responses today would seem to be:

(1) Black self organisation to turn traditional institutions, specifically the Labour Party and the unions, to the purposes of the black communities.

(2) A turning inwards to compensatory creeds such as Rastafarianism and Pan Africanism which in themselves lack a practical political dimension.

(3) Militant semi-spontaneous resistance to draw attention to the plight of the communities as in the riots in Bristol in 1980, in most major British cities in 1981 and in Handsworth and Broad Water Farm in 1985.

Racism as a political issue

Throughout the sixties and seventies, despite different emphases and rhetoric in opposition, there was a broad consensus on the 'control and integrate strategy'. This has been criticised as a strategy for combatting racism on the grounds that:

(1) The immigration legislation involved appeasing, legitimising and encouraging the racism of the electorate by identifying black people, not white racism, as the problem and by practising racial discrimination at the point of entry.

(2) This state institutionalisation of discrimination led to a system of internal surveillance of black residents. Every black was a potential criminal, as could be seen most graphically by the six police raids on workplaces in early 1980 in search of illegal immigrants.

(3) Successive governments, far from seeking to educate the electorate, have succumbed to the lowest common denominator. A high profile anti-racist campaign plus a determined attempt to provide more resources to support the new settlers in the '50s and '60s could have limited the problems we face today. The failure to grasp the nettle has helped its luxuriant growth.

(4) The anti-discrimination legislation was not only a case of too little, too late. It was contaminated by the laws on exclusion. If the government was refusing to admit people on the grounds, that their skin colour would cause problems, why shouldn't a factory owner do exactly the same?

(5) A harsher analysis depicts the race relations legislation as tokenism intended to create a 'black middle class' and suppress conflict without redressing injustice. Most critics, however, accept that the 1976

legislation and the increased role of the CRE represented a passing over from half-hearted education to more vigorous enforcement and that the legislation has some role to play in an anti-racist strategy.

With economic conditions militating against ambitious solutions to the problem of racism, such as increased resources being directed to housing, education and jobs for the black community, there is today no consensus. The differences between the main parties can clearly be seen in their response to the inner city riots, the Conservatives articulating the issue basically in terms of law and order and discipline, Labour in terms of economic and social deprivation. The Conservative party appear broadly satisfied with the status quo. They firmly resist further moves towards positive discrimination in favour of blacks as divisive. They are, however, prepared to devote more resources to 'crisis' situations and areas of particular disadvantage and to turn aside pressure from the right in favour of repatriation. It seems as if after the next election there will be six black Labour MPs. But the refusal of that party's leadership to countenance autonomous black sections within the Party has caused it problems. Labour, feeling the pressure of black activism and sensitised by the re-emergence of fascism, a historic threat to the Labour movement, has adopted its most detailed and liberal policy yet. Going a long way to accepting the criticisms outlined above, it proposes a repeal of the Nationality Act, a relatively open immigraiton policy and positive discrimination for the black communities in the context of launching 'through public education ... a major initiative aimed at changing the racial prejudice of white people'. The Alliance has adopted similar policies and its 1983 campaign laid particular emphasis on the attitudes of black voters. It is clear that the present situation in Britain represents a failure of political nerve, political strategy and political action. There *is* a need for new policies. It is also clear that the implementation of any such policies will have to take account of the growing activism of the blacks themselves and their increasing impatience with their continued standing as second-class citizens.

Reading

Martin Barker, *The New Racism*, Junction Books, 1978.
C. Brown, *Black and White Britain*, PSI, 1984.
E. Ellis Cashmore and Barry Troyna, *Introduction to Race Relations*, Routledge & Kegan Paul, 1983.

Stephen Castles *et al., Here for Good*, Pluto Press, 1983.

Peter Fryer, *Staying Power: The History of Black People in Britain*, Pluto Press, 1984.

Stuart Hall, *et al., Policing the Crisis*, Macmillan, 1978.

Charles Husband, *'Race' in Britain*, Hutchinson, 1982.

Zig Layton Henry, *The Politics of Race in Britain*, Allen & Unwin, 1984.

Robert Miles and Annie Phizacklea, *Racism and Political Action in Britain*, Routledge & Kegan Paul, 1979.

Robert Moore, *Racism and Black Resistance in Britain*, Pluto Press, 1975.

John Rex, *Race Relations in Sociological Theory*, Weidenfeld and Nicolson, 1970.

A. Sivanandan, *A Different Hunger*, Pluto Press, 1983.

Women and politics

Women are virtually invisible in textbooks on politics. Voters, MPs, even Prime Ministers are assumed to be male and are discussed as though it is not important to ask why politics remains a 'man's world'. But to ask such a question − as this chapter seeks to do − raises the much broader issue of women's position in the wider society and challenges our understanding of what politics is about.

The vote − exclusion from politics

Until nearly sixty years ago the denial of the right to vote effectively excluded women from participation in formal parliamentary politics − only women over thirty were granted the vote in 1918 and it was not until 1928 that universal suffrage was achieved. Many women saw winning the vote as the key to their emancipation. Once women had access to the system they believed that they would be able to end inequality and change the male political agenda.

The suffragists (constitutionalists) and suffragettes (militants) were not alone, for women have been arguing for women's rights and challenging men's power for centuries. But the voices of Mary Astell in the seventeenth century and even Mary Wollstonecraft in the eighteenth century have been distorted, ignored and even silenced. Women therefore have very little sense of their own history and the reasons why women were willing to sacrifice so much − their health and even their lives − to get the vote.

Separate spheres – public and private

The traditional divide between the public world of politics and work and the private world of the home and the family has been used to justify the exclusion of women from the political process and remains a strong barrier to women's equality. What does this mean for women's political participation?

(1) In the past, it was argued that the two spheres were separate but equal (rather like apartheid). Women had their own responsibilities and participation in the public sphere would 'unsex' them, making them unfit for their primary duty of motherhood and the family. Although the physical divide between public and private is not as sharp now as it was in the nineteenth century, its power persists at the level of ideas: politics is not a 'feminine' pursuit but a man's world.

(2) Psychologically, the effect of the division is to undermine women's confidence in their own abilities. The attributes which are popularly associated with politicians are seen as male: aggresssion, ambition, self-confidence. There is little for a woman to identify with as women's skills and abilities are undervalued.

(3) The stereotype of woman at the heart of the public/private split is that women are *only* mothers and carers, they are emotional rather than political. Some women accept this as natural and make a virtue of it. These arguments are used very differently by Conservative women (e.g. pro-family, anti-abortion) and by some of the women's peace movement: as mothers, women have a particular responsibility to ensure a world for future generations free from nuclear war.

Women's under-representation

Women are 51·5% of the population yet only a fraction of that number hold positions of power in formal politics. The 1979 general election on the one hand resulted in the election of Margaret Thatcher as the first woman Prime Minister but it also saw the smallest number of women MPs (19) elected since 1951. Although this number increased to twenty-three by the end of the parliament, the general election of 1983 did not produce an increase in the number of women MPs. The 14 by-elections to July 1986 have only resulted in the election of a further 4 women MPs, one for each of the main parties, bringing the total to 27. In Britain, 96% of MPs are male; a clear picture of the under-representation of women. The achievement of one woman in becoming Prime Minister has obscured the fact that there are actually very few women in parliament, no women in the Cabinet and only one woman on the Opposition Front Bench. Her role is somewhat ambiguous as she does not shadow an existing minister, but would head a Labour government's proposed Ministry of Women. The picture is much the same in the USA and Italy but much higher proportions of women participate in Sweden and Denmark.

Why are there so few women in politics?

If challenged on women's under-representation in politics, men often complain that the problem lies with women themselves: not enough put themselves forward. But the issue is not as simple as this.

(1) *Attitudes*

   (a) As girls grow up they are not encouraged to be assertive and they learn very quickly that they have to be much better than a boy at any task if they are to be taken seriously. Women therefore learn not to put themselves forward.

   (b) Men's beliefs about women's capabilities reinforce women's perception of themselves. The belief persists that women are not up to the job and that they should stick to what they are good at, i.e., being wives and mothers.

   (c) Political parties, particularly their constituency selection panels, reinforce these attitudes by a firm, if not proven, belief that the voters do not like women candidates and that votes will be lost if the standard issue male, white, middle-class candidate is not adopted.

   (d) The media's approach to women in public life reinforces stereotyped attitudes, e.g., the destruction of Maureen Colquhoun's career as an MP because she came out unashamedly as a lesbian or the criticism of Helene Hayman for breastfeeding her baby in the House of Commons.

(2) *Childcare* Domestic responsibilities, and specifically the caring for children at home, is a huge obstacle to women's equal participation in every aspect of the 'public' world, particularly paid work but also politics. Because it is assumed by women and/or their families that this is primarily women's responsibility then women are disadvantaged at work and in politics.

   (a) This is reflected in the tendency for women MPs to be single or married/divorced without young children. Of the twenty-seven women MPs elected in 1974, only two had children under ten years old.

(*b*) By the time children are old enough, women themselves are relatively old to embark on a political career. This has ramifications for what women can then achieve and can affect women's decisions on the best ways to use their skills and energies.

(3) *Paid work but no time*   Women's increasing involvement in paid work outside the home has to be combined with their domestic responsibilities. They therefore, literally, have little time for politics, with its endless meetings. In 1984, 63% of women of working age (16–59) and 61% of married women of working age were in the labour force. Although participation in the workforce can increase women's political awareness through breaking their isolation, it is much more likely, because of the practical and ideological constraints on women, to result in grass roots and community political action rather than parliamentary politics.

(4) *Unlikely to fit the model of an MP*   For the same reasons – discrimination and the division of labour – the occupational segregation of the workforce – means that it is harder for women to have the same occupational background as male potential MPs; specifically the professions. Moreover women cannot rely on the 'old school tie' or brotherly sponsorship in the way that men now take for granted.

(5) *The cost*   Women's reticence in putting themselves forward for political office may, in fact, be a rational anticipation of the obstacles involved. The costs may just be too great.

The barriers to selection as parliamentary candidates
Many women who would be eligible because of their political experience, occupation and educational background do not put themselves forward because of the constraints just discussed. But even those who are undeterred face a daunting set of obstacles.

(1) *Approved candidates*   The political parties have lists of approved candidates. The Labour Party has an A list (trade union nominated) and a B list (constituency party nominated). Those candidates with trade union sponsorship are more likely to succeed, yet because of women's under-representation in the trade union hierarchy, there are very few

women on the A list, e.g., three out of 103 in 1977 with the B list containing 9·1% women in the same year. The Conservatives similarly had only 15% women on their list of approved candidates for 1979.

(2) *The shortlist*   Having made the list of approved candidates, women then have to get on to the constituency shortlists. Here women have a better chance inasmuch as the need for a 'token' woman has become widely accepted.

(3) *Selection*   Then, the problem is actually to get selected as a prospective parliamentary candidate. There is still some prejudice – that women are an electoral liability despite the dearth of evidence to prove it – and much to show that gender is not a factor in the political outcome.

(4) *A safe seat*   Although the overall number of women candidates is increasing at general elections (from 212 in 1979 to 268 in 1983), the number elected, as we have seen, is a small proportion. Most of those women were standing either in unwinnable seats or in marginals. In 1979, of the fifty-two women Labour Party candidates, fifteen were standing for re-election, one had been selected to fight a safe seat and four were standing in marginals. Only eleven were elected, five incumbents lost and none of the women's marginal seats were won. Of the eight Conservative women elected that year, seven were standing for re-election and one out of the three women standing for a marginal was successful. Because so few women are selected for safe seats, the probability of women becoming MPs under the present electoral system remains slight. However, a reformed voting system, based on multi-member constituencies and proportional representation might increase women's chances (see Ch 5).

(5) *Re-selection*
   (a) In the 1970 parliament, over two-thirds of male MPs had been elected on the first occasion they stood for parliament whereas less than a third of women had succeeded at their first contest. So as women are less likely to win at their first attempt, it is important that they get re-selected, as that increases their chances. But only 20% of those women defeated at the 1974 elections were re-selected to fight in 1979. There is therefore a high wastage of women candidates and the length of the odds against election, combined with the practical constraints, must deter them from putting themselves forward.

(*b*) Even if a woman gets elected for a marginal seat, which may be her best option, she is then as vulnerable as any other MP sitting for a marginal seat.

In the House of Commons

This obstacle course just described ensures that few women get elected. But even when safely elected, there are limitations on women's participation.

(*a*) *A male institution* It is not for nothing that the House of Commons is claimed to be the 'best gentleman's club in Europe': its traditions, atmosphere, concerns and most of its members are male.

(*b*) *High office* The relatively precarious nature of women MPs' careers means that their chances of being in parliament long enough to become a Cabinet member are less than for men. Up to 1979, of the seventy women Labour MPs elected since women first became eligible (1918) only 7% became Cabinet Ministers, whilst for the same period, of the forty Conservative women MPs only 5% have achieved Cabinet rank. Of course, this is not the only reason for the lack of promotion of women MPs either by male Prime Ministers or indeed, by a woman Prime Minister (who now has no women in her Cabinet). Women have never held the high status office of Chancellor of the Exchequer or been Home or Foreign Secretary. Women who do succeed are therefore seen as exceptions or as Margaret Thatcher is often described − 'the best man for the job.'

Taken together there is little official, and negligible practical, aid or incentive for women to overcome their under-representation in politics.

But there's more to politics than MPs!

Politics is not just about electoral bodies and political parties. Unfortunately the picture of under-representation is as true for public bodies and for the trade unions as it is for Parliament and the parties.

(1) *Public bodies*

In terms of public bodies, whose members are appointed by ministers, only 23% of their membership was female in 1981. In keeping with the division of labour, women are to be found in far greater numbers on 'caring' bodies and on those concerned with consumer affairs than on those responsible for trade, industry or the police. So women constitute 30% of Home Office appointments whilst only 1·9% of those made by the Department of Industry are women. Many public bodies either have no women ministerial appointees (304 in 1981) or just one (159 in 1981).

(2) *Trade unions*

(*a*) There has been a large growth in women's membership of trade unions in the last twenty years as the number of women in the labour force has risen. Of the total increase in trade union membership between 1960 and 1978, over half (55%) were women, the largest growth being in the public sector. Yet this has not resulted in greater female partici-pation in the leadership of trade unions. From shop steward upwards there is no correllation in women's representation with the fact that by 1983 half of the women who work full time were unionised, as were a third of women part-time workers. Even unions with a predominantly female membership such as NUPE (63% are women) have dispropor-tionately low representation of women – eight out of the thirty four person executive, seven out of 150 full-time officials in 1981. As for the two largest unions (TGWU and GMWU) with their 657,000 female membership in 1980 – they did not have any women between them on their executives. This under-representation can be explained in the same terms as women's under-representation in formal politics.

(*b*) Traditionally women's concerns, for instance working hours, part-time workers rights and childcare provision, have been low on unions' lists of priorities when it comes to collective bargaining. This is exacerbated when the unions themselves are under attack and are losing members as jobs are lost. Although some unions, e.g. NUPE, TGWU and COHSE, are now taking up TUC proposals for positive action, they are working against a background of economic recession where women's jobs are particularly vulnerable and the family wage ideology – men need a wage to support a dependent wife and children whilst a woman works for pin money – holds as strong as ever amongst many officials and members alike.

(3) *Local government*

(*a*) There is an increasing interest among women in local govern-ment. By 1985 19·2% of all local councillors in Great Britain were women, compared to under 4% of MPs in the House of Commons.

Participation in local politics is not so disruptive to domestic responsibilities and family commitments as parliamentary politics can be but a sample survey of local councillors in England in the mid-seventies found that 91% of women councillors were housewives, retired or employed part-time. Generally the age of women councillors is appreciably older than women in the population as a whole, with a ratio of almost 2 to 1 in the fifty-five to sixty-nine age group. Local government is also concerned with questions of housing, welfare and education, for example, at a local level where the links to women's experience within their community are much stronger. Yet, once again in terms of the hierarchy, very few women become chairpersons of council committees.

(*b*) One development which is affecting both a general and a feminist perception of local government is the advent of Women's Committees, e.g. the recently abolished GLC (now the Women's Equality Group in the London Strategic Policy Unit), various London boroughs, Sheffield, Leeds and Manchester. These have involved women in local government in an unprecedented scale and pushed higher on the agendas of full councils a series of pressing issues. These include childcare, continued institutional sexual discrimination in the council's employment policies and also in the areas for which the council is responsible, e.g., education, transport, discrimination against lesbians, facilities for women with disabilities, the needs of black women and low pay campaigns. Many of the Women's Committees were formed because of outside pressure from women and all represent an attempt consciously to involve women in the local decision-making process.

To summarise the chapter so far: the popular assumption is that the under-representation of women in many of the bodies mentioned is evidence of women's lack of interest in politics, that women are apolitical and through their own choice have low levels of participation in politics. It is hoped that the foregoing has disposed of this myth: the practical and ideological constaints on women's participation are enormous.

Women's conception of politics – where do women choose to put their energies?

Clearly there are other kinds of activity seeking to influence the making of public policy and the distribution of resources which are beyond the narrow definition of politics as parliament and political parties.

It is when these less conventional political arenas are examined that the limitations of the apolitical stereotype of woman are exposed.

(1) *Women have always been politically active*

(*a*) For example – women were prominent in seventeenth, eighteenth and early nineteenth-century food riots, and the anti-Poor Law demonstrations (1837). These were local and immediate concerns for women and their families which prompted direct action as a protest.

(*b*) Women have always organised as women in campaigns to change the condition of women's lives, e.g. agitation for the repeal of the Contagious Diseases Act, for access to education and the professions, for the vote and for equal pay. Women have shown in the past that they are able to develop organisations for themselves with their own forms – such as local suffragist networks – using imaginative and often disruptive tactics. To publicise the demand for the vote for example, women disrupted meetings, held the first mass women's demonstrations and sent themselves as human protest letters to the Prime Minister.

(2) *Women and community action*

Many of women's concerns in the past focused on the community, dealing with issues of immediate need where practical organisation could be based around the many demands on women's time. Today women are very active participants in tenants' groups, childcare campaigns, health campaigns, anti-poverty lobbies, anti-nuclear groups, Women's Aid, and other campaigns. Such campaigns, prompted by women's own experience, often combine self-help projects with pressure group activity.

(3) *Women's associations*

There are many organisations of women which usually define themselves as 'non-political' (accepting the narrow party-political definition) but which nevertheless seek to influence the determination of public policy, e.g. Women's Institutes, Townswomen's Guilds, Housewives' Register, WRVS. About 3 million women in Britain are involved in these organisations, where women organise as women. They have been involved in campaigns relating to taxation policy, the payment of Child Benefit, local planning decisions and the closing of local facilities. Women's associations often act as a springboard for participation in formal politics, particularly local government.

(4) *The Women's Movement*

(*a*) Women continued to organise (on a much reduced scale) after the vote was won keeping up the pressure for equal rights and to campaign on issues which directly affected the condition of women's lives. But in the late 1960s the Women's Liberation Movement blossomed with a new generation of feminists.

(*b*) Women are self consciously organising as women to support one another through battered women's refuges, Rape Crisis Centres, Women against Violence against Women, together organising to combat male violence. The Women's Movement has also focused on a woman's right to control her own body and thus her own life, campaigning for free contraception, against attacks on abortion rights, for the extension of abortion facilities and well-women clinics.

(*c*) Women have become involved in a broad range of issues, some of which have mobilised those previously untouched by politics. Examples are the Women's Peace Camp at Greenham Common and its support network throughout the country, and Women against Pit Closures as part of the support for the 1984 miners' strike. The latter appeared in the heartland of working-class masculine culture: the mining communities. Women came together, valuing their own experience and supporting one another, to recognise and mobilise their potential collective strength. But it has proved hard to sustain these women's groups after the defeat of the miners' strike.

(*d*) The Women's Movement thrives on its lack of conventional political organisation – you cannot join, there are no leaders. The campaigns and groups of which it is composed are characterised by women organising autonomously (where only women are welcome), non-hierarchically (rotating tasks within groups and nationally using networks rather than centralised structures) and where each woman's voice should be equally valued. The intention is to live your politics: as the slogan says, 'the personal is political and the political is personal'.

But the Women's Movement remains ambiguous about politics as conventionally defined. Different types of feminism would emphasise different approaches to this question:

Liberal feminists are principally concerned with women's rights believing that under the current system women's inequality can be rectified principally through legislation and education.

The Sex Discrimination Act (1975) and the Equal Pay Act (passed 1970, into force 1975) were therefore important breakthroughs although they and the Equal Opportunities Commission (set up in 1975) have

disappointed women in key respects. The lack of teeth for the enforcement of both Acts and the weakness of the EOC has meant relatively
little progress in any absolute measure of equal rights. One problem
is of definition, particularly over equal pay, for given women's occupational segregation – i.e. women are concentrated in low paid,
low status jobs often with no direct comparison with male workers –
the initial concept of equal pay for equal work proved ineffective in
achieving its goal. Women's average pay is still less than 75% of men's
average pay. Yet the government only bowed to EEC pressure in 1984
when the Act was amended to the wider definition of equal pay for
work of equal value.

Using the law depends upon persuading sympathetic men and
women to frame legislation but it also depends upon the courts to
interpret and enforce that law in women's interests. Therefore liberal
feminists are also concerned to change sexist attitudes in the media,
in education and to promote genuine equal opportunities throughout
society.

Socialist feminists believe that women's oppression can only end
with the end of the capitalist system. In the meantime, however,
demands can be made of the state, whilst recognising that it embodies
both class and male power. Socialist feminists organise inside mixed
organisations, such as the labour movement, by building their own
support networks (women's sections and caucuses) as well as organising
in autonomous women's groups, depending on the nature and requirements of the issue. Issues of concern to socialist feminists include
statutory childcare provision, women's rights and working conditions
and cuts in the welfare state which particularly affect women. They
are very critical of male-defined politics but choose to become involved
over particular campaigns to build broader support, to gain access to
resources and influence the system without becoming enmeshed in it.

Radical feminists believe that the fight is against institutionalised
male power in all its forms. They argue that essentially men as a group
benefit from the oppression and exploitation of women as a group.
As change can only come about through women's collective action,
the convincing of men of the need for feminism is not a priority. Key
issues for women to organise around in women-only groups include:
male violence, pornography, sexuality and the building of a woman's
culture.

Radical feminists are opposed to involving themselves in conventional politics except on a very limited basis, where their own terms

can be set: in order to gain government grants, local authority support for Women's Aid, Rape Crisis lines, lesbian support groups, and so forth.

This is inevitably an over-simplified analysis and such is the richness and diversity of feminism that many women would not define themselves as belonging to any particular brand, preferring to be described as 'just a feminist'.

What can be done involve women in politics?

(1) *Positive action*

If the under-representation of women in political parties, parliament, public bodies and the unions is to be reversed then the barriers to their participation have to be removed.

(*a*) Some women are demanding that men make space for women, that some of those safe seats have to be handed over. The 300 Group has been formed to promote the election to Parliament of at least 300 women (irrespective of political party).

(*b*) It is argued, particularly by women in the Labour Party, that parties have to make good their stated commitment to women's equality and consciously recruit them to higher office with all that that may entail – for example, meetings and parliament at social hours with childcare provision.

(*c*) Most importantly, attitudes have to change – women have to be welcome not just as tokens or as proxy men but as themselves.

(*d*) Women are also demanding power e.g. the campaign in the Labour Party to empower the Women's Conference to bring forward five resolutions onto the full conference agenda and that women should elect the five women's representatives on the party's National Executive Committee.

(*e*) There is also a debate on whether more seats should be reserved for women on the executives of unions and political parties, for it seems that only by women being seen to do the work, can other women's confidence be raised and an example be set to remove prejudice.

(2) *Valuing women's issues*

(*a*) The stereotype of women as carers means that women tend to be given responsibility for education, social services, and consumer issues. These are therefore regarded as 'soft' and have less status than the 'hard', masculine issues of finance and foreign affairs. So, it is argued, the identification of politics with maleness alienates many women and reinforces a belief that politics do not relate to their experience, life and immediate concerns.

(*b*) It has also been suggested that the small number of women MPs should not be seen as a failure of womens' nerve: the large number of women involved in community politics, pressure groups and voluntary bodies indicates that women are consciously choosing *not* to get involved in Parliament. There is a cynicism amongst these women about MPs – their lack of real power, their isolation from the grass-roots, their conception of politics as compromise and committees. A valuing of women's issues and a commitment to real change for women is needed, it is argued, to end this possible abstention by women and their clear under-representation.

(3) *Domestic responsibilities*

(*a*) A practical demand now made by women is for statutory provision of childcare for both pre-school and school-age children, in and beyond school hours. Women would then have far wider options in terms of paid work and political participation. Equivalent support would also be needed for women caring for other dependents, e.g. the elderly and handicapped adults.

(*b*) As challenging is the observation that unless domestic work ceases to be women's prime responsibility, despite 'help' from men, then paid work continues to be a second job for a woman and politics a third. The key point in this argument is that women will not have enough time unless men give up some of theirs.

Together these changes could alleviate a woman's perennial choice between family and career, and allow her to make real choices about what she does with her life.

Concluding comments

This chapter has argued that women's position in society, specifically the division of labour, fundamentally inhibits women's participation in formal politics. It is therefore suggested that only major changes in society will allow women to participate equally. At its most challenging, some women are now arguing that women have to get men to give up some of their power and make space for women. So women have to be organised and although some women are self-consciously choosing not to participate in parliamentary politics that does not mean that they are not political. Women *are* actively organising, particularly in grassroots and community politics, over issues which directly affect their experience as women. When formal politics deals more with women's concerns and priorities and rids itself of the structural barriers to women's participation, then we may see something approaching equal representation of women and their interests. Of course, this would transform politics itself.

Reading

Vicky Randall, *Women and Politics*, Macmillan, 1982.

Jill Hills, 'Britain', in Lovenduski and Hills (eds.), *The Politics of the Second Electorate*, Routledge & Kegan Paul, 1981.

Margaret Stacey and Marion Price, *Women, Power & Politics*, Tavistock, 1981.

Barbara Rogers, *52% – Getting Women's Power into Politics*, Women's Press, 1983.

KEEPING THE PEACE

Chapter Fifteen   *Peter Byrd*

Northern Ireland

This chapter begins with a brief outline of Britain's involvement in Ireland and then examines various explanations of the 'Irish question'. It reviews a number of the alternative policies for resolving Britain's problems in Northern Ireland that have been discussed since the problem became acute at the end of the 1960s, and concludes by discussing the latest British initiative, namely the Hillsborough agreement with the Republic of Ireland made in November 1985.

Britain in Ireland: an historical overview

Henry II intervened in Ireland in 1172. During the Middle Ages the deployment of English power in Ireland was part of a complex process of expanding the realm of the Crown, and defending the English state from internal and external subversion. The Reformation in England added a new dimension because Ireland remained Catholic and hence the potential ally of England's continental Catholic enemies. Catholic uprisings led to a more systematic English reaction by the establishment of Scottish Presbyterian plantations, primarily in Ulster, in order to maintain a Protestant ascendancy. Renewed Catholic resistance was violently put down by Cromwell and after further rebellion in 1689 – again with a strong continental element – London enacted penal laws against Catholics, a purely Protestant parliament was established in Dublin and Ireland became a sort of colony governed through Anglo-Irish protestant 'collaborators'.

In 1800 this indirect rule broke down and a formal union with Great Britain was established, the United Kingdom of Great Britain and Ireland, with an enlarged parliament at Westminster. Integration failed, despite the emancipation of Catholics, to meet the growing demands of Irish Catholic nationalism which focused around the issue of Irish home rule. Gladstone's decision to concede home rule split the Liberal Party in 1886 and led to two decades of Conservative domination in government. When Asquith's Liberal government resurrected home rule it also faced a political crisis which spilled over the Irish sea into Britain. Ulster's Protestants, led by Carson, made clear their absolute determination to fight home rule. In March 1914 British army units based at the Curragh near Dublin displayed a sympathy for the protestants which was tantamount to defiance of the government.

During the First World War the issue was first put successfully on ice but in 1916 the Easter Rebellion revealed the growing strength of a more extreme nationalist movement Sinn Féin. After the war the government was confronted with incompatible demands from the protestants of Ulster and Sinn Féin which had displaced the old moderate parliamentary nationalist party. The 1920 Government of Ireland Act offered the compromise of two home rule parliaments for Ireland within a looser United Kingdom state. Ulster reluctantly conceded but Sinn Féin refused, demanded complete independence for a united Ireland and began an armed insurrection against British rule.

In 1921 the government conceded quasi-independence to the south on a basis similar to that enjoyed by the White Dominions of Canada and Australia. The treaty split Sinn Féin and erstwhile comrades fought a bitter civil war. Although the moderates won, in 1932 one of the extreme republicans, De Valera, came to power as leader of a new party called Fianna Fáil and he was forced to outlaw the old rump of Sinn Féin and its military wing, the Irish Republican Army (IRA). De Valera successfully exploited the ambiguities of dominion status so that by 1939 he was able to remain neutral in the Second World War. In 1949 full independence with a republican constitution, and withdrawal from the Commonwealth, was easily achieved.

In the north the six counties of Ulster with a Protestant majority remained within the United Kingdom and, in return for agreeing to the 1920 Act, were given a devolved parliament at Stormont. The London government, exhausted by Irish affairs, was anxious to concede to Stormont control of events in Northern Ireland. The Protestant majority of Unionists enjoyed almost unfettered freedom to act outside the usual conventions of British politics. The Prime Minister of Northern Ireland, Lord Craigavon, established a protestant ascendancy on the basis of a 'Protestant parliament and a Protestant state'.

The Catholic minority, about one-third of the population, was treated as a potential enemy of the regime. Laws discriminated against Catholics and were enforced by a largely Protestant police force and a wholly Protestant paramilitary force called the B Specials. These arrangements, reinforced by economic discrimination, were both massively unjust and surprisingly stable so long as the Catholic community was too weak to challenge them.

In the 1960s the Northern Ireland political system became unstable. Catholic demands for civil rights culminated in a major demonstration in 1968 which provoked the inevitable Protestant backlash. The Prime Minister, Terence O'Neill, pursued a moderate policy and attempted to modernise this anachronistic system, even opening up a dialogue with Dublin, but he failed to satisfy either community and in 1969 he resigned. His successor, Robin Chichester-Clark, could only maintain order by requesting assistance from London and troops were dispatched by Harold Wilson's government. The British government was now drawn into the situation and began to enforce reforms on the Protestants. Two consequences followed. Firstly, conflict emerged between the London and Belfast governments over the pace of reforms and control of security policy culminating in Edward Heath's decision to suspend Stormont in April 1972, ushering in what has become known as 'direct rule'. Secondly, the IRA renewed its campaign against British rule by launching a campaign of terrorism and guerrilla war. In 1972, the more politically-inclined factions of the IRA called a truce but their more violent colleagues in the Provisional IRA intensified the struggle. Violence has continued both in Ulster and from time to time in Great Britain, and the Provisional IRA has itself been factionalised with the emergence of the Irish National Liberation Army. The Provisional IRA has also engaged in political struggle through the Provisional Sinn Féin which has gained some of the Catholic vote. The British army remains, its strength having fallen from a peak of about 20,000 to about 9,000.

Politics in the north has thus been dominated by military and security problems. Direct rule has continued since 1972 except for a short and unsuccessful experiment with devolution in 1973–4 (discussed below). A solution to the problem appears further away then ever. Indeed it is the essence of Northern Ireland that there is no agreement on what the problem is, let alone any agreement on a solution.

Explaining the problem: six languages of analysis

Different 'languages of analysis' (a term I owe to my colleage, Jim Bulpitt) define the nature of the problem quite differently. Each has something to contribute to our understanding and together they give something of the flavour of the complexity of the issue.

1. *Religion*

Church attendance is high in Northern Ireland, religious leaders are drawn into politics and some (though by no means all) self-professed Christians are bigoted, intolerant and unpleasant. For Protestants, the privileged status of the Catholic church in the Republic is a familiar bogey. Hence the communal conflict in Northern Ireland does have a religious dimension; it has persisted for four centuries, and exhortations of goodwill from Great Britain are fatuous. But religion does not completely explain the problem. Some Christians co-exist across the divide and, when removed from the particular context of Northern Ireland — to, say, Liverpool or Glasgow — the religious conflict loses its political bitterness.

2. *Nationalism*

The conflict in Northern Ireland can be seen as the clash of competing national identities claiming exclusive control of territory. Irish nationalism can be traced back to nineteenth-century theories and politics of national self-determination. The two communities perceive themselves as distinct ethnic groups and one advantage of this explanation of the conflict is that it helps explain not only Catholic Irish nationalism but also Protestant Ulter nationalism. Some of the more extreme Protestants see an Ulster identity and separation from Great Britain as an alternative to the Union and a better basis for re-establishing a Protestant ascendancy.

The re-emergence of the conflict in the 1960s, viewed from a perspective of nationalism, also fits in with the more general re-emergence of ethnicity and nationalism as a political phenomenon. Peripheral nationalism became a potent force in Scotland, Wales, Britanny, the Basque lands, Catalonia and Quebec.

Does a nationalist perspective point to a solution of the problem? Protestants can point to their 2 to 1 numerical superiority in Northern Ireland as the justification for rejection of a united Ireland. Catholic nationalists strongly emphasise the natural unity of the island of

Ireland – nationalists have traditionally seen islands as natural national units. Of course, not all Catholics in the north favour unification with the south and it is very difficult to establish how many of them actively favour unification as opposed to espousing a traditional opposition to Britain. Nor should we assume that the population in the south is enthusiastic about unification, an aspect of the problem discussed briefly below.

The IRA draws analogies between its struggle against British colonial rule in Ireland and Third World nationalist movements, particularly in Algeria and Palestine. The Jews of Israel are portrayed as alien settlers in Palestine comparable with the Protestant settlers in Ulster. However, Jews can make a reasonable claim to Israel based on a long period of settlement before an enforced diaspora. The Algerian cause is probably more compelling, with the Protestants seen as comparable with the French colonial settlers, the *pieds noirs*. However, the *pieds noirs* were in a 1 to 7 minority in Algeria whereas the Protestants are in a 2 to 1 majority in Ulster, though of course Irish nationalists would place the Protestants within the context of Ireland as a whole and not merely the 'artificially contrived' statelet of the six counties of Ulster. Ulster, Israel and Algeria also raise the question of the time required to legitimise a presence. Jews claim a presence back to Abraham in 1000 BC and a small continuing presence even through the diaspora. Ulster's protestants, who naturally tend to sympathise strongly with Israel, can claim only the relatively brief period of four centuries, although this is much longer than the one century of French settlement in Algeria. In any case, national self-determination cannot be determined solely by historical claims – if so, then what of the original inhabitants of North America or Australasia? Another interesting analogy drawn by the IRA is with South Africa. Many British liberals would be shocked by a solution to the South African problem on the basis of self-determination which would permit continued white rule in the towns and countryside in which whites constituted a local majority.

In short, while the conflict in Northern Ireland can be viewed from a nationalist perspective, that perspective does not point unambiguously at a particular solution.

3. *Marxist analysis*
There is no single Marxist view of the issue. The advantage of Marxist views is that they concentrate on the relationship between Britain and Ireland and hence may tell us more about Northern Ireland as a problem

for Britain than, for instance, the two perspectives of religion and nationalism.

One view, fashionable in the 1970s but now in tattered retreat, is that the United Kingdom has always constituted an 'internal colony' of the English in which Scotland, Wales and Ireland were exploited by England. The internal colonialism thesis, which is associated particularly with the work of Michael Hechter, also argued that the economies of the peripheries were shaped by the English to be export-orientated and tied into a larger imperial colony. Linen and ship-building, the two traditional industries of Ulster, could be viewed as fitting into this category of vulnerable export-orientated industries, now seriously in decline. From this perspective, Catholics are a sort of 'sub-class' similar to the blacks of the United States.

'Dependency analysis' is a closely related variety of Marxist analysis which explains the development of capitalism in terms of 'cores' and 'peripheries'. The core exploits the periphery but conflict between the two is mediated by 'semi-peripheries' or local metropoles which are exploited by the main core but in return exploit the periphery – relations between the core and the periphery are thus indirect. Most dependency analysis has focused on the underdeveloped economies of Latin America. The Belfast area can be seen as a sort of local metropole, exploited from the core of capitalism in Britain but in turn exploiting the periphery of Ulster, which would include both the Catholic and Protestant working classes.

A more simple-minded Marxist view might simply regard the state in Northern Ireland as an agency of British imperialism, protecting the interests of British capital. However it is difficult to take this view very seriously today because from any calculation of economic interests Northern Ireland is a major drain on the British state and it is difficult to imagine British capitalists conceiving of any advantage from continued British rule there.

Tom Nairn, a rather unorthodox Marxist, who strongly sympathises with nationalist movements, argues that nationalism is caused by uneven rates of economic growth. He argues, following Gellner's argument, that there are two varieties of nationalism: firstly, that associated with relative under-development and relative deprivation *vis-à-vis* a political and economic core (Wales, Britanny, the west of Scotland, Ireland in the nineteenth century); secondly, that associated with relative over-development and relative prosperity *vis-à-vis* a political core (the Basques, the Catalans, the east of Scotland, the Ibos).

Ulster's Protestands fit into this second category and Nairn thus regards them not, as do most people on the left, as peculiarly reactionary but as an historically progressive force whose bourgeois values are a necessary precondition for eventual proletarian emancipation.

4. *Modernisation thesis*

The argument here is relatively simple: traditional societies are stable (clear hierarchies, little social dynamism, strong power centres); modernised societies are stable (pluralistic, affluent, secular); modernising societies are unstable as the old order painfully gives way to the new. Although this argument can be applied powerfully to African societies it also seems to fit Northern Ireland. The Protestant domination of 1921–60s was a continuation of a pre-modern Protestant ascendancy in Ulster. Catholics were badly treated but were powerless to challenge and the usual Catholic political response was a sort of abstention from the state. In the 1960s society changed. Firstly, a nascent Catholic middle class demanded proper civil rights, inadvertently offering a covert opportunity for the IRA to re-establish itself. Secondly, the Protestant middle and working classes faced the decline of the province's traditional industries. Thirdly, from 1963 Prime Minister O'Neill pursued an ambitious policy of trying to modernise Northern Ireland. In a society as deeply divided as Northern ireland, these social changes were bound to produce complex conflict.

5. *Liberal analysis*

Liberal analysis of Northern Ireland would probably focus on two ideas. The first is that industrialisation and modernisation will bring about an inevitable softening of old antagonisms and lead to an integration of the communities or to mutual tolerance. From this perspective, high unemployment makes matters much worse because it slows down the process of modernisation and secularisation and allows minds to concentrate an old and irrelevant struggles. The second idea is that political institutions are important – get good institutional arrangements and the rest will follow. The British government after 1969 forced liberal reforms on the Ulster government and the worst grievances of the Catholics were resolved. The classic case of the liberal analysis being applied is the set of institutions established by the Sunningdale Conference in 1973.

The conference was attended by, and produced agreement between, the British and Irish governments and the two major Catholic and

Protestant parties of Ulster. Four sets of institutions were established which, from this liberal perspective, ought to have resolved the problem. Firstly, there would be regular referenda in Ulster on the question of union with Britain in order to meet the fears of the Protestants about having a united Ireland forced onto them. Secondly, a new assembly would replace Stormont, elected on the basis of proportional representation and hence 'fair' to both communities. Thirdly, from the new assembly would be drawn a political executive to exercise devolved governmental power in Ulster. The executive would include Catholic as well as Protestant ministers − the principle of 'power sharing' (or *consociational democracy*). Fourthly, a Council of Ireland would provide a forum for the discussion of matters affecting both Ulster and the Republic, for instance energy co-operation. The assembly was elected and the new executive established but these arrangements proved unacceptable for many Protestants. By a stroke of bad luck for these new arrangements, a general election was also immediately held and in Ulster it was naturally fought on the issue of Sunningdale. The Unionist Party of Brian Faulkner was humiliated in the election and the legitimacy of his party's position in the new assembly and executive called into question. In May a political strike of the Protestant working class finally smashed the new institutions. The British government of Harold Wilson condemned the strike but did not intervene to save the situation, presumably because Northern Ireland was not a major priority.

Nevertheless, British governments have continued to try to establish new liberal institutions in Northern Ireland. In 1975/6 Merlyn Rees established a convention to prepare new power-sharing institutions, but the convention collapsed because 45 of the 75 seats were held by Protestant parties opposed to power sharing. In 1979/80 Humphrey Atkins attempted a similar policy, though with a less ambitious amount of power sharing. This also failed. In 1982 Jim Prior finally re-established an assembly but with extremely limited powers (and no executive governmental powers). However some Protestant parties boycotted even this assembly. Perhaps more seriously from a liberal perspective, the moderate Social Democratic Labour Party lost significant support from the Catholic community and gained 14 seats to the 5 seats gained by Sinn Féin. Both parties boycotted the assembly.

Thus successive attempts by British governments to find acceptable institutional arrangements for Northern Ireland have failed. While moderate Catholics may prefer power sharing and most Protestants favour a revival of the old Stormont, both groups may find continued direct rule from London an acceptable second best. However, one of the objectives of the British governments in pursuing new institutions has undoubtedly been to relieve themselves of the burden of involvement in Northern Ireland. While direct rule may be acceptable from a liberal perspective, direct rule is clearly a poor policy for a government wishing to reduce its involvement in Ireland.

6. *The territorial politics of a 'Dual Polity'*

Jim Bulpitt in *Territory and Power in the United Kingdom* argues that the United Kingdom is a 'dual polity'. By this he means that two relatively independent political systems have existed alongside each other. A London-based political elite (which includes of course provincials who orientate themselves to London), constituting a sort of Court Party, has controlled the 'high politics' of the state, defence and foreign affairs in particular. A distinct set of local elites has managed the 'low politics' of the periphery. The implicit bargain in this arrangement has been mutual non-interference, allowing each a good deal of autonomy within its own sphere. When the English state incorporated the Celtic peripheries within the realm it did so on an informal basis, relying largely on local elites or 'collaborators'. Formalisation of state power, involving a formal union and an enlarged Westminster parliament, was implemented only when there was either a breakdown of informal rule or a severe external crisis in which the ambiguous position of the periphery might be exploited. Normally these two factors tended to coincide. This model helps explain the politics of union with Wales in the 1530s, Scotland in 1707 and Ireland in 1800. Even after formal union, the dual polity system meant that London allowed a high degree of local autonomy.

The dual polity perspective helps explain two aspects of Britain's Irish policy in the twentieth century, namely a lack of consistency and lack of commitment to Northern Ireland. In 1921 Lloyd George was prepared to sell out the northern Protestants to a united Ireland in return for Ireland remaining within the Empire, a pressing high political objective which overrode the interests of Ulster. Perhaps more strikingly, in 1940 Churchill offered De Valera Irish unity in return for an alliance against Germany, another case of high politics requiring a sacrifice of an expendable part of the realm. Towards Ireland itself Britain has first pursued a policy of subjugation, followed by colonial rule, followed by union. After 1921 the government allowed a free hand to Stormont, an extreme case of the dual polity system, because intervention in Ireland spelt trouble. The bipartisan policy of the two parties since 1969 has likewise aimed at keeping Irish problems out of British politics so far as possible, but the chosen instrument of that policy, namely an assembly for Ulster commanding support from both communities has failed and Britain now finds itself bereft of acceptable or powerful collaborators in Ulster.

The implicit conclusion of the dual polity model is that the British would be prepared to abandon Ulster if this could be done without incurring great costs — a very big 'if', of course. Already, Ulster has a formal right to secede from the United Kingdom, a privilege granted no one else. Less dramatically, this model forces us to ask: what interests of Britain are served by remaining in Northern Ireland? We have already argued that the interests of capital in Britain are not much affected and might favour withdrawal. Secondly, the political parties have no interest since they do not organise in Northern Ireland. The Labour party has always been emotionally hostile to the Union, has never organised in Northern Ireland and favours a united Ireland as the best possible outcome. The Unionist Party of Northern Ireland, when it was the organised political instrument of Protestant power, aligned itself with the Conservative party at Westminster. However since Sunningdale the Unionist Party has fragmented and most unionists have become virulently anti-conservative — the Official Unionist party going so far as to keep the Callaghan government in power after 1977. Thirdly, few bureaucratic interests are served by Britain remaining. For the Treasury, Northern Ireland is a major liability; the province consumes much and provides little. For the Ministry of Defence, it is a major and thankless commitment which places strains on the resources of the army. Northern Ireland is also an unwelcome obstacle to the Foreign and Commonwealth Office's conduct of diplomacy with Ireland, the European Community and the United States. Enoch Powell has accused the FCO of attempting to ditch the province. The Northern Ireland Office itself has weak links with any organised interest or constituency and, in obvious contrast to the Scottish or Welsh Offices, a necessary claim to high ministerial office is to have no local connection.

Each of these different languages of analysis contributes something to our understanding of the problem, indeed each defines the problem itself quite distinctly. The Marxist and dual polity models are particularly helpful because they analyse Northern Ireland both from a peripheral and also a metropolitan perspective. The liberal analysis should offer a clear warning to well-intentioned people in Britain who think that better institutions will help resolve the imbroglio. The nationalist perspective suggests that the conflict will remain intractable while two distinct communities lay claim to the same territory.

Alternative policies for the future

The best source for starting to consider alternative policies is Richard Rose, *Northern Ireland: A Time of Choice*. However, it should by now be clear that there is no solution to this problem and that all alternative policies bear massive costs. Any policy has to recognise two fundamental characteristics of the system. The first is that there is no consensus on the rules of the game, no agreement on means let alone on ends. The second is that the state lacks not merely a monopoly over the means of violence and coercion but even lacks a monopoly over what is regarded as legitimate violence. These two characteristics incline one to conclude that there is in fact no 'state' existing in Northern Ireland in any meaningful sense. In these circumstances everything becomes difficult.

1. *Direct rule/integration with the rest of Britain*
Enoch Powell favours this course, but few Ulster people because it means, in effect, rule by non-Ulster people. For Britain it would mean that Ireland became a permanent ingredient of politics. On the other hand, this might be a second best for both communities in Ulster and it enjoys the enormous advantage of representing the status quo. At the moment, all other alternatives appear in contrast fanciful.

2. *Independent Ulster*
Some 'extreme' Protestants favour this course. Those on the left in Britain who demand the withdrawal of British troops, such as Tony Benn, also favour this course, at least by implication, because it would be the consequence of a unilateral British withdrawal. An independent Ulster state would probably be born in civil war and if it survived would be poor and oppressive.

3. *Unilateral British withdrawal*
This policy would probably lead to an independent Ulster. Richard Rose terms a unilateral withdrawal 'Doomsday' with consequences even

worse than a form of negotiated or planned establishment of an independent Ulster. The Protestant community is alleged to be heavily armed and would probably defeat the IRA and many innocent Catholics would die. The Republic would probably be drawn in. Quite aside from considerations of political morality, a British government would fear that the fighting would spill over into Great Britain.

4. *Unification of Ireland*

Unification is a romantic myth of Irish nationalist history. But in practice it is the goal of few people. In Ulster the idea is anathema to Protestants, the Social Democratic Labour Party tolerate British rule and have in effect postponed unification to some remote point in the future and only the IRA actively work for a united Ireland. Viewed from Dublin, unification is hardly less attractive. The Republic is stable, peaceful and relatively prosperous. The tax burdens of unification would be enormous and living standards would fall in north and south. All the achievements of the Republic would be threatened by incorporating a million hostile Protestants – the existing Protestant minority in the south is no precedent for what would happen with unification. Above all for southern politicians, the only united Ireland imaginable in the short term would be one in which the IRA held power.

As if to confirm this view, until recently the Republic made no efforts to overcome the opposition of Ulster protestants to unification. The present government has taken a modest step with the publication in May 1984 of the *New Ireland Forum* which emphasises that the goal of unification can only be reached with consent. This effectively rules out unification for the foreseeable future. The Forum report also discusses federal and confederal systems of government as alternatives to the classical nationalist idea of unity. The British Labour party favours unification by consent as the ideal long-term policy but it also has yet to discover how consent is to be achieved.

5. *Redrawing the border/repartition*

The border could be redrawn to transfer Catholic-dominated areas near to the existing border into the Republic. However these areas are not homogeneously Catholic and there would remain Catholic areas in Ulster, particularly in West Belfast and around Ballycastle in the north, whose relative position would be worse. Protestant opinion opposes conceding a single inch of territory while the IRA, though not necessarily more moderate nationalist opinion, demands unification not border realignment. This alternative is therefore more attractive to British liberal opinion than to Ireland.

6. *Devolution to Northern Ireland*

This remains probably the preferred British solution, certainly for the Conservative party and in practice probably also for a Labour government. But it is very doubtful whether there is a consensus in Ulster for power sharing and this is bound to be a necessary requirement for any significant restoration of powers back to Ulster. Unionists favouring power sharing won only 5 of the 49 unionist seats in the 1975 convention. In 1982 both the SDLP and Sinn Féin boycotted the assembly and later the Official Unionists, the largest party with 26 of the 78 seats, walked out in protest at inadequate British security policies. This left in the assembly only the centre-party Alliance with 10 seats, favouring power sharing, and Ian Paisley's Democratic Unionists with 21 seats, violently opposed to power sharing. In May 1984 the Official Unionists re-entered in order to protest against inadequate British security policies.

Devolution without power sharing is not really a realistic option for Britain, however strong the attractions of partial withdrawal from responsibility for Ulster. In any case, while the army is deployed to combat the IRA, Britain is tied into Ulster's politics and devolution could displace partially but not remove this involvement.

7. *Anglo-Irish condominium*

This is a superficially attractive idea which involves Britain and Ireland assuming a joint responsibility for Ulster. The two communities in Ulster could look either to Britain or the Republic and have a choice of citizenships. The idea is based on the close and growing links between Britain and Ireland in such areas as trade, travel, population movements, enhanced by shared membership of the European Community. The hope would be that the practical significance of territorial and sovereignty questions would be gradually submerged by a growing network of co-operation. The *New Ireland Forum* gives some support to this approach to the problem. An extreme variant of the condominium idea is a broader confederation between Britain and Ireland which would of course undo the 1921 separation of the two states.

The Hillsborough Agreement of November 1985

In the 1980s closer inter-state relations between Britain and Ireland, a modest version of condominium-type arrangements, became an important element in Britain's policy for Ulster. Three factors helped shape this development. The first was the replacement of Charles Haughey's Fianna Fáil government in Dublin by a less overtly nationalist, and anti-British, government of Fine Gail and Labour led by Dr Garret Fitzgerald. The second was the prospect of co-operation between the security forces in the two states to combat the IRA including, on the British side, the prospect that Dublin would accede to the European Convention on the Suppression of Terrorism, allowing the extradition of IRA criminals to Britain. The third was the need of both states to offer tacit support to the SDLP to enable it to remain as the vehicle for nationlist aspirations in Ulster. Sinn Féin gained 5% of the vote in the 1982 assembly elections and subsequently did better. In the May 1985 local elections the party gained 12% compared with 18% for the SDLP.

In November 1981 Margaret Thatcher and Dr Garret Fitzgerald held a first summit meeting and agreed to a system of regular political meetings (the 'Anglo-Irish Intergovernmental Council') and to the possibility of a parliamentary forum involving London, Dublin and the Northern Ireland Assembly. This initiative was denounced by unionists and the IRA but, following a short and difficult period when Charles Haughey resumed the premiership, a second summit was held in November 1983. A third was held a year later and a process of intense bureaucratic and political exchanges then culminated in a fourth summit in November 1985 at Hillsborough Castle. A formal treaty was concluded between the two states, embodying two principles to govern the future relations concerning Ulster. The first principle was that there was to be no change in the status of Northern Ireland without consent; consent which, it was agreed, did not exist. The second principle was the involvement of the Irish government in the government of Northern Ireland through an 'Intergovernmental Conference'. The conference established a permanent machinery, located in Northern Ireland, whereby the bureaucratic, security and political agents of the Irish state were given consultative status in Britain's government of Ulster. Four aspects of co-operation were emphasised: security; economic and social co-operation across the border; administration of justice (including extradition); political development in Ulster where Dublin would help represent the interests of the minority community in the absence of an agreed and widely supported system of devolution. Although the treaty claimed to leave undisturbed the question of sovereignty in Northern Ireland, the treaty represented an unprecedented acceptance by Britain of Dublin's legitimate interests in Ulster and the need to safeguard the interests of the minority community. The Irish government also agreed to accede to the convention on terrorism.

The agreement found many staunch enemies and few strong friends. In Dublin it was opposed by Fianna Fáil. In Westminster the political parties of Great Britain supported it except for tiny minorities on the extreme left of the Labour party and the extreme right of the Conservative party. In Northern Ireland strong support came from the SDLP (which had played a role, behind the scenes, in the whole process) and the Alliance, but the agreement was denounced by the IRA and the unionist parties. The Unionists vilified the agreement as a major extension of the Republic's influence and as a step towards a united Ireland. The Unionist parties returned to the Assembly to demand a referendum on the issue. When this was refused all fifteen Unionist MPs at Westminster resigned and fought a concerted set of by-elections over the issue. In these elections, in February 1986, fourteen of the fifteen MPs were re-elected. In June the British government dissolved the Assembly, leaving Northern Ireland once again under direct rule, though now supplemented by the advisory role of Dublin in the Intergovernmental Conference.

The Unionist campaign against the agreement led, for the first time, to major and sustained violent attacks on the Royal Ulster Constabulary which thus faced opposition from both communities and terrorist attacks from two sets of extremists.

The Hillsborough agreement had promised much but, after its first few months, produced little for the British government. The bolstering up of the SDLP at the expense of Sinn Féin was a gain, but the outbreak of protest and popular unrest a major loss. Relations with the Republic had been consolidated but the future of the Fine Gail-led coalition appeared very uncertain, especially after the failure of its referendum campaign on divorce which revived the importance of the religious divide within Ireland.

Conclusion

By the summer of 1986 the British government had exhausted each of the routes towards 'normality' in Northern Ireland, confirming that there is almost certainly no solution to the problem which is achievable in existing political circumstances. A broader consensus in Northern Ireland, British willingness to accept a major Irish dimension to its internal politics, British readiness to confront the unthinkable option of withdrawal – none of these appears even remotely on the horizon. Direct rule, modified by the Hillsborough Agreement, is therefore likely to remain almost indefinitely as a temporary non-solution to the problem.

However, in contemplating the future two facts should be considered, and in the complexities of Ireland they are probably two of the very few indisputable facts. The first is that the inter-communal conflict in Ulster has an integrity stretching over four centuries and will not easily be resolved or wished away by British politicians exhorting the communities to 'behave reasonably'. The second is that British policy in Ireland has displayed a marked lack of consistency or stability, other than in the negative sense of wishing the problem away. In the long run therefore it is more likely that some form of Irish than some form of British solution will endure.

Reading

D. Birrell: 'Northern Ireland: the obstacles to power sharing', *Political Quarterly*, 1981.

J. G. Bulpitt, *Territory and Power in the United Kingdom*, Manchester University Press, 1983.

A. H. Birch, *Political Integration and Disintegration in the British Isles*, Allen & Unwin, 1978.

R. Rose, *Northern Ireland: A Time of Choice*, Macmillan, 1976.

Cmnd. 7950, *The Government of Northern Ireland: Proposals for Further Discussion* (1980) and Cmnd. 8541, *Northern Ireland: A Framework for Devolution* (1982) are the Conservative government's two main contributions to the problem of devolved government.

New Ireland Forum, Irish Government Publications, Dublin, 1984 (the British press discussed the report extensively in May 1984).

The Hillsborough Agreement of 15 November 1986 is contained in Cmnd. 9657 and was discussed extensively in the British press at the time.

Crime and punishment

This chapter examines the perennially topical problem of law and order, seeking to place it within the context of the current political debate. Law and order in relation to political ideas is examined together with the extent of crime, its causes and society's responses to it.

Law and order and political ideas

The attitudes we have towards law and order depend to a substantial degree upon our assessments of what human nature is really like. Some philosophers have taken a pessimistic view. For Thomas Hobbes human nature was such that in a state of nature, life would be, in his famous phrase, 'nasty, solitary, brutish and short'. Machiavelli was more specific: 'it may be said of men in general that they are ungrateful, voluble dissemblers, anxious to avoid danger and covetous of gain'. Others were more sanguine. Rousseau, for example, believed that 'man is naturally good and only by institutions is he made bad'. Similarly, Marx, following his precept that 'environment determines consciousness' believed that it was the harshness of the capitalist economic system which was responsible for man's shortcomings.

For pessimists like Hobbes, chaotic anarchy could only be prevented through the agency of an all powerful state, a 'Leviathan' which could impose order through overwhelming force. For optimists like Marx the problem of lawlessness could only be solved by fundamental changes in society which would refashion human nature and produce laws based upon fairness and justice rather than the interests of the capitalist ruling class.

The debate about law and order still revolves around these familiar and ultimately unresolvable themes. Conservatives tend to support the pessimistic or what they would call 'realistic' analysis. They believe 'respect for the rule of laws is the basis of free and civilised society' (1979 Manifesto) and,

(1) See the problem of crime primarily from the viewpoint of its victims rather than its perpetrators.

(2) Support a deterrent strategy, i.e. stiffer penalties.

(3) Believe individuals have free will and should be accountable for their actions. Everyone, rich and poor, has the choice of obeying or breaking the law but if they take the latter course they should be in no doubt as to the penalties they must face.

Labour and the SDP—Liberal Alliance tend to take a more optimistic, some would say, idealistic line. They believe that:

(1) Crime has social cause e.g. poverty, poor housing, unemployment, which are remediable through social policy.

(2) Deterrent strategies involving greater police powers and penalties should not be pursued to the point when civil liberties are unacceptably eroded.

(3) The criminal has rights too: penal policy should be humanised and more emphasis placed on rehabilitation rather than punishment.

In the late seventies Mrs Thatcher took up a tough right-wing stance, stating in the run up to the 1979 election that: 'The demand in this country will be for two things: less tax and more law and order' (*Daily Telegraph*, 29 March 1979). The manifesto reflected this emphasis on law and order, claiming that 'Labour has undermined it'. During the campaign, 87% of Conservative candidates mentioned this subject in election addresses. There is little doubt that all this rhetoric struck a resonant note: an ITN election night survey indicated that 23% of respondents who had switched their support to the Conservatives had done so primarily over this issue. The Conservatives have clearly succeeded in making themselves the party of 'law and order'. A MORI poll for the *Sunday Times* in November 1985 revealed that 45% of those questioned judged the Tories best equipped to deal with increasing crime, compared with 19% for Labour and 9% for the Alliance. The irony here is that, according to some analyses, (see below) it is Conservative economic and social policies which are exacerbating the causes of crime in the first place.

The extent of the problem: is there a crime wave?

'The number of crimes in England and Wales is nearly half as much again as it was in 1973' stated the Conservative 1979 Manifesto. Mrs Thatcher's government, however, did not stem the tide; notifiable offences rose by 44% from about a quarter of a million offences in 1979 to about 3·6 million in 1985. Table 5 gives the details.

Table 5 *Notifiable offences recorded by police by offence group*

	Percentage increase					
	1981	*1982*	*1983*	*1984*	*1985*	*1985 ('000s)*
Violence against the person	+ 3	+ 8	+2	+ 3	+ 7	121·7
Sexual offences	− 8	+ 2	+1	− 1	+ 6	21·5
Burglary	+16	+12	−	− 1	+ 6	871·3
Robbery	+35	+ 3	−3	+13	+10	27·5
Thefts & handling stolen goods	+10	+10	−3	+ 6	+ 4	1,884·1
Fraud and forgery	+ 1	+15	−1	+ 7	+16	134·8
Criminal damage	+ 8	+ 8	+6	+ 8	+ 3	539·0
Other offences	−	− 7	−	+19	+17	12·2
TOTAL	+10	+10	−1	+ 8	+ 3	3,611·9

Source: Home Office Statistical Bulletin, 12 June 1986.

The increase in violent crime is particularly worrying. The number of notifiable offences recorded by the police in which firearms were reported to have been used increased, according to Home Office figures in August 1985, from under 3,000 in 1974, to over 9,000 in 1983. The inner city riots in the autumn of 1985 also alarmed the British public. Hundreds of police were injured in all three riot areas, two Asians died in Handsworth, a policeman was murdered in Tottenham and pistol shots were fired on the police.

Furthermore, the Home Office sponsored *British Crime Survey* (BCS) of 1981 suggested that large numbers of offences are never reported and hence never recorded, e.g. half of all burglaries,, over 90% of vandalism, nearly 90% of robberies and over 70% of sexual offences. The 'dark figure' of unrecorded crime in fact may be four or five times higher than official police figures.

In statistical terms these figures might well be interpreted as the 'crime wave' of which the Conservatives and the popular press make so much. However, a number of important qualifications have to be made which challenge this conclusion.

(1) It is far from clear whether the level of unrecorded crime has increased by the same proportions as recorded crime. One Home Office survey of burglary and theft concluded that the actual rise in these offences was only *1% per year* from 1972–80 compared with the officially recorded figure of *4% per year*. It was the *proportion* of crimes recorded which had sharply increased, in this instance possibly because of more widespread use of property insurance.

(2) Much crime is relatively trivial, recorded or not. The 1984 BCS showed that 62% of vandalism cases, 60% of motor vehicle thefts, 63% or burglaries and 51% of thefts from the person were not reported to the police because no damage was involved and no property taken. In 1984 65% of home burglaries committed involved thefts of property worth less than £100.

(3) Britain is less violent now than it used to be. A report (E.G. Dunning *et al.*) from Leicester University revealed that whilst reported violent disturbances in the UK (excluding Northern Ireland) had increased since the war years the rate in 1975 was less than a third of that of 1900, *despite* a 46% increase in the population during that period.

(4) In a society of material plenty and the 'hard sell', the opportunities for crime are much greater and the motivation sharper. And the growth of more plentiful laws and regulations — especially at work — means that there are more crimes now to commit.

(5) More efficient police recording procedures also help explain the increase together with the 10% increase in police manpower since 1979 available for such duties.

(6) When placed in certain perspectives the chances of being the victim of crime is remarkably low. The 1981 BCS (p. 15) showed that

a statistically average person of 16 or over can expect
   * a robbery once every five centuries (not attempts)
   * an assault resulting in injury (even if slight) once every century.
   * the family car to be stolen or taken by joyriders once every sixty years.
   * a burglary in the house once every forty years.

As the BCS observes, 'small upward changes in either reporting or recording can all too readily create a "crime wave"' (p. 14). Can we conclude then — as some on the left do — that the crime wave is merely a creation of the press and politicians playing upon popular fears for political gain? Perhaps. Some experts use the above factors to explain the fifteen fold increase in crime in 1981 compared with the early 1930s. Others disagree and assert that sharp real increases have occurred particularly in violent crime, burglary, robbery and theft. Moreover, statistical averages mask the fact that for certain people, i.e. young, working-class males, especially blacks, living in areas like the inner cities, the risks are much higher. For example survey evidence indicates that you are twice as likely to be burgled if you are an unskilled worker than if you are a professional (Lea and Young, p.26).

Crime wave or not, crime is indeed a major problem as anyone, especially old people, who have suffered the trauma of a burglary know only too well. Certainly statistics can lie, newspapers sensationalise and politicians exaggerate but there is a legitimate cause for concern. Moreover, the principal victims of crime are not, as one might expect, the propertied middle classs, but those least able to afford loss: working-class people themselves.

Fear of crime is arguably as much of a problem as crime itself, blighting peoples' lives and causing yet more crime through emptying streets at night and thus removing social constraints upon criminal actions. The BCS (p.23) revealed that 60% of elderly women living in inner city areas felt 'very unsafe' when walking alone in their locality after dark. Over half of all women in inner city areas sometimes avoided going out at night and 8% of all respondents *never* went out alone at night through fear of crime.

The irony is that fear of crime seems to be experienced in inverse proportion to actual risk; for example, only 1% of men aged 16−30 felt 'very unsafe' yet they are the group most likely to be victims: women over sixty, on the other hand, are the least likely to be victims of crime. Again, statisticians, the press and politicians, can be blamed for whipping up unnecessary and morbid fears but it is also understandable that the old and frail should fear what, for them, might be catastrophic − even if rare − events.

The causes of crime

What are the causes of crime? Two broad analyses can be identified which typify positions on the right and left; many 'centrist' positions, of course, exist in between them.

The right-wing analysis

This approach sees crime as fundamentally a matter of values.

(1) Human beings have a natural disposition towards acts which give personal pleasure or advantage, even at the expense of others; as Mrs Thatcher asserts, 'man is inherently sinful'. This predilection is kept in check by the ideas and habits of self-discipline which have been inculcated by the church, family life, social institutions, the law and those entrusted with authority.

(2) The ideas and actions of the left, so the analysis runs, have eroded this self discipline by rejecting religion, crucially weakening the role of the family and undermining both the law and traditional institutions like schools. This misguided permissiveness, combined with the over-protective institutions of the welfare state have created an atmosphere in which citizens have abandoned self restraint and discipline for free licence and reliance upon the state.

(3) Excessive immigration of alien peoples, say the right, has created tensions and further weakened cultural restraints against lawless behaviour.

(4) Trade unions, aided actively by extremist left wing groups and tacitly by the Labour Party, have increasingly ignored the law and used violence and intimidation − 'the rule of the mob' to quote Mrs Thatcher − to achieve their industrial and political objectives.

The left-wing analysis

This puts the blame for crime principally at the door of capitalism. This approach:

(1) dismisses right-wing arguments as a mere rationalisation of ruling-class interests; many of the 'values' which workers are enjoined to embrace are those which favour not them but the ruling middle class.

(2) asserts that capitalism produces great inequalities of wealth and gives vastly inferior life chances to the poor whilst imbuing them with an ideology of material acquisition and career success. Because capitalism denies what it induces people to pursue it causes crime. American radical Angela Davies puts the argument in its purest form: 'The real criminals in this society are not all the people who populate the prisons across the state but those who have stolen the wealth of the world from the people'.

(3) sees the law as protecting the privileges of the rich through prosecuting and punishing 'working-class crime' such as robbery and vandalism with much greater energy than 'middle-class crime', e.g.

fraud and expenses fiddling. For example, in 1981 the state lost £4 million a week through social security frauds and made 576 prosections, yet lost £80 million through tax evasion and made only two prosecutions per week. Moreover, since 1979 the Conservative government has taken on one thousand social security investigators yet has actually reduced the size of the tax inspectorate (Downes: p. 5).

(4) The racial allegation is deliberately used by the right to stir up ill-informed prejudice and divert attention from the real causes of crime.

Unemployment

These rival analyses have clashed bitterly in recent years over the issue of unemployment. The left point to the close correlation between soaring unemployment and mounting crime and see a natural causal relationship. The right wing, typified by Mrs Thatcher, vehemently deny the connection, attributing rising crime to the growing lawlessness which Labour's policies have helped to bring about. They point out that in the thirties unemployment increased whilst crime figures actually decreased. More moderate Conservatives however accept that some connection is bound to exist, for example, Michael Heseltine, William Whitelaw, and Francis Pym who observes that unemployment has helped produce an 'increase in crime and lawlessness and occasional outbreaks of anger and frustration as evidenced in the riots of 1981' (Pym, p. 19).

Inner City Riots

The contrasting political explanations were clearly displayed at the time of the 1981 and 1985 inner-city riots:

Conservative politicians, newspapers and police officers ... ascribed the riots to criminality and greed, hooliganism and 'mindless violence', extremists and subversives, imitation, base impulses in human nature, or to a failure in education and a breakdown in family life and proper values. Douglas Hurd said after the Handsworth disorder that it was 'not a social phenomenon but crimes': it was 'not a cry for help but a cry for loot'. Mr Norman Tebbit ... said after the Tottenham riots that they were the result of 'wickedness', and he later suggested that the moral degeneration was a legacy of the permissive society of the 1960s (Benyon, p. 6).

Labour politicians pointed instead to the 50–60% youth unemployment in the riot areas, police harassment of young blacks and a breakdown of trust in the police, environmental decay, poor schools, social services and leisure provision, racial discrimination in employment, and the fact that inner-city communities lacked representation on the decision-making bodies which could affect their lives and determine their futures.

Responses to crime

Just as political opinions differ over the causes of crime, so there are sharp disagreements as to the most effective and morally acceptable responses to it.

Changes in values
At the most fundamental level, politicians argue, society must change so that values will alter and crimes be reduced. The extent of this change usually constitutes the ideological aims of the political creed involved. For right-wing Conservatives this would entail the creation of a free market economy and the dismantling of the welfare state; this would help facilitate a return to the law-abiding virtues of the Victorian era with its emphasis upon family life and obligations, self-reliance and personal accountability. For the socialist the necessary changes in values will only occur when the economy is based upon cooperation not competition, with more equal distribution of wealth and life opportunities. How long will it take to effect these changes? As long as rival political ideologies are locked in insoluble conflict neither side will win; even Mrs Thatcher's huge 1983 majority has not enabled her to move very far towards her stated goals. It does not follow either that any political analysis is correct, that any wholly victorious political ideology will substantially reduce crime. Inevitably, in the meantime much emphasis is placed upon effective police action.

Policing
Conservatives believe a strengthened police force is an essential high priority response to the increase in crime. Accordingly, between 1979–83 they raised spending on the police by over 20%, increased the number of police in England and Wales by 9,500 to 120,000, raised police pay by some 30%, improved anti-riot equipment and put more policemen back on the beat. Mrs Thatcher and her ministers were emphatic in their praise for the police throughout the extended bitterness of the 1984 miners' strike and were keen that police powers should be increased through the Criminal Evidence Bill. This measure extended powers for the police regarding: stop and search (including body

seaches); road checks; the searching of premises; and, most contentiously, detention of suspects without trial for up to ninety-six hours instead of the previous twenty-four hours, and for the first thirty-six hours incommunicado without access to legal advice. On the other hand, the Act created, against fierce police criticism, an independent authority to investigate complaints against the police instead of the previous procedure controlled by the police themselves. In 1986 a new public order act gave the police more power and discretion to curb or control demonstrations, marches and picketing.

Criticisms of this pro-police line are offered by left and centrist socialists, the Alliance, academic experts and many others.

(*a*) Labour left-wingers assert that the police pay awards were a deliberate ploy by Mrs Thatcher to buy their support for their role in containing the social disruption which she knew her policies would cause.

(*b*) Some experts point out that spending on the police is not especially cost-effective in that (i) only a tiny part of their time is spent on crime fighting – the major part of their time being spent on other duties (Downes, p. 12); (ii) increased beat duty – according to a 1984 Home Office Study – offers only a negligible deterrent to crime.

(*c*) Other critics believe that all is not well in the police force, pointing out that:

(i) the 'clear up' rate of reported crimes has actually dropped from over 40% in the late seventies to 35% in 1984.

(ii) despite vigorous earlier denials by the police and their supporters, investigations in the seventies revealed extensive corruption especially in the Metropolitan Police. 'Altogether eighteen men of varying ranks from constable to commander were sentenced to over a hundred years imprisonment, including terms of 12, 10 and 8 years in the worst cases' (Sir Robert Mark, *In the Office of Constable,* 1978, ch. 20).

(iii) a report into the Metropolitan Police by the Policy Studies Institute revealed widespread racist and sexist attitudes together with frequent drunkenness on duty. Yet despite this, and the occasional well publicised incompetence – e.g. the shooting of the innocent Stephen Waldorf in mistake for the wanted David Martin in 1983 – only 10% of Londoners registered complete lack of confidence in their police. The majority were satisfied with the service provided.

(*d*) At present the police are allowed to arrest and prosecute. Critics have long called for an independent prosecuting service for England and Wales, rather like the system used in Scotland.

(*e*) Those concerned with civil liberties identify a worrying erosion since Mrs Thatcher has been in power. The Police and Criminal Evidence Act was seen to give the police a frightening amount of power and the new public order act was criticised as more draconian than any similar legislation in America, France or West Germany.

(*f*) The received wisdom that the best policing is done by forces in close touch with local communities was strengthened by the 1981 riots in Brixton where it was obvious that relations had collapsed. Labour and Alliance critics stress the importance of this approach and urge that local police forces be made formally accountable to local communities.

(*g*) The specially trained Special Patrol Groups for use in public order roles have been condemned by many critics as provocative and aggressive. Moreover, the use of police – again specially trained – in support of disturbances caused by government industrial relations policy – most notably the 1984 miners' strike – has been condemned by left-wing critics as a quasi-political role for what should be a wholly non-political body. Gerald Kaufman, Labour's Shadow Home Secretary, was particularly worried by the formation of the National Reporting Centre, the centralised body which coordinated action against the flying pickets. He feared the 'embryonic growth of an uncontrolled national police force ... a potential national police militia' (*Guardian*, 7 September 84).

(*h*) Concern has also been voiced that the police have been allowed to use a wide range of surveillance techniques, e.g. phone taps, which constitute severe erosions of civil liberties.

Penal policy

Once offenders have been apprehended by the police and found guilty by the courts, they have to be dealt with in some suitable fashion. What principles should underlie their treatment?

Right-wing Conservatives believe in retribution and deterrence. Wrongdoers must be punished according to the severity of their crimes to the extent that they – and other potential criminals – will be deterred from committing such acts in the future. If crimes continue to increase notwithstanding, then penalties clearly need to be increased even further. Mrs Thatcher told a conference of the American Bar

Association in July 1985 of 'the very real anxiety of ordinary people that too many sentences do not fit the crime'. No doubt she had in mind the reintroduction of the death penalty for murder and longer sentences for serious or persistent offenders. The Conservative Party Conference regularly calls for such measures and Mrs Thatcher has appeared to endorse some of these previously unfashionable ideas. This has placed recent Home Secretaries in a more than usually difficult position in that, when faced with the complex reality of crime and punishment in society, they have been trapped by their own vote-winning rhetoric. William Whitelaw – Home Secretary 1979–83 – was unable to conceal his relatively liberal proclivities behind his right-wing conference pronouncements and was consequently much criticised for his alleged softness. He must have felt a good deal of sympathy with many Labour and Alliance critics of his own right wing, especially over the issue of capital punishment.

(*a*) *Capital punishment* Mrs Thatcher, who favours capital punishment but believes it to be a matter of conscience rather than party policy, promised a free vote on the issue if she returned to power after the 1983 election. Throughout July a lively public debate took place. Against the retributive and deterrent arguments were adduced the following: it would be a retrograde step for a civilised society; Britain in any case has a low level of murders – 616 in 1985 compared with over 18,000 in the USA; there is little or no evidence to suggest that murders have increased appreciably since the death penalty was abolished; it would put added pressures upon judges and juries; would remove the possibility of freeing those wrongly convicted; and in the case of political terrorists would merely play into their hands through making them martyrs.

When it came to the debate, the reinforced Conservative right wing proved less resolute than many expected and the proposals were emphatically rejected.

(*b*) *Prisons* The tendency of courts in recent years to commit more people to prison – from 16% of adult males convicted of indictable offences in England and Wales in 1973, to 20% in 1983 – has created a number of problems and occasioned much criticism along the following lines:

(i) to deprive people of their liberty is a very severe punishment which should be used rarely e.g. 'only where there is extreme danger to the community' (Lea & Young, p. 267).

(ii) The aim of prison should be to rehabilitate, not merely to punish. The Barlinnie Special Unit in Glasgow revealed that even hardened criminals — Jimmy Boyle is the best known — can be reclaimed for society given appropriate attitudes and resources.

(iii) Less than 10% of those in prison are murderers, rapists and armed robbers whilst about one half are there for persistent, non-serious offences: alternative sentences could and should be found for the latter.

(iv) A wealth of respectable evidence suggests that prison is not only very expensive — £639 million in 1985–6 — but also ineffective in that recidivism (the rate at which offenders return to crime) is high. The Advisory Council on the Penal System reported 'Neither practical experience nor the results of research in recent years have established the superiority of custodial over non-custodial methods in their effect upon renewed recidivism'. Indeed there is evidence to suggest that the enclosed criminal sub-culture of prison actually encourages recidivism. A NACRO report produced in 1985 revealed that the UK imprisons 274 people per 100,000 of the population compared with 207 in Italy, 199 in West Germany, 140 in France and 78 in Portugal. Only the USA, USSR and South Africa imprison more. The report concludes that our use of prison is 'both excessive and ineffective'. The fact that one-third of our prison population is there for burglary and that 68% of them are re-convicted within 6 years would appear to support this view.

(v) According to Whitelaw himself, the conditions in our prisons are an 'affront to civilised society'. In 1978 there were 42,220 prisoners: 9·7% more than the prisons had been designed for. By February 1986, despite a much publicised prison-building programme the figure had risen to 46,617: 14% over the top limit. Conditions are insanitary and desperately overcrowded. Five thousand or so live three to a cell designed for one, often without toilet or washing facilities. To deprive offenders of their liberty is one thing but to lock them up in such conditions for up to twenty-three hours a day with minimal work and educational opportunities is to add an inhuman dimension to an already harsh punishment. Many reformers call for: legislation to protect prisoners' rights regarding conditions — especially cell space; better leisure services inside prisons and better resettlement care for those leaving prison.

(vi) Some research by criminologists and polling organisations suggests that public opinion is less retributive than right wingers claim. The 1984 British Crime Survey revealed that 67% thought fines were better than prison for non-violent offences. And a 1985 NACRO poll showed that only a third of people burgled believed that the offenders concerned should have been imprisoned.

(*c*) *Non-custodial alternatives*   Opponents of prison as the answer to crime look to alternatives which will reclaim offenders for the law-abiding majority in society and will also do something to help their victims.

(i) *Victim restitution* schemes have been very successfully experimented with in America: offenders are brought face to face with their victims and required to make amends.

(ii) *Community service orders* whereby offenders work off their debt to society through undertaking worthwhile tasks have been in existence for some time. In 1981 only 5% of indictable offenders were dealt with in this way but many urge its more extensive use.

(iii) *Other alternatives* to prison like fines, probation, supervision orders are also urged as preferable, more effective alternatives to prison. Whitelaw's attempt to introduce a supervised early release scheme for short-term prisoners was nipped in the bud by opposition from the senior echelons of the judiciary and his own right wing. Some critics, such as Downes, also point out that prison is used more for working-class crimes; middle-class crime which is largely financial and occupational is 'almost invariably dealt with informally or by negotiation rather than by the police and the courts' (p. 9).

(*d*) *Juvenile crime*   The response to the worrying growth in crime by 14–16 year olds, by both Labour and Conservative governments, has been greatly to increase custodial sentences: they actually rose at *four times* the rate of juvenile crime during the seventies. The present Conservative government has reinforced this trend by its establishment of four detention centres with tough military regimes to deter young offenders from a life of crime by a 'short sharp shock'. Critics argue, however, that such treatment is mostly counter-productive: it merely serves to alienate young people and socialise them into the alternative sub-culture of the criminal world. The recidivism rate from detention centres is over 70% and from Borstal over 80%.

(*e*) *Crime prevention*   This approach asks whether money spent on preventing crime might not be more cost effective than policing and punishment of offenders. It lays some responsibility upon individuals and the community to make crime more difficult and therefore less likely. The need to rehabilitate offenders and thus reduce recidivism has already been mentioned but a number of other possibilities exist.

(i) A greater sense of community awareness and repsonsibility could be inculcated, especially in young people. In Cuba and China, for example, regular street meetings put moral pressure on people to be law abiding and greater efforts are made to re-absorb offenders into society.

(ii) Property can be made more secure by individuals, companies and public services. In West Germany car thefts plummeted after the introduction of steering column locks in the sixties; in Sweden cheque card frauds did likewise when affixed photographs were introduced as a requirement; crime and vandalism on tube trains are reduced when closed circuit television is installed.

(iii) Neighbourhood Watch schemes, whereby residents undertake to keep a look-out for and report crime in their area have burgeoned in recent years. Some 8,000 schemes have been created, encouraged by Sir Kenneth Newman (Commissioner of the Metropolitan Police) – half of them in London. One negative result, however, appears to have been a compensating increase in street crime. A variation on this approach was worked out in a valley near Caerphilly where residents marked valuables with their postcode and indicated the fact with window stickers. The result? A 40% decrease in burglaries.

A penal policy which gives more emphasis to crime prevention seems sensible but how far should it go before our quality of life is adversely affected? Should we, for example, turn our houses into fortresses or never go out at night? Should all customers be searched before they leave shops? Some people may justifiably opt for a greater risk of crime in exchange for maintaining a tolerable way of life.

Concluding comments

Despite the protestations of right-wing Conservatives, common sense – as well as Lord Scarman and others – tells us that deteriorating socio-economic conditions must be causally related to the increase in crime. As the inner cities continue to decline and more young people join the long-term unemployed (or even unemployable), then we can expect vandalism, robbery, burglary and other forms of crime to proliferate.

But there is one reason why crime might begin to decline in a few years' time, and it has nothing to do with increased policing, or alleviation of social deprivation. Nearly 50% of convicted offenders are aged 15–19. During the seventies this age group increased by 16%, explaining, perhaps, the crime wave from a demographic point of view. Between 1985 and 1993, however, this crime prone age group will decrease by 26%. As *The Economist* commented (9 November 1985),

> Maybe an even higher proportion of them will commit crimes. Maybe the extra, more expensive policemen will record a higher proportion of the crimes they do commit. But it will be very odd indeed if recorded crime does not rise much more slowly than in recent years. The government will be able, at last, to justify the electorate's faith in its ability to control crime – thanks not to greater public spending in the 1980's, but to a change in the British people's breeding habits 20 years ago.

Reading

J. Lea & J. Young, *What is to be done about Law and Order? Crisis in the Eighties*, Penguin, 1984. (A clear and interesting discussion by two sociologists.)

David Downes, *Law and Order: Theft of an Issue*, Fabian Tract 490, Fabian Society, 1983. (An excellent informative essay written from a committed position.)

Colin Moore & John Brown, *Community Versus Crime*, Bedford Square Press, 1981.

National Association for the Care and Resettlement of Offenders (NACRO), *The Use of Imprisonment – Some Facts and Figures*. (169 Clapham Road, London SW9 0PV.)

Mike Hough & Pat Mayhew, *The British Crime Survey*, A Home Office Research and Planning Unit Report, No. 76, HMSO, 1983.

Home Office Research Unit, *Fear of Crime*, HMSO, 1984.

Home Office Statistical Bulletins, Issue 5/84, (15 March 1984) & 16/86 (12 June 1986).

John Benyon, 'Turmoil in the Cities', *Social Studies Review*, Vol. No. 3, January 1986, pp. 3–8.

John Benyon & Colin Bourn (eds.), *The Police: Powers, Procedures and Proprieties*, Pergamon, 1986.

The Economist regularly publishes excellent analyses on law and order.

I am grateful to Dr Ken Pease for useful comments on this chapter.

The peace movement

This chapter examines the growth of the peace movement in recent years. It concentrates upon the nature and tactics of the British movement and analyses the problems it seeks to overcome.

Factors behind the rise of the peace movement

(1) *Deteriorating East–West relations*

The 1977 proposal by the Carter administration to deploy the neutron bomb in Europe was an important one – the concept of a weapon that emitted more radiation to kill people, without as much damage to buildings through blast, seemed immoral to many and focused attention upon shifts in Pentagon strategy which appeared to bring nuclear war nearer. However, the strongly negative European response to the neutron bomb (1 million signatures to a Dutch petition) led to its deferment and an important success for the protestors.

The election of Ronald Reagan in 1980 produced further alarm. Committed to increased defence spending and viewing Soviet Communism as 'evil', Reagan had repudiated Carter's SALT II (Strategic Arms Limitation Treaty). In 1981 he spoke of his belief in the possibility of a 'limited' nuclear war in Europe and Secretary of State Haig, mentioned the possibility of dropping a 'demonstration' bomb on the East. The deployment of Cruise and Pershing II missiles, agreed in 1979, seemed to make war a more feasible option and in 1982 the *New York Times* released US Defense Department plans for a protracted nuclear war.

In March 1983 President Reagan issued his 'Star Wars' directive to scientists for the development of laser defence systems – a potentially seriously destabilising measure – and during the year the Soviets broke off three sets of arms limitation talks – on intermediate range nuclear weapons, the Strategic Arms Reduction Talks (START) and on accidental nuclear war. Threatening to 'launch on warning' the USSR increased its stocks of SS20 and SS22 missiles and moved the latter into East Germany and Czechoslovakia – in range of Britain. The Bradford University School of Peace Studies predicted a doubling of arsenals within ten years. In 1980 BBC Radio announced an opinion poll showing that 40% of respondents thought nuclear war likely within ten years.

While distrust of the Soviet Union remained high in the light of its policy towards Poland and invasion of Afghanistan, more people questioned the US relationship. Plans for a new nuclear war bunker (1982) and the possible deployment of Minuteman missiles in Britain (1984) were revealed, and a central issue became the control of Cruise missiles based in Britain. The SDP, in particular, pressed for a real 'dual key' arrangement, i.e. a British veto over firing the missiles. A 1981 *Observer*-NOP poll showed 53% wanting American bases removed from Britain, and a 1983 poll showed 73% distrusting American guarantees of joint control of Cruise missiles (*Sunday Times*, 30 October 83).

(2) *New weapons*

(*a*) *Accuracy* Not only was the number of weapons increasing in the late 1970s and early 1980s, but they were undergoing a technological change: Pershing II and Cruise missiles were deemed to be highly accurate. Cruise, SS20s and the MX system (an American plan to install 200 intercontinental ballistic missiles under 6,000 square miles of desert) were all mobile systems. Mobility and accuracy against military targets were said by many experts to increase the likelihood of use.

(*b*) *Accidents* The Americans estimated that thirty-six accidents involving nuclear weapons had occurred since 1945, including the very near explosion of a twenty-four megaton bomb in North Carolina and the contamination of Palormares, Spain, after three ten-megaton bombs were dislodged in 1966. Between 1950–76, sixteen submarine collisions occurred in Soviet waters.

Technological advances have not improved the risks – it was disclosed that the US Airforce Defense computer, NORAD, produced two false alarms every three days by 1983. Cruise and Pershing had development problems, and in August 1984 the US Navy recalled a third of its Trident missiles because of faulty microchip mechanisms. During one year, 3,647 people with access to nuclear weapons were moved due to alcoholism, drug abuse, mental illness or indiscipline (US Congressional evidence). And in May 1986 the US Navy admitted to 628 incidents and 2 accidents involving nuclear weapons over 20 years, including submarines running aground near Gibraltar and in the Irish Sea.

(c) *Cost*   Critics have claimed that defence spending in the UK, which exceeds expenditure on the NHS, has a distorting effect on the economy. Besides the 10% of government income, it takes 60% of technological resources – the Ministry of Defence alone employs 25,000 of our best scientists and engineers.

Trident has been particularly singled out for criticism, as original costings soon doubled to 10–12 billion. CND translate this into £200 for every man, woman and child, or the yearly food bill for 7 million families. Alternatively, for the price of two Trident submarines half the Third World could be given primary schools and teacher training facilities and Britain's 385 Tornado bombers would build 320,000 new homes (Kennard & Sissons). Doubts about the usefulness of Trident by Conservatives and military figures e.g. Field Marshall Lord Carver, have reinforced their arguments.

(3) *Wider movements*
Peace groups in Britain have been assisted by being part of a wider opposition, which did not exist during the 1960s period of CND activity.

(a) *European Nuclear Disarmament (END)*   END was formed in 1980 when it was decided that national protest was insufficient. The culmination came in October 1981 with rallies of 250,000 in Bonn, 100,000 in Oslo, 50,000 in Paris, 50,000 in Potsdam (E. Germany), 80,000 in Helsinki, 120,000 in Brussels, 150,000 in London and a similar number in Rome. The demonstration in Amsterdam brought out 500,000 (one-thirtieth of the Dutch population). END's role is one of publication and communication – linking groups as diverse as the Campaign Against Military Bases in Iceland, West German Greens, Dutch Interchurch Peace Council and Italian Eurocommunists.

In July 1982 END organised its convention to press for a nuclear-free western Europe. Three months later two million protested against Cruise and Pershing II missiles.

(*b*) *US Freeze Campaign*   Gaining publicity and strength at the same time was the American Nuclear Weapons Freeze Campaign, supported by Senators Kennedy and Hatfield. Only months before, American protest was confined to a few groups such as SANE and Pax Christi; by 1982 60% of US voters, the bishops and the House of Representatives supported the 'freeze'. In November 1985 a Freeze Campaign was launched in the UK, with the support of senior politicians from all parties, but under the chairmanship of actress Jane Asher. They organised a Marplan poll showing 72% support, with an interesting 84% in favour of a test ban if the USSR offered one – they were not told they already had done.

(*c*) *Multilateralism*   An example of such movements was the launch in November 1984 of an international programme based on the Aspen Institute in New York. In the UK former Prime Ministers Heath and Callaghan joined Shirley Williams of the SDP on the same platform.

(*d*) *Environmentalists*   The rise of Friends of the Earth, Greenpeace and the Ecology Party in the early 1970s coincided with a lull in CND activity. Indeed, the latter had favoured 'atoms for peace' in its early days. Gradually their aims began to coincide as the effects of radiation were explored. *Non-Nuclear Futures* by Amory Lovins, and the Flowers Report of 1976 drew attention to the link between civil and military nuclear processes. The 1977 Windscale inquiry and the 1977 Anti-Nuclear Campaign cemented the alliance. CND and FOE now give mutual support at demonstrations, and in 1984 jointly campaigned aginst the Sizewell nuclear reactor.

British activities

(1) *Information*
Information about preparations for and the effects of nuclear war is the lifeblood of the peace movement. Governments' habit of secrecy often stores up trouble – such as the revelation in 1980 that a secret £1 billion modernisation of Polaris missiles (Chevaline) had been undertaken.

Perhaps the most effective impact came through film. In 1976

CND's membership increased as it staged 'All Against the Bomb' on BBC 2's *Open Door* programme. In the same year they purchased *The War Game*, commissioned by the BBC in 1965 but not shown for fear of 'irrational reaction'; this still powerful film was shown to 20,000 people over the next two years. Recent dramas have included *The Day After*, seen by 70 million in America and 15 million in Britain, and *Threads*, a two-hour British production showing the devastation of Sheffield and ensuing horrors. Such programmes generated considerable debate. On the documentary side were *QED: A Guide to Armageddon* (July 1982), *The Truth Game* (ITV October 1982) and Panorama's screening of the official pre-war film for the public (spring 1982).

The Civil Defence pamphlet 'Protect and Survive' was a restricted document but was released for sale by the Home Office. Its practical DIY advice on building a shelter includes the removal of potentially incendiary newspapers and the disposal of dead members of the family. By 1982 E. P. Thompson's riposte *Protest and Survive* had sold over 100,000 copies.

The Home Office also provided predictions of the holocaust through its civil defence exercises – Operation Square Leg envisaged twenty-nine million dead, and Hard Rock was said to have been scaled down to an unrealistic three million to preserve morale. CND sold the maps of devastation. In November 1983 a copy of the computerised training course on post-nuclear Britain 'reached' the *Sunday Times*, and Granada TV released details of the most vulnerable areas to attack from a Whitehall scientific seminar the following month.

The GLC commissioned a £475,000 study which reported in March 1986 after 2 years that in an attack on London one-third would try to leave amid panic, food-hoarding and desertion of jobs.

The British Medical Association assisted the process by conducting a two-year study into the effect of nuclear war and reported, in March 1983, that even one bomb would overwhelm the health service and any more would mean chaos. Doctors then demanded non-co-operation with government plans, and a Royal College of Nursing report saw no role for their own service. Plans to use private hospitals, store medical supplies and issue a new NHS war plan showed the government was pressing ahead regardless. A survey helped by the World College of Physicians revealed in March 1986 that 20% thought war plans a waste of time, over half favoured them to show they were impossible, 45% of health authorities had not started planning and 10% did not intend to.

(2) *The tactics and organisation of the peace movement*

(a) *Resources* Their most important asset is expertise. Like the 1960s CND, the 1980s version is predominantly middle class and professional. The main developments seem to have been the greater involvement of women and the perception of disarmament as a moral rather than a political issue. Contributions of time, money and organising skill could be offered in ample measure.

The rise of the CND was phenomenal — a tenfold increase in membership between 1980–2. By 1983 there were 54,000 national members, joining for £9, with some 250,000 members attached to local groups, plus Youth CND. The turnover of CND's thirteen booklets was £250,000 (half its income), it sold a million badges (at 20p) in two years, and sales of stickers and necklaces increased at 50% per month. Its journal, *Sanity*, with a print order of 60,000 and monthly advertising worth £4,000 improved in quality. Expanding into three buildings and employing twenty-eight full-time staff, CND clearly had the financial resources it required (statistics: *Observer*, 20 June 1982).

The peace movement can call on respected names to give credibility to its policies — citing Lord Mountbatten on the effects of a nuclear war, Lords Carver and Zuckerman on 'limited' nuclear war, and the supreme Allied Commander, General Rogers on conventional containment. Within its own ranks are credible and renowned authorities: Scientists Against Nuclear Arms (SANA), Christian CND (a Church of England working party under the Bishop of Salisbury produced a report in October 1982 advocating unilateral nuclear disarmament), and even Generals for Peace led by Brigadier Harbottle. The involvement of personalities such as actresses Susannah York, Julie Christie and others also attracts publicity.

(b) *Diversification* As already indicated, there are several strands to the 1980s peace movement. National CND itself expanded its Council in 1981 to include five delegates from each region and there is representation there for specialist sections — Youth, Christian, Trade Union, Student, Labour, Liberal and Green CND. In addition to the independent groups referred to already, there are Journalists Against Nuclear Extermination, Tories Against Cruise and Trident, and many others, 1,000 organisations including trade unions such as NALGO, NUPE, TGWU and ASTMS, are affiliated. But much of the strength of CND is at local levels where 'Against the Missiles' groups organise and act. This combination means CND is stronger than the 1960s version, which was overtly dependent on key personalities, and had no central organisation until 1966, envisaging only a short campaign.

Other parallel groups include the Greenham Common peace camp women, who retain their independence from CND, and the local authorities who have declared their areas 'nuclear free zones'. Seventy-three local councils attended a meeting in Manchester in 1982, and to date 155 zones have been declared. Sheffield agreed a pact with its Soviet 'twin' while the five counties declared Wales 'nuclear free'.

(c) Tactics

(i) *Arguments:* as in the case of cost the peace movement has been adept at enabling people to understand the scope of the subject. Hence a Trident submarine is described as being able to reduce 160 cities to the state of Hiroshima, and that the UK's Trident force could produce 7,000 Hiroshimas. Accepting that the electorate was not yet persuaded on nuclear disarmament or leaving NATO, CND has concentrated on softer targets — Trident and Cruise. In 1982 63% disapproved of Trident (ORC, *The Guardian*, 27 February 1982) and in September 1985 in a Gallup poll this was still 64%. Three-quarters of a December 1985 Gallup poll sample disagreed with a NATO strategy of first nuclear use, and 60% said Britain should leave if there was no change.

(ii) *Marches and demonstrations* — in June 1982, for example, 250,000 people attended a Hyde Park rally and two years later CND filled Trafalgar Square and blocked off the US Embassy in Grosvenor Square in a disciplined first attempt at non-violent direct action. Conscious of the criticism of 1960s CND for 'Trafalgar Squarism', other approaches to publicity have been followed. In 1983 a human chain, over fourteen miles long, of 70,000 people linked three nuclear establishments, and the following year attention was switched to the Barrow warship yards. In 1982 200 Scandinavian women marched from Stockholm to Minsk in the USSR. In October 1985 CND could still organise a march of 100,000 people in Hyde Park and form a peace symbol from 20,000 people.

(iii) *Non-violent direct action (NVDA)* — often involving civil disobedience, such action has an honourable tradition which includes Gandhi and Luther King. The division between constitutional CND and the Direct Action Committee (DAC) and then the Committee of 100 in the 1960s (which organised sit-down protests at bases and in Trafalgar Square) cost the movement dearly. The issue does not seem such a problem today, as CND accepted NVDA in 1981 and reaffirmed the decision in 1982 and 1984 with a call for a four-year guerrilla campaign at Molesworth. As with the Greenham women, it is left to members to decide to take such action and whether to agree to be 'bound over' or go to gaol. A *Peace News*/CND booklet gives advice on how to organise and cope with the consequences of NVDA, a Legal Advice Pack was produced in 1984 and seminars have been held. A notable victory for CND was the occupation and halting of construction of a nuclear bunker at Bridgend, Wales. The Greenham women have conducted several operations – climbing silos, cutting the perimeter fence and camping inside. The arrival of Cruise in November 1983 led to 141 arrests at Greenham and 300 at the House of Commons. The Americans conceded two years later that cruise deployment had been disrupted by protests.

(iv) *Emotional protest* – The women of the peace camps believe they have added a new emotional dimension to the campaign, rejecting the rational, 'male' game of bargaining over numbers and types of missiles. There can be no doubting the powerful symbolism of toys, clothes and pictures of children hung on the Greenham wire in 1982. It was largely to ensure non-violence that men were excluded from their protests.

(v) *Local campaigns* – An action manual, 'What do we do after we've shown *The War Game?*', provides CND members with detailed advice on the mechanics of organising meetings, finding information, writing to the press and on the psychology of attitude change. Particularly effective is an acetate bomb blast measuring device which can be overlaid on any Ordnance Survey map.

(vi) *Debate* – CND have constantly sought debate and have disarmingly offered to distribute the government's material with their own and to use their films too.

(vii) *Party politics* – CND voted against adopting party status at its 1980 conference. Canon Collins and the early leaders of CND made winning the Labour Party to unilateral nuclear disarmament a key objective and this they achieved at the 1960 conference. The refusal of Labour's leaders to accept it, the reversal in 1961 and subsequent acceptance in government of Polaris all precipitated CND's decline. Today more realism attends the relationship, but the adherence of the Labour Party to unilateralism in 1980, 1981, 1982 and at the 1983 general election was a major fillip for CND. Labour's 1984 'Defence and security for Britain' envisages the UK disposing of its own nuclear weapons and of US nuclear bases, strengthening conventional forces and campaigning for 'no first use' and then abolition of nuclear weapons in NATO. In May 1985 Mr Gorbachev offered Neil Kinnock to reduce weapons on a one-by-one basis and not target Britain if all nuclear weapons were removed.

The ecologists and nationalists similarly support unilateralism and indeed the SNP are closest to CND policy in wishing also to leave NATO. The Alliance has had difficulties, though these have attracted attention to the issues. The division within the Liberal Party which existed at the time of the general election was continued in 1984 and 1986 when the Assembly again voted against the leadership. Both the Liberals and SDP oppose buying Trident. Dr Owen's views on limiting the number of CND-supporting Alliance candidates did not go down with Liberals, suspicious of atempts to impose a freeze policy on them. Most serious was the attempt by senior SDP spokesmen to replace Polaris by sea-launched cruise missiles. First suggested by John Cartwright in November 1984, the issue developed into a major row by June 1986 with Dr Owen at odds with the Liberals and SDP President Shirley Williams, who accused him of selected reading of a policy document. A Gallup poll showed 51% of SDP candidates favouring replacement, while 83% of Liberal candidates were against. CND kept its own members active and interested prior to the 1983 general election by conducting a Peace Canvass. At the election itself they took legal advice about the Representation of the Peoples Act 1948 and then, to the anger of Conservatives, they encouraged voters – especially in marginal constituencies – to vote only for candidates opposed to nuclear weapons. Such an attempt to bring a 'sanction' to bear is rare for a cause group (in contrast to an interest group with economic power such as a trade union). CND also tried to use the 1983 European elections as a referendum on Cruise and Pershing, and attempted to 'black' Tarmac for its airbase construction work.

(viii) *The law* – nuclear free zone councils have tried to use the law and its loopholes to stop the transportation of nuclear materials and delay planning applications, and they achieved a notable success in 1982 when their non-co-operation with operation Hard Rock forced the cancellation of the civil defence exercise. And just as the Committee of 100 wanted to 'fill the gaols', there were fears that the Greenham arrests would clog both courts and gaols. The Court of Appeal did, however, restore their right to vote in Newbury.

Factors operating against the peace movement

(1) *Opposition*

(a) Government   Having been taken off guard by the anti-nuclear movement, the Conservative government gradually organised opposition. Elements of the public relations campaign included:

(i) *Ministers speeches* – speeches and their reproduction in the press emphasised the Soviet nuclear build-up as SS20's were installed, that Soviet intentions had to be doubted and that nuclear weapons had preserved peace in Europe for some forty years.

President Reagan's initiative of November 1981 of a 'zero option', whereby deployment of Cruise and Pershing II missiles would be halted if SS missiles were removed, was seized upon as proof of NATO's good intentions. And the Prime Minister saw the Falklands war as demonstrating a need to deter aggressors, and chided CND that in a Soviet dictatorship they would have no freedom to voice their views. NATO was sufficiently disturbed by 1981 to try to co-ordinate its response to the peace movements.

(ii) *Counter information* – in November 1981 the Conservative Party issued a briefing document on the advantages of multi-lateral disarmament. Mr David Trippier, MP, published 'Defending the Peace' through the Conservative Political Centre in February 1982. This defended both the acquisition of Trident and deployment of Cruise. The Ministry of Defence commissioned a twenty-minute film at a cost of £70,000, called *The Peace Game* which emphasised Soviet expansion. And a pamphlet called 'The balanced view' was prepared by the Central Office of Information for distribution to schools and colleges. It warned against neglecting defences, 'as in the 1930s'. In 1982 the Foreign Office had published a leaflet 'The Nuclear Debate' in response to requests from organisations for an alternative view to nuclear disarmament. 'Protect and Survive' was to be reviewed and replaced, and by July 1984 the Home Office was issuing more credible documents on nuclear and chemical attacks.

(iii) *Bolstering civil defence* – the government sought to re-establish the credibility of civil defence in the aftermath of the abandonment of Hard Rock 82. It was argued that peacetime emergencies as well as conventional attacks warranted civil defence and a free Home Office pamphlet warned that nuclear fallout from a war elsewhere could spread over Britain. The National Council for Civil Defence pointed to terrorism. Even in a nuclear war involving the UK, it was asserted that millions could be saved by preparation.

To assuage public opinion the government let it be known in January 1983 that the Home Office was working on radical plans to evacuate 12 million people or more from high-risk areas in the event of war, conceding that the previous 'stay put' policy lacked credibility. At the same time the government sought to exercise its authority and in October 1983 new regulations were issued obliging local authorities to carry out civil defence duties under the 1948 Civil Defence Act, and providing 100% grants for communications, training and expenses. In November 1984 the Home Office threatened to send in its own experts and bill ratepayers.

(iv) *Direct criticism and action* – a reason advanced for the appointment of Michael Heseltine as Secretary of State for Defence in 1983 was his ability to mount a vigorous campaign for Trident and Cruise missiles. He established a unit, Defence Secretariat 19, to combat the rise of CND. In one of the first speeches, drafted for Mr Peter Blaker, Armed Forces Minister, unilateralists were described as 'woolly people in woolly hats' (*The Guardian* 3 March 1983). CND were soon claiming that a 'smear' campaign was being waged against them. As early as 1981 Conservatives had said that the KGB had spent 100 million dollars on its anti-neutron bomb campaign in the west. It was asserted that Soviet Spetsnaz had infiltrated the Greenham camps (*Jane's Defence Weekly*, 1986). In March 1983 the Conservative Bow Group and German Adenauer Foundation published a study dubbing CND's leadership as communists or Tribune Group members, and in April Michael Heseltine wrote to all Conservative MPs and candidates in marginal seats setting out biographical details of CND's national council and naming thirty officials said to be past or present Labour or Communist Party members. He had to deny that he had put pressure on Cardinal Home to remove Monsignor Bruce Kent from the general secretaryship of CND and confine him to church duties. Similarly the Lord Chancellor had to deny that there was a direct ban on CND members being magistrates, after a dismissed magistrate was not allowed to take her case to the High Court. Government scientists were told in 1986 that they would not be promoted unless they worked on the Trident missile. In February 1985 it was alleged that MI5 had tapped the telephones of leading members of CND.

The strong new line could be seen when the Ministry of Defence resorted to a 19th-century statute to draft a new by-law making trespass a criminal offence. Learning from Greenham, 1,500 Royal engineers, 600 MOD police and 900 civilian police (supported by Mr Heseltine in a flak jacket) evicted the 150 Rainbow villagers at Molesworth without warning over Easter 1985. Local passes were issued and people stopped 20 miles away, as in the miners' strike. Meanwhile the MOD was trying to buy land at Greenham to close the peace camp.

Citizens' Advice Bureaux suffered a cut to their grant partly because of 'inappropriate political activity' – Joan Ruddock, chairperson of CND, was an employee (*Sunday Times* 10 April 1983) and membership of CND was said to be a relevant factor during positive vetting of civil servants for sensitive posts. Besides open criticism, the government continued to use what CND describe as 'repressive tolerance', treating them as a temporary, misguided phenomenon – as an outsider, uninfluential pressure group.

The authorities contifnued to withhold information where possible – a booklet on advice to farmers after a nuclear war was not put on sale at the time of the general election of 1983. The BBC, which had not shown *The War Game*, withdrew its invitation to E. P. Thompson to give the Dimbleby Lecture of 1981. Two years later Mr Heseltine persuaded Caspar Weinberger, US Defence Secretary, to withdraw from a televised debate with Thompson because of the impending election and, it was claimed, fear of embarrassment. The full power of the state, through the Official Secrets Act, was used against Sarah Tisdall – a civil servant goaled for six months for leaking Cruise arrival information to *The Guardian* in March 1984. Many described the story as merely politically embarrassing to the government and the sentence as harsh.

Dilemmas

Through acting against the peace movement in such a robust manner the government had some success but it also raised some sensitive issues. The Defence Ministry had intended to spend £1 million on a campaign for nuclear weapons run by J. Walter Thompson, an American agency, but the project was dropped. The politically controversial work of the ministry's special unit raised doubts about civil servants' involvement – such work was suspended during the election and the unit was dismantled in September 1983. By impugning the motives and delving into the background of CND leaders, ministers left themselves open to countercharges of factual errors and unworthy manoeuvres. The central dilemma was inescapable – by responding to and criticising the peace movement, the government gave it what it wanted most – publicity.

(2) *Pressure groups*

By definition, the main problem facing pressure groups opposing the
policies of the peace movement is not to appear to be pro-war. It is
not therefore surprising that countervailing groups have been slow to
emerge and flourish, but having done so they were able to go further
in their criticisms and language.

(*a*) *The British Atlantic Committee*   Established twenty-eight years
ago, its grant from the Foreign Office (half its revenue) was doubled
in 1982 to £40,000. It insisted that it was pro-NATO rather than pro-
government. The Disarmament Study Trust, seeing the rejection of its
own application, objected to the Committee's twelve-year registered
charity status.

(*b*) *The Council of Arms Control*   Launched in November 1981 by
academics, bishops, Conservative and Liberal MPs and former am-
bassadors, the Council intended to distribute bulletins in schools.

(*c*) *The Coalition for Peace Through Security*   Created in 1981, Mgr
Kent described it as 'the most offensive, unjust, and aggressive group
around' (*Guardian* 30 April 1983). It organised a secret briefing of
political, military and business figures on lobbying, mailing and opinion
forming techniques. CND claimed that spies had come to CND offices
under false pretences, and some had joined CND. CND lost a High
Court copyright action against the Coalition for parodying its symbol
with a hammer and sickle.

(*d*) *The Committee for Peace with Freedom (CPF)*   The Coalition
(above) merged with Mr Winston Churchill's CPF when he was
appointed by Mrs Thatcher to coordinate the reply to CND.

(*e*) *The Campaign for Defence and Multilateral Disarmament (CDMD)*
Mr Churchill also has close links with the CDMD formed in October
1982, which is funded and run from Conservative Central Office. CND
claimed that smears of 'communists' were used against them in the
United States by CDMD.

(*f*) *Youth for Multilateral Disarmament*   Formed by the Young
Conservatives in 1981, one of its leaflets read 'The Soviet Union Needs
You! Support Unilateral Disarmament'.

(*g*) *National Council for Civil Defence*   Whilst the prime purpose of the Council is to obtain sponsorship for civil defence, it turned to blaming CND.

(*h*) *Women for Defence*   This group was founded by Lady Olga Maitland and others who were 'incidentally Conservatives' in March 1983. While some activities, such as an attempted Trafalgar Square rally and visit to the 1984 Labour Party Conference were not successes, they did attract considerable publicity.

(*i*) *Conservative Medical Association*   Counterbalancing 'defeatist' sectional and professional groups, some, like the CMA, offered advice on how to survive.

(3) *Local authorities*
Far from being nuclear free zones, some Conservative-controlled councils restricted peace group activities. In 1982–4 CND was banned from selling its literature in Penzance market, its exhibition at Tunbridge Wells was closed, Cardiff City Council stopped its campaigning in a shopping centre, and Devon banned its meetings in schools and colleges. Newbury District Council persistently tried to evict the Greenham women, who by September 1983 were said to have cost the public £2 million, mainly through police costs.

(4) *Individuals*
Prominent critics included papal envoy Archbishop Helm who rebuked Mgr Kent and disarmers as 'useful idiots' for the Russians. Two members of the Civil and Public Services Association took their union to the High Court over its decision to affiliate to CND in 1982. There were also acts of violence by individuals and groups against peace groups and offices, and local interest groups, such as Ratepayers Against Greenham Encampments, were formed.

(5) *The press*
News coverage, particularly of the Greenham women, has not always been favourable. It has dwelt upon the squalor of the camps, with pictures of punks, stories of a 'starving baby' and a baby born at Greenham, of families abandoned, 'scrounging' social security payments, and 'strident feminists', 'burly lesbians' (*The Sun*, 14 December 1982).

(6) *Internal problems*

(*a*) *Digression*   The 1960s CND turned its attention to the Vietnam war and in doing so weakened its message and lost the support of pacifists. There was a similar attempt in 1981 to line the movement up against the government in a 'Jobs Not Bombs' campaign. By 1985 there were divisions in CND between the END supportes who favoured a cross-party coalition for non-nuclear defence, and who also wanted stronger support for Nicaragua, and those who oppose NATO member-ship – concentrated in the Youth, Green and Labour organisations. Feeling that CND had lost its way – towards education and away from resistance, 500 'activists' met in Manchester in 1985. By this time Rainbow Villagers, Peace Convoy hippies and broader teenage move-ments were involved, with the Greenham Women producing literature called 'Widening the Web' on Namibia, prison conditions, South Africa, sexism and inner cities.

(*b*) *Infiltration*   As a successful vehicle, entryists try to take control of its direction. Just as the Anti-Nazi League had to deal with members of the Socialist Workers Party and Socialist League, so CND in 1981 and 1982 saw attempts to link it to wider struggles, industrial action and more public opposition to NATO. In August 1983 to combat this all the officers and executive committee of its Youth Section were suspended. During the 1985 Easter weekend, Class War, an anarchist group, infiltrated the demonstrations at Molesworth.

(*c*) *Co-option*   Too close an identification with the Labour Party and its problems would be damaging. The Party remains its likeliest way to implementation and there is a large overlap of membership.

(*d*) *Public opinion*   A fundamental problem is that the majority of British people are not yet ready to abandon nuclear weapons, nor to ensure greater 'safety' by leaving the nuclear alliance, NATO. In 1981 23% wished to abandon nuclear weapons, 56% to maintain them and 18% improve them (*Guardian*/Marplan, 22 April 1981). In October 1983 16% wished to abandon, 63% to maintain, and 14% to improve (*Guardian*/Marplan, 22 October 1983). To try to change this CND launched a campaign in 1986 to convince the public of the futility of nuclear weapons in clear language, based on the same approach as CND in Bristol and Cheltenham. But an October 1985 Gallup poll showed a first-ever majority of 52% to 35% for keeping cruise missiles. CND blamed some of this on Labour's performance in the House of Commons and employed a second lobbyist.

(e) *Momentum*   In view of government indifference and public implacability there is danger that members lessen their efforts or accept partial successes. This befell CND in its early phase as fatigue set in and the 1963 Test Ban Treaty was agreed.

By 1985 the superpowers were talking again and attention had switched to other issues, such as famine in Africa. While incidents could still revive interest, e.g. the Chernobyl disaster, US abandonment of SALT 2 in May 1986 or their raids on Libya the month before (£20,000 donated and many membership applications) – the pre-cruise intensity could not be maintained. The Star Wars issue seemed too complex and to worry governments more.

(f) *Alienation*   Non-violent direct action runs the risk of alienating both peace movement members and the general public. CND had problems in 1984 with a splinter group, Peace Anonymous, which organised a 'die-in' at the Cenotaph and wanted to blockade the Lancaster House Summit of May 1984. Similarly, the activities at the peace camps can lessen public support.

One dilemma that seems a long way off for the peace movements is one sometimes faced by issue campaigns – e.g. the Anti-Corn Law League or the Anti-Slavery Society – what to do when their goal is attained. Future success or failure will depend on a combination of imponderables – East–West relations, proliferation to other countries, our knowledge of technological systems or 'nuclear winters' and the fortitude of volunteers as they wait in the rain for a missile launcher.

Reading

J. Minnion and P. Bolsover (eds.), *The CND Story*, Allison & Busby, 1983.

H. Clark, S. Crown, A. McKee, H. MacPherson, *Preparing for Non-Violent Direct Action, Peace News*/CND 1984.

P. Webber, G. Wilkinson, B. Rubin, *Crisis Over Cruise*, Penguin, 1983.

A. Cook and G. Kirk, *Greenham Women Everywhere*, Pluto, 1984.
P. Kennard and R. Sissons, *No to Nuclear Weapons*, Pluto, 1981.
The Nuclear Debate, Central Office of Information, 1982.
Andrée Shepherd, 'The politics of nuclear protest in the fifties: CND
    and the early New Left', *Teaching Politics*, September 1986,
    pp. 476–91.

Chronology of development

1945 Only 21% of British disapprove of use of A-bomb against Japan.
1950 British Peace Committee claim 1 million signatures on Stockholm
      Peace Appeal.
1952 Sit-down protest at War Office and Aldermaston.
1954 H-Bomb National Campaign founded. Coventry City Council
      disbands Civil Defence Committee as 'waste of time and public
      money.
1957 Protest boat sails to stop H-Bomb test at Christmas Island.
      Labour Party H Bomb Campaign Committee rallies 4,000 in
      Trafalgar Square.
      National Committee for Abolition of Nuclear Weapons Tests
      transfers funds to new body – CND. Members: Bertrand Russell,
      Sir Julian Huxley, Michael Foot, James Cameron, J. B. Priestley.
1958 Britain agrees to four US Thor missile bases in E. Anglia.
      Gallup poll – 80% expect half UK population to die in war.
      Gerald Holtom invents symbol   . Aldermaston march.
1959 Aldermaston march – 20,000 in Trafalgar Square.
      Direct Action Committee organises civil disobedience at bases.
      Voter's Veto in election campaign.
      Support risen from 25% to 30%.
1960 Committee of 100, led by Russell, breaks away from CND.
1961 Sit-downs and arrests – 1314 in Trafalgar Square.
      Arrest at bases, including 100 at Greenham Common.
      450 CND groups; *Sanity* – 45,000 circulation.
1962 150,000 in Hyde Park Rally.
      Cuban missile crisis.
1963 'Spies for peace' reveal bunkers and HQs.
      Partial Test Ban Treaty signed.
1970 Festival of Life in Hackney attracts 20,000.
1973 Weeks of action in Scotland.
      Labour Party Conference votes for unilateralism.

1978   Neutron bomb petition.

1980   Chevaline modernisation of Polaris revealed.

      Panorama shows 'Protect and Survive'.

      Manchester City Council declares nuclear free zone.

      80,000 at Trafalgar Square rally.

1981   Women for Life on Earth march from S. Wales to Greenham Common.

      42 nuclear free zones.

      CND membership 30,000.

      Demonstrations in European cities by over one million people.

      President Reagan offers zero option.

1982   140 nuclear free zones.

      Operation 'Hard Rock' abandoned.

      Greenham women ring base. Eleven women gaoled.

      Hyde Park demonstration by ¼ million.

1983   Cruise arrives – 700 arrests.

      Human chain between bases.

      National membership of CND 54,000. Total membership 110,000.

      CND non-violent action in Grosvenor Square.

1984   Liberal Assembly again votes to remove cruise missiles.

      Labour reaffirms unilateral nuclear disarmament.

      Several attempts to evict Greenham women.

      Nuclear free zones cover ½ to ⅓ of England, all Wales.

1985   100,000 march to Hyde Park.

      20,000 demonstrate at Molesworth, proposed second cruise missile site.

      Greenham Peace Camp numbers fall to 40.

      CND Secretary General Bruce Kent and Chairwoman Joan Ruddock stand down.

1986   CND membership falls to 91,000, 25% not renewing subscriptions. No large Easter rallies.

      Alliance dissension over replacement of Polaris support slumps in opinion polls.

      Amalgamated Engineering Union disaffiliates from CND.